WOMEN-WRITERS

OF

THE NINETEENTH CENTURY

WOMEN-WRITERS
OF
THE NINETEENTH CENTURY

BY

MARJORY A. BALD

New York
RUSSELL & RUSSELL

SHED IN 1923

USSELL & RUSSELL, INC.

BY ARRANGEMENT WITH CAMBRIDGE UNIVERSITY PRESS

L. C. CATALOG CARD NO: 63—8356

PRINTED IN THE UNITED STATES OF AMERICA

PREFACE

THIS collection of studies does not aim at giving an exhaustive account of the contribution made by women to Nineteenth Century literature. Neither does it profess to be in any sense a "feminist" treatise. The writers selected were in all cases remarkable women; but they were something more —remarkable human beings. I have endeavoured throughout to concentrate, not merely on questions of sex, but on the complete humanity of each woman. So far as possible all preconceived theories of the literary woman have been deliberately excluded. There is no initial attempt to determine what the woman of letters should be like. After looking carefully at these particular women, we may see what she has sometimes been like; and we may also discern certain characteristics common to different women of literary instinct. That is all the "theory" which this book professes to give. For its aim has not been the evolution of a principle. It has attempted something more elusive, and to many minds far more satisfying—to look at individual writers, as it were face to face, with a quickened sense of kinship and reverence.

With regard to the proportional length of the separate sections, it may be necessary to make special reference to the study of Mrs Gaskell. Though it is the longest of the sections, this does not imply that Mrs Gaskell is to be considered as the most important of all the writers in question. The length of the section is due to the fact that she was many-sided, whereas the other women of stronger idiosyncracy—and it may be, of profounder genius—were more limited in their outlook; and it takes longer to describe a varied treasure hoard than a single peerless gem. The extent of the study was also determined by the fact that Mrs Gaskell has often received less than her deserts; thus it seemed not only generous, but fair, for me to make some little compensation in at least the quantity of my words.

I should like to express my gratitude to Professor Grierson for his help and interest all through the preparation and development of these studies; and also to Professor Saintsbury, who gave me several valuable suggestions.

M. A. B.

OXFORD,
November 1922

CONTENTS

PAGE

JANE AUSTEN . . . . / . . I

  I. The Utilisation of Small Resources . . I

    Static Quality—Limitation—Life in miniature and a style to fit it

  II. Elements of her Appeal—Cheerfulness and Moderation 9

    The Will to be happy—Reserved and private humour—Life as a game—Vitality—Relationship of author and reader—Dislike of Excitement or Sensation

  III. The Study of Human Temperament . . . 17

    Some types of character—Satire—Treatment of her own Sex—Value and Influence of her achievement

THE BRONTES 28

  I. General Introduction. Family Characteristics 28

    Environment, Tradition and Escape—The Medium of Personal Experience

  II. Anne Bronte, 1820–1849 35

  III. Charlotte Bronte, 1816–1855 38

    The Reader and Student—The Deliberate Artist, her Theory and the artistic result—The Woman, her experience, opinions, and emotions—Summary

  IV. Emily Bronte, 1818–1848 77

    Introductory. Charlotte and Emily compared—*Wuthering Heights*—The Poems—Summary

MRS E. C. GASKELL 100

  I. Introductory 100

  II. Atmosphere and Setting 103

  III. Humour 107

  IV. Pathos 122

  V. The Woman's Point of View 136

  VI. The Social Problem 145

  VII. Moral Theory or Moral Effect . . . 151

PAGE

GEORGE ELIOT 162

   I. Introductory 162

   II. The Expression of Temperament . . . 166

      The Woman—The Student—Her religious stand-point—Her attitude to Convention—The Doctrine of Retribution

   III. The Impersonal Artist 184

      Vocation—Irony—Pathos—Atmosphere—Character-Study—The Poems—Comparison with Charlotte Bronte—Summary

MRS BROWNING 209

   I. The Negative Approach 209

      Self-consciousness—Lack of self-control

   II. The Positive Approach 221

      The Feminine Element in the *Drama of Exile*—The Consequences of her Marriage—Summary

CHRISTINA ROSSETTI 233

   I. Personal Experience reflected on her poetry 233

   II. Sources 239

   III. Symbol, Allegory, and Dream 254

   IV. Emotional Quality 260

   V. General Considerations 267

CONCLUSION 275

INDEX 285

JANE AUSTEN
1775-1817

I

THE UTILISATION OF SMALL RESOURCES

JANE AUSTEN, the daughter of a Hampshire clergyman, was born in 1775, and died in 1817. Of her unsensational life there is little to chronicle. Neither is there much to detain us in the story of her literary career. *Northanger Abbey*, her first novel, was bought by a publisher in 1797, but was published after her death. In order of publication her novels form the following series: *Sense and Sensibility* published in 1811; *Pride and Prejudice* published in 1813, but written in 1797; *Mansfield Park* published in 1814; *Emma* published in 1816; *Persuasion* and *Northanger Abbey*—her last book and her first—published in 1818. It seems a meagre record of insignificant facts; and these are precisely the terms which might be applied by a short-sighted person to Jane Austen's experience. Yet from this experience, apparently so meagre and insignificant, there sprang an art finished in every detail, filled with life, and therefore filled with meaning. This result could be brought about by no other means than the unique personality of the artist. Always while reading Jane Austen, we feel that she possessed "the magic touch." This touch of hers—so unhesitating and unerring—was the outcome of another touch—the contact of her temperament with her own experience.

Jane Austen was not a Victorian; nor can she be regarded as a herald of the coming age. When she looked back it was mainly to the tradition of "Fanny" Burney. But she was the kind of person who seldom glanced to past or future. Hers was chiefly the outlook of the present tense. Like her own Miss Bates, but with a different signification, she might have said, "What is before me, I see." This gives to her art a certain static quality. Unlike the women who came after her, she had nothing of the pioneering instinct. She neither wished nor feared to startle the world with revolutionary achievements. We find in her no trace of Charlotte Bronte's hunger for liberty, no yearnings for wider horizons. She took her world as she found it, wishing for nothing better. Nobody could call her an idealist, for this term implies a looking forward to some future perfection; and Jane Austen would have found little zest in an ideal world so perfectly cured of folly as to be completely deprived of matter for laughter. She satirised people, but from no passionate motives of reformation. Though she did not like Mrs Bennet or Lady Catherine de Bourgh, she would not have had them different. In their unreformed absurdity they had at least this merit—they afforded some amusement. If they had become all that they should have been, nobody would have wanted to laugh at them any more; and for this reason Miss Austen wished to keep them, and all others of like kind, in a state of unredeemed, original folly. We cannot help feeling that in certain cases Jane Austen enjoyed her own dislikes. It would have been a keen sorrow to her if she had been deprived of her delight in hating people like Mrs Elton. Of Emma's feelings at the ball she wrote with a kind of exhilarated sympathy: "Emma must submit to stand second to Mrs Elton, though she had always considered the ball as peculiarly for her. It was almost enough to make her think of marrying."

This static quality appears very strongly in Jane Austen's portrayal of individual characters. Very few of them contain, like Emma, any suggestions of enigma, or references to the future. "There is an anxiety, a curiosity, in what one feels for Emma," said Mr Knightley; "I wonder what will become of her." This, as we have said, is a very rare type in Jane Austen. We know most of her characters after the first introduction; and though we cannot anticipate what they are going to do next, we are hardly ever taken by surprise. Mrs Norris is one who makes a very strong first impression. We cannot forget her characteristic tendency to tell her relations every now and then "in an angry voice that Fanny had got another child." After that first chapter of *Mansfield Park* we are quite prepared for different aspects of her temper. In fact we are put into an expectant attitude; and our expectations are never disappointed—certainly not at the Grant's dinner-party. "(Mrs Norris) did always contrive to experience some evil from the passing of the servants behind her chair, and to bring away some fresh conviction of its being impossible among so many dishes but that some must be cold." Mrs Norris, it is true, has about her something emphatic which might be expected to leave a strong indelible mark, but even the feebler characters resemble her in this single quality of making a constant impression. They do nothing to contradict our first expectations of them. Their dispositions undergo no growth or change. They simply stand where they were.

All this implies a measure of restriction. Limitation, indeed, is an outstanding characteristic of Jane Austen's workmanship. But a limitation may be voluntarily imposed. She defined her own boundaries, and never stepped beyond them. Like Charlotte Bronte, she had a narrow experience; but she adopted an entirely different attitude towards it. About Charlotte's work there clings a great wistfulness; it is incomplete, tentative, always striving for something vaguely out of reach. Her writings create a sense of distance, and open vistas in the mind of the reader. This may be partly due to that atmosphere of wild and open nature in which her stories are set; but the essential reason lies deeper. Charlotte Bronte had a limited external experience; yet within her own spirit there lay a mysterious power uncalculated and incalculable. No matter how small the external incidents, they were apprehended by a human mind—"the intense atom" of which Shelley sang. This atom,

> This, which imagined God and is the soul,

has magnifying powers. We quote again from the words of a modern poet:

> O little self, within whose smallness lies
> All that man was, and is, and will become,

Atom unseen that comprehends the skies
And tells the tracks by which the planets roam;
That, without moving, knows the joys of wings,
The tiger's strength, the eagle's secrecy,
And in the hovel can consort with kings,
And clothe a God with his own mystery.

Charlotte's mind was like that. It was at once the setting of her experience and her means of escape from its limitations. Jane Austen was entirely different, for she desired no escape. Looking out from herself she scrutinised her small experience. Charlotte Bronte made the same investigation constantly glancing inwards. As a natural result Charlotte always found it easy to describe what she herself had felt or done; but Jane Austen concentrated upon the deeds and sentiments of other people. It has been said of Romantic art that it leaves the impression of something incomplete and unstated,

Which into words no virtue can digest.

Whereas it suggests infinity, classical art brings with it a sense of something finite and flawless, carried through to its utmost limit of perfection. We know how to place the two artists—Charlotte Bronte with her suggestions of infinity, and Jane Austen with her unerring perfection of craft.

Miss Austen adjusted her vision, and focussed it to a very small perspective. This involved the blurring of her larger prospects; but she knew what she was about. It is impossible at the same moment to look through the lens of a microscope and to study the contours of a mountain range. The choice of one excludes the other. Jane Austen chose the microscopic method of observation. In the mental as in the physical vision of every human being there is a blind spot; and Jane Austen's was a large one. She was blind, for example, to any democratic idea. The modern reader is rather taken aback at her almost naïve treatment of Emma's snobbishness; it is practically impossible to discern any ironic touch in her handling of class prejudices. We read that Emma rather disapproved of Frank Churchill because "his indifference to a confusion of rank bordered too much on inelegance of mind." It is never safe to assert of a demure person like

Miss Austen that she wrote any sentence with an unimpaired gravity. She *may* have been laughing at Emma; but it seems easier to believe that in this point she quite seriously agreed with her. In other directions Jane Austen was not born blind, but she deliberately shut her eyes. As we shall see, she refused to look towards the high passions or excitements; but she refused on perfectly rational grounds. Generalising on her mental vision we must come to a definite conclusion:— either by nature, or from want of exercise, her long sight was defective; but this was compensated by a short sight of keenness unsurpassed and well nigh unexampled. She confined her thinking within very strict limits. She never went beyond her frontiers. But within bounds she allowed herself an almost unparalleled freedom of criticism. In that small world there was nothing immune from her laughter. Indeed "world" is too large a word to suggest the compass of Jane Austen's authority. A room would describe it better —a small room, comfortable and elegant, but not ostentatious. There would be no obtrusive decorations in that room, no parade of its delicate, priceless curios. Many of its treasures would be in odd corners, readily overlooked. Jane Austen was a connoisseur in human nature—a collector of fine quaint specimens. That is the charm of her small room. Outside her casements lie the dusty streets of a coarser, fiercer world. Sometimes we feel impelled to open her windows, and get some tidings of a stern work-a-day life, more robust in its laughter and tears. At other times we are glad to indulge in the luxury of forgetting—to close the windows, and draw the curtains, and sit very still. Far below us are throbbing the harsh noises of the street; but we do not hear them, or only so faintly as to rejoice in our aloofness. There is a great sense of security in closing our doors against storm or tumult. Jane Austen invites her readers to share in that satisfaction.

"All our adventures were by the fireside," wrote the Vicar of Wakefield, "and all our migrations from the blue bed to the brown." In all Jane Austen's novels life is described from the same standpoint of minute simplicity. Her writings come as a revelation of the fineness and clearness of touch requisite for miniature painting. Beauty is, after all, something quite independent of bulk. It requires colour, outline, character; and these may be found in small measures.

Jane Austen's mastery of apparent trifles is nowhere more evident than in her unique employment of words. It takes searching to find in her books long words, long sentences, or even long paragraphs. For sheer brevity she has few, if any, equals. Like a clever needlewoman who can manufacture garments out of odd pieces of cloth, Jane Austen can convey her complete meaning in a few common words. Of Lady Catherine de Bourgh, we read: "Whenever any of the cottagers were disposed to be quarrelsome, discontented, or *too poor*, she sallied forth into the village to settle their differences, silence their complaints, and scold them into harmony and plenty."—"Too poor!"—It is almost incredible that a couple of words should have such possibilities of suggestion.—It is in the chronicles of the same evening, that shy Maria Lucas, sitting at Lady Catherine's table, "thought speaking out of the question"—another far-reaching phrase. A sentence taken from *Emma* sums up three love-stories in little more than thirty words: "(Mr Elton was) in the same room at once with the woman he had just married, the woman he had wanted to marry, and the woman he had been expected to marry."—Another sentence from the same book gives a complete picture, full of expression and movement: "Mrs Elton was first seen at church; but though devotion might be interrupted, curiosity could not be satisfied, by a bride in a pew."—Take again another sentence from *Emma*, and we receive most adequate enlightenment as to the bride's popularity: "Mr Knightley seemed to be trying not to smile (at Emma's raillery); and succeeded without difficulty upon Mrs Elton's beginning to talk to him."—It is easy to accumulate examples, but such delights call for restraint. Three more must suffice. The first is a miraculous delineation of character in about five lines: "(Mrs Bennet) was a woman of mean understanding, little information, and uncertain temper. When she was discontented, she fancied herself nervous. The business of her life was to get her daughters married; its solace was visiting and news." The second example is an equally wonderful setting forth of a dilemma: "Oh, Mr Bennet," cried his wife, "you are wanted immediately; we are all in an uproar. You must come and make Lizzie marry Mr Collins, for she vows she will not have him, and if you do not make haste, he will change his mind and not have *her*." The third example brings before us the atmosphere of Mrs Price's household: "Whatever was wanted, was hallooed for—and the servants hallooed out their excuses from the kitchen." These instances, all except the last, have been taken from two novels only; they might be multiplied indefinitely from every book that bears Jane Austen's name.

Before leaving the subject of her diction, it is necessary to refer briefly to her use of figures in speech. Similes and metaphors are almost entirely absent. But her style is strongly antithetic.—Mr Elton had gone away, as we are told, "not only losing the right lady, but finding himself debased to the level of a very wrong one." Mrs Bennet's attitude to Charlotte Lucas's engagement is described in a most suggestive climax: "A week elapsed before she could see Elizabeth without scolding her, a month passed away before she could speak to Sir William or Lady Lucas without being rude, and many months were gone before she could at all forgive their daughter." Dramatic irony appears quite frequently—especially in *Pride and Prejudice*, the richest of all the novels. We find it in Mrs Bennet's artless exclamation: "My dear Mr Bennet, you must not expect such girls to have the sense of their father and mother." Mr Collins' proposal displays the same innocent blindness to his own self-revelations: "My reasons for marrying are...I am convinced it will add very greatly to my happiness." The same unconscious humour appears in *Sense and Sensibility*, where Mrs Palmer exposes unawares the character of her husband: "Poor fellow! it (that is, electioneering) is very fatiguing to him! for he is forced to make everybody like him."

The above examples have been restricted to phrases or sentences; but Jane Austen showed an equal command of the paragraph. We need only refer to the description of Lady

Catherine's dinner party, and the demeanour of her guests. There is a most vivid piece of narrative in Mrs Jennings' breathless report of the Dashwood family thrown into "uproar" by the discovery of Edward Ferrars' engagement to Lucy Steele. We have space here for only a single quotation, and this one which acquaints us at once with the most intimate tone and spirit of a scene. It is a description of the reception given at Mansfield Park to William Price's stories: "Though Mrs Norris could fidget about the room, and disturb everybody in quest of two needlefuls of thread or a second-hand shirt-button, in the midst of her nephew's account of a shipwreck or an engagement, everybody else was attentive; and even Lady Bertram could not hear of such horrors unmoved, or without sometimes lifting her eyes from her work to say, 'Dear me! how disagreeable! I wonder anybody can ever go to sea.'"

II

ELEMENTS OF HER APPEAL—CHEERFULNESS
AND MODERATION

ALL these things may be acknowledged of Jane Austen, and yet they do not seem to touch the inmost secret of her charm. It is possible to assent to much praise without feeling any quickening of the heart. Many readers remain on the outside edge of Miss Austen's acquaintance. Hardly any of them enter into a real intimacy on a first, a second, or even a third reading. She "takes a great deal of knowing." We grow very slowly into her fellowship, and it is a long time before we can account for her extraordinary fascination. But most of her lovers come to feel—it may be subconsciously—the magnetism of her joy. She had the will to be happy. She possessed the mark of a keen intelligence—an incapacity for being bored. "I emphatically deny," says a modern essayist, "that anything is, or can be, uninteresting." There is no doubt that Jane Austen would have agreed with him. She seemed to find spice in everything.—"A fine Sunday in Bath," she wrote, "empties every house of its inhabitants, and all the world appears on such an occasion, to walk about, and tell their acquaintance what a charming day it is." She knew very well that there is a great deal of fun to be got out of life, if a person will only take the trouble to look for it; and she set out on a deliberate quest for mirth. Her mind was like a sensitive plate prepared to receive impressions of amusement. Because of this prepared surface of her expectations, she was stirred to delight by ordinary matters which left other people in a state of blank indifference. Of all her books *Northanger Abbey* shows most clearly this readiness to be pleased. Catherine Morland's happiness is of a robust, invincible type. Almost at random we take a few quotations: "Catherine could not at all get over the double distress of having involved her friend in a lecture and been a great simpleton herself, till they were happily seated at the dinner-table, when the General's complacent smiles, and a good appetite of her own restored her to peace." Or: "Her mind being made up on these several points, and her resolution formed, of always judging and acting in future with the greatest good sense, she had nothing to do but to forgive herself and be happier than ever." Her family partook of the same incurable optimism. They were "far from being an irritable race," and when they could not understand the reason for Catherine's sudden dismissal from the Abbey, they decided to acquiesce in a happy ignorance. "'My dear, you give yourself a great deal of needless trouble,' said her mother at last; 'depend upon it, it is something not at all worth understanding.'" They were always prepared for pleasant news and pleasant estimates of character; and Catherine's lover was accepted in all good faith.—"Having never heard evil of him, it was not their way to suppose any evil could be told." The book closes with a remark quite in keeping with the family tendency to regard all vexations as blessings in disguise. The course of Catherine's love had run by no means smoothly, but all came right in the end: "The General's interference had conduced to their felicity, improved their mutual knowledge, and added strength to their attachment."

In every book Jane Austen showed the same willingness to appreciate the good things of life. Others might consider it their business to study human sorrow; she specialised in happiness. In *Mansfield Park* she wrote: "Let other pens dwell on guilt and misery. I quit such odious subjects as soon as I can, impatient to restore everybody not greatly in fault themselves, to tolerable comfort, and to have done with all the rest." It is quite possible to condemn such an utterance on the score of superficiality. Can we imagine what George Eliot would have said to it? But nobody could endure to live for ever with George Eliot. Surely in this great world of ours, and in the affections of large-hearted people, there is room for both types. It is a fine and a brave thing to confront, like George Eliot, the formidable things in life; but all life is not formidable. Much of it is extremely delightful. And why should we waste these delights by deliberate neglect? There is much to be said for the person who, like Jane Austen, resolves to cherish and develop to their utmost capacity all opportunities of happiness. It is a brave thing to face sorrows, but it is sometimes as brave to cast them aside like "unconsidered trifles." The optimism which looks on the bright side is sometimes very shallow; yet it is often very unselfish. Miss Bates, we are told, was "a standing lesson of how to be happy." And what are we to say for her cheerful, comfortable philosophy? Is it not true, no matter how the pessimists may grumble?—"It is such a happiness when good people get together—and they always do."

Nevertheless Jane Austen had one source of joy quite beyond the compass of worthy Miss Bates. This was the joy of her furtive laughter. There are some people who cannot live in this imperfect conventional world without the solace and support of a few private jests. It is a great stand-by to feel amused, and not look it. Mr Bennet was one person of that type; and we are fairly safe in saying that his creator was another. Her humour, like Chaucer's, was implied rather than articulated. We can easily imagine Chaucer, grave-faced and composed, reading to the Lady Eglantine his "impressions" of her personality. Assuredly she would not have laughed; it is quite as certain that she would not have taken offence; most probably she would have been flattered. Jane Austen's humour, though equally sly, was not quite so ingratiating. If Mrs Bennet had been privileged to read certain chapters of *Pride and Prejudice*, she would not have felt any flutterings of personal vanity. I am inclined to think that she would have felt nothing at all—only a sense of boredom. The difference between the two types of humour lies here:—on a dull apprehension Chaucer would have made an impression entirely distinct from that which he himself was feeling; on a dull apprehension Jane Austen would have made no impression whatever. That is why some people say there is "nothing" in Jane Austen. There is a great deal in her; but it can be discerned only by the freemasonry which binds all humourists into a secret fellowship. In almost every secret there is an element of romance.

When Stevenson and his boyish companions established the cult of "the Lantern-bearers," they dimly apprehended this truth. They took no delight in the bull's-eye lantern for its own sake; it was merely a token of something unexpressed, and well nigh inexpressible. "The essence of this bliss was to walk by yourself in the black night; the slide shut, the top-coat buttoned; not a ray escaping, whether to conduct your footsteps or to make your glory public; a mere pillar of darkness in the dark; and all the while, deep down in the privacy of your fool's heart, to know you had a bull's-eye at your belt, and to exult and sing in the knowledge." To the reader unendowed with a sense of humour, Jane Austen is as "a mere pillar of darkness in the dark." But she has her private circle of comrades. Any reader, on production of a very simple credential, may join that company. The credential is the bull's-eye lantern at the belt—a flame of laughter burning within the heart.

Authors often give themselves away by the metaphors, implied or expressed, which they apply to life. To some it appears as a pilgrimage or quest; to others an evolution or process; to others a conflict; and so on. Jane Austen did not deal in metaphors; but it is possible to read between the lines, and find an unwritten phrase which sums up the entire subject-matter of her novels. She described life as a matrimonial game. Every novel is the report of a series of games, grouped into a set; the characters are members of the teams. It is true that something of the charm of *Emma* lies in the fact that it possesses two prominent characters—Miss Bates and Mr Woodhouse—who, standing aside from the game, refresh our minds with the remembrance of other matters. But even they are deeply affected by the play. Miss Bates watches it eagerly, and Mr Woodhouse is disturbed by it. They cannot live their lives apart from its influence. It is hardly saying too much when we assert that anybody on the look-out for a game could not have chosen one of more absorbing interest. It has been more universally adopted than any other game played by human beings—than politics, chess, golf, or patience. It combines elements of skill and

chance; and it is a game of hazard. With a light heart Jane
Austen chose this game, and calculated all its resources. It
proves to us that even a pre-Victorian woman could possess
an unusual form of our "modern" sporting instinct.

We have said much about Jane Austen; and yet it seems
to express but a fraction of her appeal. There is something in
this dainty flawless art which grows upon the reader. It
possesses an inexhaustible magic. In contrasting Jane Austen
and Charlotte Bronte, we noted that the work of the former
artist suggests perfection, and that of the latter infinity. But
Jane Austen also has her suggestions of infinity. We do not
get to the end of her people; their vitality never runs dry.
They are not like delicate machines set going for an allotted
course of chapters. We feel that they could go on for ever.
This quality of an everlasting freshness is a token of human
reality. For human beings, even the dullest of them, are
something like that. At no time can we say of any living
persons that their interest is exhausted. The more we know
of them, the more we feel that we shall never know everything about them—we shall never grasp their entire secret.
We come to commas or semi-colons in the paragraph of their
lives, but never to the final full-stop. We have said that Jane
Austen's characters were "static"; still they were not monotonous, as they might easily have been. If they were unchanging, they were also unique. Miss Austen realised that
a circle of very humdrum people can supply material of infinite human suggestion; and in apprehending this secret,
she was well equipped for joy.

People like Jane Austen, who are not afraid of a "humdrum"
existence, are usually easy to live with. This may account
for something of the charm which she casts over the relationship of author and public. She does not put herself about to
entertain her readers; they are expected to make themselves
at home. We feel this in every book—most especially,
I think, in *Mansfield Park*. There we are welcomed into the
home circle. We are told all the little things which should
never be repeated "out of the family." There is no ceremony
or excitement; everything goes on as usual. We are not

constantly amused; we have to share the dull days and the bright ones. Life in an ordinary house can be extremely monotonous; but nobody "fusses" after us to see that we are not bored. It is taken for granted that we will settle down to the usual routine; and most of us do, with an absolute satisfaction. It is all a part of Jane Austen's exquisite courtesy. No well-bred hostess allows her guests to feel that they are in the way. Nobody feels quite comfortable to be tended by a Martha cumbered with much serving. On the other hand, if it is unpleasant to be incessantly entertained, it is certainly no less disagreeable to be neglected. The ideal hostess escapes both extremes. While she takes extra trouble to set her guests at ease, she tries to keep from their knowledge all strain or effort. Jane Austen makes us contented, but not by sheer virtue of amiability. Her quiet narrative and clear, pleasant style is not quite so easy as it looks; it is all the result of a drudgery and discipline taking place behind the scenes.

Jane Austen's good breeding and dislike of sensation went side by side. It is usually considered the mark of "a perfect lady" that she should wear nothing to make her unduly conspicuous. This principle of good taste in dress was extended by Miss Austen to cover good taste in narrative. She wished to avoid anything like a startling impression. She liked things to be so normal and wholesome that the observer would receive pleasure almost unawares.

"I like a fine prospect," said Edward Ferrars to Marianne Dashwood, "but not on picturesque principles. I do not like crooked, twisted, blasted trees. I admire them much more if they are tall, straight, and flourishing. I do not like ruined, tattered cottages. I am not fond of nettles or thistles or heath blossoms. I have more pleasure in a snug farmhouse than a watch-tower—and a troop of tidy villagers please me better than the finest banditti in the world."

Undoubtedly Edward was voicing his creator's opinions. Indeed, before creating him at all, she had written a book with these opinions implied on every page. *Northanger Abbey* is a sort of feminine counterpart to *Don Quixote*. Catherine Morland, like the immortal knight-errant, had

her head turned with reading of a high-coloured, sensational
type, till she found—or expected to find—everyday life
brimming with all sorts of thrilling and impossible adventures.
—"Are they all horrid?" she asked before deciding on a new
set of novels, "Are you sure they are all horrid?"—She
hoped to find life as "horrid" as Mrs Radcliffe's stories.
Jane Austen's narrative is a treatment of her lapses from the
ordinary ways of ordinary people, and her final restoration
to *common* sense. Charlotte Bronte herself could not have
chosen a less impressive heroine.—"No one who had ever
seen Catherine Morland in her infancy, would have supposed
her born to be a heroine."—In fact, Catherine was, if anything, even less remarkable than Jane Eyre. Her ordinary
prettiness could not weigh in the balance against Jane's
extraordinary piquancy. Catherine, it must be admitted, had
very little in her.—"Provided that nothing like useful knowledge could be gained from them, provided they were all
story and no reflection, she had never any objection to books
at all."—History made no appeal to her.—"The quarrels of
popes and kings, with wars or pestilences in every page; the
men all so good for nothing, and hardly any women at all—
it is very tiresome."—Of course Catherine might have been
a noteworthy woman without being a profound student of
history; but in the most ordinary accomplishments she seems
to have reached an extremely low average.

Though she could not write sonnets, she brought herself to read
them; and though there seemed no chance of her throwing a
whole party into raptures by a prelude on the pianoforte, of her
own composition, she could listen to other people's performance
with very little fatigue.

Even upon her lover she made no overwhelming impression.
A persuasion of her partiality for him had been the only cause of
giving her a serious thought. It is a new circumstance in romance,
I admit, and dreadfully derogatory of a heroine's dignity; but if
it be as new in common life, the credit of a wild imagination will
at least be all my own.

Charlotte Bronte may have chosen Jane Eyre as a plain and
insignificant heroine; but she could not keep her insignificant.
About her women there was an intellectual or persistent

quality which could not be hidden. Jane Austen chose an
ordinary type, and never allowed it to become extraordinary.
This is by no means an attack upon Catherine Morland, for
it is a delight to read about her. It is simply an illustration
of Jane Austen's determination to avoid the unusual.

There are two sides to every question. In her efforts to
describe usual life Jane Austen sometimes made herself quite
unusual. After all, excitement is quite as common as tranquillity. In refusing to become excited, she became uncommon. She did not seem to believe much in intensity of
feeling. Most of her people could change their affections
without any severe strain. Edmund Bertram, for instance,
did not pay heavily for his disillusions.

After wandering about and sitting under trees with Fanny all the
summer evenings, he had so well talked his mind into submission
as to be very tolerably cheerful again....I purposely abstain from
dates on this occasion, that everyone may be at liberty to fix
their own, aware that the cure of unconquerable passions, the
transfer of unchanging attachments, must vary much as to time
in different people. I only entreat everybody to believe that
exactly at the time when it was quite natural that it should be so,
and not a week earlier, Edmund did cease to care about Miss Craw-
ford, and became as anxious to marry Fanny as Fanny herself
could desire.

Jane Austen does not appear to have recognised the existence
of incurable griefs. She believed that all *bad* things come
to an end. It depends upon our mood whether we find this
a poor or a satisfying consolation. Most people with any
breadth of experience have sampled two forms of comfort.
They have taken the relief of knowing the worst, or the
relief of forgetting it. There is a great solace in high impassioned thinking. It has something of the refreshment
which we feel in attaining a lofty, difficult summit; though we
rest on top of the mountain, mind and eyes are alert. There
is also the solace of a still and tranquil heart; and this is more
like the soothing influence of scented meadows, or dim, grave
forests. When we turn to books we can choose the form of
solace which our moods require. In Jane Austen we find
the repose of the quiet valleys and cool shadowed waters.

III

THE STUDY OF HUMAN TEMPERAMENT

In monotony there is no relief; but Jane Austen seemed incapable of monotony. She never repeated herself. Her books are all alike in spirit, but subtly different in matter. She handled the same type of character, only to produce entirely distinct individuals. Mrs Allen and Lady Bertram both belong to the insipid order of human beings; but we should never mistake one for the other. There is an almost indescribable difference in tone. We can take a few lines from the description of the ball-room at Bath:

"How uncomfortable it is," whispered Catherine, "not to have a single acquaintance here!"

"Yes, my dear," replied Mrs Allen with perfect serenity, "it is very uncomfortable indeed."

Place that beside the description of Lady Bertram, "One of those persons who think nothing can be dangerous, or difficult, or fatiguing to anybody but themselves."—At once we see that each woman has something which marks her out from the other. Though very much alike, they are not identical.—In the same way we never get confused among the different varieties of brusque, or critical, or outspoken characters. Even if the proper names were erased from the printed page, we should soon learn to recognise the utterances of Mr Darcy, or Mr Bennet, or Mr Knightley. In this connection it is interesting to note that the harsher figures in Jane Austen usually confine their harshness to speech. With Charlotte Bronte it is entirely different. Mr Darcy, for instance, is a brusque man, but he gives offence chiefly by his words or silences. On the other hand Mr Rochester is equally brusque, but he repels by actions as well as words. In fact Jane Austen portrays her characters mainly through conversation; and it is noteworthy that their conversation is nearly always personal.

It is rather surprising that Miss Austen's affection for

little things did not lead her to a fuller comprehension of children. Occasionally she grouped a few of these small people as part of a suggestive background. "The little Perrys" were used in this way to throw up the figures of their father and Mr Woodhouse. It will be remembered that the latter had tried to extract from the former a condemnation of wedding-cake. But—"There was a strange rumour in Highbury of all the little Perrys being seen with a slice of Mrs Weston's wedding-cake in their hands; but Mr Woodhouse would never believe it."—We see Lady Middleton's children from an entirely adult point of view.—"On every formal visit," remarks the writer, "a child ought to be of the party, by way of provision for discourse."—Of little Anna Maria we hear that she was scratched with a pin, and "inconsolable," but Lady Middleton remembered that last week "some apricot marmalade had been successfully applied for a bruised temple."—We throw only a passing glance at Anna Maria. She is brought forward for the sole purpose of casting some light upon her mother's temperament.—Sometimes we get a swift flashing picture with a child as its subject. Of Catherine Morland's childhood we read: "She was noisy and wild, hated confinement and cleanliness, and loved nothing so well in the world as rolling down the green slope at the back of the house."—But the picture never merges into a story. Usually when Jane Austen is telling us of children, we gather that they are coddled or troublesome. (Against this we should perhaps place the fact that many of her favourite characters have "a good way" with children.) Mrs Price's household was remarkable for "such a superfluity of children, and such a want of almost everything else." There the children were an encumbrance. In other places they appear as ornaments or playthings. But they are hardly ever raised to the status of companions.

This consideration of certain types of people brings us back to the type of mind which delighted in them. In all Jane Austen's work there is a peculiar ironic flavour. Sometimes she appears quite serious, but in dealing with such a "deep" person, it is never safe to trust to appearances. It is

certain that she allowed herself license in no matters; and
even her irony was subject to discipline. She thought that
Mr Bennet had gone too far in his pursuit of absurdities; and
there were certain subjects safe from her laughter. She would
never have "let herself go" like Charlotte Bronte, in making
fun of her father's curates. Still the fact remains that Jane
Austen was "nothing if not critical"; and her criticism was
steeped in laughter.

Her satire pursued many objects, and took many forms.
It sometimes sprang from a kind of fellow-feeling. This
was the case when she portrayed any figure of the cynical
type. She and Mr Bennet had a common hobby—the delighted observation of human eccentricity. In his attitude
of amused detachment he was very close to the standpoint of
his own creator, and well qualified to take a share in her
private diversions. "Sympathy with her characters she
frequently has," wrote the late Sir Walter Raleigh, "identity
never." This is undoubtedly true; but in the case of Mr
Bennet her sympathy was based on kinship.

It is perfectly obvious that much of her satire was completely sympathetic. "I love a fool," declared Charles Lamb
in a burst of infectious fervour. This is a point upon which
he and Jane Austen could have shaken hands; for there is
a mysterious bond of union between all lovers of fools.

> Love reflects the thing beloved,

sang Tennyson. In this case, however, his sentiment is far
from the truth. The love of fools is not always a symptom of
folly. An instinctive delight in absurdity often goes with a
singular delicacy of insight. The temperament of Shakespeare supplies proof of this contention. Jane Austen was
absorbed with the comedy of human folly; Thackeray viewed
it more from the standpoint of tragicomedy. When we come
to Thomas Hardy the blind foolishness of men is surveyed
from the aspect of tragedy.

But Jane Austen provides us with a shelter from tragedy.
We return to consider her happy investigations of eccentricity.
Mr Woodhouse we might take to be a kind of specialist in
prudence. Of his supper-parties we read:

Upon such occasions poor Mr Woodhouse's feelings were in sad warfare. He loved to have the cloth laid, because it had been the custom of his youth; but his conviction of suppers being very unwholesome made him rather sorry to see anything put on it; and while his hospitality would have welcomed his visitors to everything, his care for their health made him grieve that they should eat.

We always think of him in connection with basins of gruel. He welcomed his daughter Isabella with the prospect of this joy.—"You and I will have a nice basin of gruel together. My dear Emma, suppose we all have a little gruel." When his son-in-law had been ill-humoured, peace was restored on the basis of gruel. Mr John Knightley was, "if not quite ready to join him in a basin of gruel, perfectly sensible of its being exceedingly wholesome."—The same prudential considerations lay at the back of his dislike to parties. It will be remembered how he dreaded the Coles' party:

"My dear sir," cried Mr Weston, "if Emma comes away early, it will be the breaking up of the party."

"And no great harm if it does," said Mr Woodhouse, "The sooner every party breaks up the better."

Why, we naturally ask?—A clue is obtained a few chapters ahead, where Mr Frank Churchill's gay preparations for a ball stirred Mr Woodhouse to protest:

That young man (speaking low) is very thoughtless. Do not tell his father, but that young man is not quite the thing. He has been opening doors very often this evening, and keeping them open very inconsiderately. He does not think of the draught. I do not mean to set you against him, but indeed he is not quite the thing.

By way of compensation for timidity, Mr Woodhouse was spared the pains of anticipation.—"Though always objecting to every marriage that was arranged, he never suffered beforehand from the apprehension of any; it seemed as if he could not think so ill of any two persons' understanding as to suppose they meant to marry till it were proved against them."—It is hard to take leave of Mr Woodhouse; and he is only one of many absurd people dear to Jane Austen's heart.

In passing we may observe her peculiar fondness for people who make fools of themselves. She was nowhere more pleased with Catherine Morland than at the moment when her candle went out, leaving her in uncanny darkness, with the mystery of the black chest unsolved; she "sought some suspension of agony by creeping far underneath the clothes." —We also love Catherine best when she is most ridiculous.— The absurd side of a matter usually struck Jane Austen first, and this acts as a good preservative to the milk of human kindness. When Miss de Bourgh drove past the vicarage, Sir William Lucas, "to Elizabeth's high diversion, was stationed in the doorway, in earnest contemplation of the greatness before him, and constantly bowing whenever Miss de Bourgh looked that way."—A few pages later we hear that he was uncommonly silent at Lady Catherine's table.—"Sir William did not say much. He was storing his memory with anecdotes and noble names."—Thackeray often shows more venom in his studies of "toadyism." Major Newcome, for instance, appears in a less amiable light than Sir William Lucas.

Nevertheless it is most rash to generalise on the comparative harshness of the two satirists. Towards certain failings Thackeray exhibited a tenderness quite beyond Jane Austen; and this possibly, because of his wider vision. At times he was more gentle, because more aware of the risks which are to be run. Similarly, if we compare Jane Austen and George Eliot, we find the same difficulty in setting up rigid compartments. Certainly George Eliot was the more compassionate woman, but there were limits to her pity. She would not have tolerated Willoughby's excuses; and hers is an intolerance which commands respect. There would be some hope and satisfaction in having George Eliot for a judge; but most people would fight shy of Jane Austen. She did not see every side of the question. She made up her mind once and for all. She was constant in her affections, but merciless in her dislikes. If she had become thoroughly angry, there would have been more hope of a reaction towards leniency; but she neither lost her temper nor changed her estimates. She did not like the social insincerity shown by Sir John and Lady Middleton in their attitude to Marianne's music. She heartily disapproved of Mr John Dashwood, who "never wished to offend anybody, especially anybody of good fortune." In passing we may notice that the satire of his worldliness is undoubtedly more stinging than anything in Thackeray.

His manners to *them* (that is, his sisters) though calm, were perfectly kind; to Mrs Jennings, most attentively civil; and on Colonel Brandon's coming in soon after himself, he eyed him with a curiosity which seemed to say that he only wanted to know him to be rich to be equally civil to *him*.

We feel that when Jane Austen has found something bad to say about these people, it will be very hard for her to think anything good of them.—She showed the same rooted antipathy to Mrs Norris;—"Her love of money was quite equal to her love of directing, and she knew quite as well how to save her own as to spend that of her friends."—She was equally frigid in her disapproval of the Miss Bertrams' indifference to their father's departure.—"The Miss Bertrams were much to be pitied on this occasion; not for their sorrow, but for their want of it."—Without doubt Jane Austen enjoyed her pet aversions; and so do we. But that is not the point. The matter for emphasis is this:—*we* would not enjoy being included among her pet aversions. The firmest of us would run a long way to escape such a penalty. However, placed as we are, we can afford the bliss of her "imperfect sympathies." We can treat ourselves to a thoroughly long quotation:

After a proper resistance on the part of Mrs Ferrars, just so violent and so steady as to preserve her from that reproach which she had always seemed fearful of incurring, the reproach of being too amiable, Edward was admitted to her presence, and pronounced to be again her son.

Her family of late had been exceedingly fluctuating. For many years of her life she had had two sons; but the crime and annihilation of Edward a few weeks ago, had robbed her of one; the similar annihilation of Robert left her for a fortnight without any; and now, by the resuscitation of Edward, she had one again.

So far we have been considering Jane Austen's satire without any specific reference to sex. But all her writings are in their own way, a treatment of the "sex question"; and speaking broadly, her satire is particularly directed against women. Beginning at this point, we shall try to discover something of her outlook upon the woman's problem. It would be easy to draw up a long list of feminine weaknesses subjected to her attacks. She had no mercy on people like Mary Musgrove or Lady Bertram with their affectations of ill health. She was equally severe on the affectation of excitement, and there is a distinct note of approval in her remark that Catherine Morland driving with John Thorpe, was "too young to own herself frightened." She struck through the second Miss Thorpe at another form of insincerity—the affectation of friendship.—She was loitering "between two of the sweetest girls in the world, who had been her dear friends all the morning."—The mere sincerity of an emotion was no passport to her favour; she condemned outright any taint of pampered "sensibility":

Marianne (we are told) would have thought herself very inexcusable had she been able to sleep at all the first night after parting from Willoughby. She would have been ashamed to look her family in the face the next morning, had she not risen from her bed in more need of repose than when she lay down in it.

She was hard on these lurking excesses and insincerities; and she had a keen eye for the petty spites which are generally comprehended under the term "cattishness." It has been said of Shakespeare's Beatrice that she was "neither a kitten nor a cat"; and in Jane Austen there is the same indefinite feline suggestion. She had within her a cat-like strain which sharpened her perception of its existence in other people. There is a distinct prick behind the velvety smoothness of this sentence: "Human nature is so well disposed towards those who are in interesting situations, that a young person who either marries or dies, is sure of being kindly spoken of."—The sharp claws came out swiftly whenever Miss Bingley or Mrs Hurst was anywhere within reach.—"Their powers of conversation were considerable. They could describe an entertainment with accuracy, relate an anecdote

with humour, and laugh at their acquaintance with spirit."—
The smallness of small talk was to Jane Austen an unfailing
subject of irony; so also was the littleness of prejudice.
Mrs Price, so harassed with the problems of domesticity,
responded immediately to the stimulus of her servant's
millinery; on her way to church she was "only discomposed
if she saw her boys run into danger, or Rebecca pass by with
a flower in her hat."

Though by no means a "new woman," Jane Austen had
sufficient proper pride to uphold the virtues of her own sex.
Her women were obsessed by the game of matrimony, but
some of them, anyhow, played it without desiring any
handicap. Her clever women were on a practical equality
with her clever men; and even Fanny, though not at all
a brilliant heroine, claimed a right to her own point of
view. "I think," she said, "it ought not to be set down as
certain that a man must be acceptable to every woman he
may happen to like himself." Elizabeth acted on the same
principle when she refused Mr Collins.

Generally speaking, Jane Austen's women were not at all
simple. They all had a game in hand, and many of them
were "crack" players. Their apparent artlessness was often
the result of a carefully studied pose:

Where people wish to attract (we read), they should always be
ignorant. To come with a well-informed mind, is to come with
an inability of ministering to the vanity of others, which a sensible
person would always wish to avoid. A woman, especially, if she
have the misfortune of knowing anything, should conceal it as
well as she can.

It will be admitted that, as a whole, the men were more
transparent than the women. They were not so careful to
conceal their cards.

This is chiefly the negative side of the picture. If we turn
to the portraits of Jane Austen's heroines, we shall obtain
a more positive impression. It is sometimes assumed that
Fanny Price was the author's favourite; but Fanny was too
fragile of temperament to stand as an adequate representative.
The portrait which seems to have approached most closely
to Jane Austen's ideal type, is that of Anne Elliot. She had

common sense, and "a good deal of quiet observation."
Ingenuous herself, she "prized the frank, the open-hearted,
the eager character beyond all others." She possessed an
innate delicacy of feeling; and Captain Wentworth discovered
in her what he wanted—"a strong mind and sweetness of
manner." It will be found that Jane Austen's heroines usually
answer in a greater or less degree to this description; they
were quiet-voiced, but not insipid. It has been said that
brave men are "all vertebrates; they have their softness on
the surface, and their toughness in the middle." Jane Austen
and Charlotte Bronte were at one in their dislike of the
invertebrate woman. What they most appreciated was an
unobtrusive efficiency. They both described aspects of life
where the woman's touch is strongly in evidence. It is true
that Charlotte went further and would have given to the
woman privileges and functions which her predecessor neither
claimed nor desired. From the standpoint of the "woman's
movement," Jane Austen is sadly out of date. Still there are
certain things in her conception of womanhood which will
never pass out of fashion. She like Mrs Gaskell was saved
from the theories which make for an unsettled equilibrium.
Thus she wrote with a quiet wisdom—of sense as well as
sensibility; of shrewdness as an essential part of grace.

*   *   *   *

Literature, we are told, should teach us to enjoy life or to
endure it. It may be that the moments of joy are a good
preparation for the hours of endurance. In that sense Jane
Austen will surely be admitted as a cultivator of both joy and
endurance. Though her books are restful companions, there
is in their influence nothing drowsy or listless. The tranquillity
of some people is extremely vacant and bloodless; it gives
no refreshment. But Jane Austen had in some measure the
gift of healing; her disciplined vitality exerts a soothing
power. There is some light reading acceptable to none but
invalids, and yet it is lacking in all medicinal quality. Jane
Austen does not drug her readers; but she supplies them
with a tonic. There is a distinction between a tonic and a
daily food; and it is by no means certain that she can be
accounted a "giver of bread." Nevertheless it sometimes

happens that we need a tonic to restore our appetite for plain fare. At times like these, when the mental taste is jaded, Miss Austen's novels are remarkably efficacious.

To change the metaphor:—we do not usually choose to live with Jane Austen; we go to call on her. She is not altogether one of us. Perhaps it is that she is too much of a recluse, living apart from the pulse and conflict of great movements; it may be simply that our modes of etiquette have changed. However that may be, it is always a pleasant change to spend some time with her. It gives us respite from the strain and puzzle of our fuller modern days.

That is how Jane Austen appeals to us of the twentieth century; but this is only one point of view. We leave a great deal unsaid if we make no attempt to determine her position as a maker of literary history. There are some people whose social influence is almost inappreciable; without argument or self-advertisement, simply by living their lives, they raise the tone of their society. Jane Austen's literary influence worked after the same fashion. Without making any sensation she achieved her own purposes. By showing what could be done, she helped to maintain the standard of literary excellence. She has made it impossible for any woman to put forward her sex as an excuse for slipshod writing. She did not "teach" the writers who came after her. As we have said, she rarely looked forward. At heart she belonged to the eighteenth century; still she never appeared to look back with any sense of survival or superannuation. She would have "drawn" well with Pope or Addison, Goldsmith or Sheridan. With Fanny Burney she could have found much in common. Those people of the past age would have attracted her, because they never went too far. The Romantic writers of the nineteenth century were too disturbing for her. The Brontes would have made her uncomfortable; and it would have been a strain for her to live beside George Eliot. She would have liked Thackeray; but he, also, had in his blood a certain admixture of the eighteenth century instinct.

Jane Austen was eminently fitted to take her place in an age of transition. While she helped to keep alive the former excellences, she did nothing to retard the processes of new birth. In the midst of a period restless, curious, and impassioned, she preserved her faith in moderation and discipline. Quiet writing such as hers must have had a steadying effect upon a hot-headed and hot-blooded generation. Without obtrusive effort or exertion of visible influence she gave to her world what it most required—an example of reserved and ordered serenity.

THE BRONTES

I

GENERAL INTRODUCTION. FAMILY CHARACTERISTICS

THERE are some things in the Bronte story which fall into the memory, and quietly, firmly, take root. We do not learn them; we hear them once, and then we always remember. One of these unforgettable things is the picture of a simple room, its bareness softened by the flickering shadows of firelight; in it we see three girls pacing the floor, and talking with the strange zest and absorption of those who discern a momentous future. We cannot imagine the sisters sitting by the fire and speaking out the thoughts which stirred within them. They had to keep moving, as it were, in sympathy with their restless dreams and yearnings. They clung to this habit, as to most things, with a wonderful persistence. Even when Emily and Anne were dead, Charlotte could not shake off the old custom, but paced the floor alone. There is something in the spirit of that room which draws us into sympathy with the Brontes' achievements; it was there, in the dusk, that their hopes were most fully and frankly declared; it was there that they felt a secret exhilaration, harmonising in mood with the red glow of firelight, or the stress and cry of the winds—yet leaping far beyond them; it was there that they found the joy, almost bitter in its intensity, of those who are called to be pioneers.

In their own restricted sphere they experienced something of the eagerness felt by Milton as he wrote the opening lines of *Paradise Lost*. They were doing, or about to do, "things unattempted yet." Almost every day of the year they must have realised that they were unlike other people. Nobody in Haworth, nobody whom they had ever met, seemed to speak—not as they spoke, for words often failed them—nobody seemed to *speak* in the same way as they *thought*. Yet they who were struck dumb before their father's parishioners or curates, meant to risk setting down their thoughts in writing for all the world to read them; but at the same time they cherished their incognito with the overwhelming shyness of those who can never forget their own singularity.

For one thing they could never shake off the sense that they were handicapped by sex. Other women had written before them, but never in their way. They did not scrutinise the difference, they did not attempt to bring themselves into line with womanly traditions. It is remarkable that Charlotte published *Jane Eyre* before she had read a line of Jane Austen; and when, later on, she read her books, she did not like them. How could she? There could have been no more incompatible fellowship. Jane Austen could have sat with ease in a drawing room full of her own characters, and would not have put them out of countenance. Who can imagine Charlotte Bronte—or worse still, Emily—talking to Mr Bingley, Mr Darcy, or even Mr Bennet? We may be sure that under these circumstances neither sister could have found a word to say. Still, they would have felt like the speaker in the familiar poem—

> I would that my tongue could utter
> The thoughts that arise in me!

Such thoughts uttered in such a place would have produced a very definite sensation. It would have been something more vital than a case of simple misunderstanding. Everybody in that room would not have understood Jane Austen, but they might have been happy in their dullness—happy because she did not disturb them. We know how she establishes between herself and her readers a sort of dramatic irony. She says things of which only we, who are outside the room, can catch the point. As the late Sir Walter Raleigh put it, "The kingdom of Lilliput has its meaning only when it is seen through the eyes of Gulliver"; and Jane Austen would be the only Gulliver in that room. But such a dramatic irony requires no close friendship before it can be established; it may spring up between casual acquaintances.

Jane Austen commands the interest of her readers without giving herself away in personal confidences. With the Brontes it was different. They had to speak intimately, and with a frank daring. On no other terms could they bring words to their lips. In a modern anthology there is a little poem which might be applied with slight reservations, to the manner of Jane Austen:

O why do you walk through the fields in gloves,
  Missing so much and so much?
O fat white woman whom nobody loves,
Why do you walk through the fields in gloves,
When the grass is soft as the breast of doves,
  And shivering-sweet to the touch?
O why do you walk through the fields in gloves,
  Missing so much and so much?

Assuredly Jane Austen was not a fat, white, and unloved woman; but she touched life daintily with gloved fingers. Straining to miss no part of their heritage, the Brontes gripped it with bare, vigorous hands.

Thackeray has spoken somewhere of the absurdity of raising "a tempest in a slop-basin." Jane Austen never did anything absurd. She would have loved a slop-basin made of rare and delicate china; but she allowed no tempests to sweep through her fragile domain. The Brontes disregarded slop-basins, because they preferred tempests. In those days the avowal of such a taste demanded considerable courage; for it shattered any claims to ladylike decorum. No great winds blew in Jane Austen's quiet retreats; like Mr Worldly Wiseman in Bunyan, she had no fondness for "desperate ventures." This is what distinguishes her satire from much akin to it in Thackeray; in her neat miniature world, there are hardly any risks. Contrast Elizabeth Bennet and Ethel Newcome disentangling themselves from the conventions of their society. We never feel that Elizabeth is in any danger, but we are afraid for Ethel. It is this element of peril that makes Thackeray's presentation of life so much more alluring. The Brontes also felt the magnetism of danger. It will be remembered how Robert Moore met the rioters with a "deep dancing ray of scorn" in his eyes. Still more remarkable is the place where Rochester describes to Jane the menace of his destiny:

During the moment I was silent, Miss Eyre, I was arranging a point with my destiny. She stood there, by that beech-trunk— a hag like one of those who appear to Macbeth on the heath of Forres. "You like Thornfield?" she said, lifting her finger; and then she wrote in the air a memento which ran in lurid hieroglyphics all along the house-front, between the upper and lower row of windows, "Like it if you can! Like it if you dare!"

The Brontes all liked the sensation of holding their heads high when destiny defied them.

It is customary to exalt Jane Austen at the expense of the Brontes. Everybody must admit that the former never attempted anything which she could not achieve, whereas the latter were for ever reaching after ideals beyond their grasp. Yet are we to say nothing for the courage which pursues an elusive ambition? Can we not praise the motive even while we admit defects in the achievement? After all it is with books as with people; we have most fellow-feeling with those which exhibit slight flaws. We are such heretics by nature that we rarely give our whole hearts to the unimpeachable person or the unimpeachable book. Jane Austen is an excellent acquaintance; she flatters us with the sense that we are clever in appreciating her subtleties. Few can hold out against her delicate charm of manner. Still we could not bear to live with her always. She could not be a daily comrade. She and the Brontes were alike in the fact of limitation; this, in itself, may be one of the conditions of originality, for it implies selection. Jane Austen's stories have the scintillating appearance of a drab texture shot with silver; she describes a grey life softly coloured with humour. The Brontes also handled a dull texture, but they dyed it with the glowing colours of passion. Each method is excellent for its own purpose; and without doubt there are some flaws in the deeply coloured texture. Yet we should not be so early Victorian as to turn aside from the high colours of passion. Ruskin has told us that it is a sign of artistic health to like rich primitive colours. Primitive colour is sometimes crude; so is primitive emotion. The Brontes were sometimes crude; but they were always fully alive. This gives to their books a warm living quality, which glows all the brighter when it is placed beside the cool and disciplined serenity of Jane Austen's perfect achievement.

The Brontes were pioneers in the sense of being out-spoken women in a world which tolerated direct speech from the lips of men alone. They were also pioneers in another and more weighty manner. They spoke of life in a relative fashion —not as scientific facts stated impersonally once and for ever, but as truths brought into relation with their own lives, and coloured with their own emotions. However interesting any truth may be in the abstract, it gains a new impetus and grace when we see it through the eyes of another. The Brontes described realities, and reflected on them their own fervour. Their conceptions of reality cannot be exactly our conceptions. But the object described remains permanently, and the mind reflected on the object is also a reality. "The true poem," said Emerson, "is the poet's mind." This is what Hazlitt meant when he made his plea for the imagination which deepens and intensifies the value of common experience.—"Poetry then," he said, "is an imitation of nature, but the imagination and passion are a part of man's nature." In other words, there is something non-human and incomplete in a delineation which does not contain in it some elements of the humanity of the delineator. That theory had been consciously applied to poetry by Wordsworth and Coleridge. It was Coleridge who compared the "modifying colours of imagination" to "the sudden charm which accidents of light and shade, which moonlight or sunset diffused over a known and familiar landscape." It was Wordsworth who carried the theory into practice, and endeavoured to enrich with his own spirit and sympathy the bareness of trivial incidents. By the time the Brontes wrote, these things were becoming recognised in the domain of poetry; but they had not been applied to novels. The Brontes were not entirely original. In their novels they adopted the method which Wordsworth had applied to poetry; but in their hands the method was transformed. While the personal element was deepened, the imaginative outlook was shifted from cool reflection to strong passion.

Charlotte, who was the most conscious artist among the three sisters, avowed her preference for books expressing an author's personality; and she acknowledged in Emily's love of nature, the presence of an inborn sympathy which made things better than they seemed. She said plainly that only those who carried within them a latent beauty could find any beauty in the Yorkshire moors. The passage is long to quote, and yet wonderfully significant.

If she (that is Imagination) demand beauty to inspire her, she must bring it inborn; these moors are too stern to yield any product so delicate. The eye of the gazer must itself brim with "a purple light" intense enough to perpetuate the brief flower-flush of August on the heather, or the sunset-smile of June; out of his heart must well the freshness, that in latter spring and early summer brightens the bracken, nurtures the mosses, and cherishes the starry flowers that spangle for a few weeks the pasture of the moor-sheep. Unless that light and freshness are innate and self-sustained, the drear prospect of a Yorkshire moor will be found as barren of poetic as of agricultural interest; where the love of wild nature is strong, the locality will perhaps be clung to with the more passionate constancy, because from the hill-lover's self comes half its charm.—My sister loved the moors. Flowers brighter than the rose bloomed in the blackness of the heath for her; out of a sullen hollow in a livid hill-side her mind could make an Eden.

What was true of Emily's attitude to Nature was also true of both Charlotte and Emily in their outlook upon human life; within them they carried something which transformed the common experience. It is remarkable that Anne, who never attained to genius, had least of this transforming quality. Her representation of life is more average and normal than anything in the work of her sisters. Huntingdon in *The Tenant of Wildfell Hall* is admittedly nearer to the actual Branwell Bronte than Emily's Heathcliff or Charlotte's Rochester. Anne was content to copy nature, but she could not create. She told a story clearly and simply, but her personality was too faint to colour the ordinary record. She did not survey life, like Charlotte and Emily, through the medium of passion; for she had no passion. Nevertheless we feel that it is the use of a passionate medium which gives the work of Charlotte and Emily its quality of genius. Christina Rossetti's figure dreaming the dream of death, had a veil before her eyes—

> Through sleep, as through a veil
> She sees the skies look pale.

Charlotte and Emily Bronte had a veil of emotion hung between them and the external reality; but it was of no soft uniform rose-colour, it glowed with iridescent lights—

> Innumerable of stains and splendid dyes
> As are the tiger-moth's deep-damask'd wings.

Although this veil lends new shades to the external facts, it does not keep out the air. The spirit of the outside world passes through its fragile texture. Tennyson, it has been said, saw nature through glass, which is a stronger barrier than a veil; it satisfies the eye, but checks all other senses. If there is any twist or unevenness in its surface, it gives a distorted picture, and only by shattering the glass can we escape from the distortion. A veil may give colours which are not in the actual objects under observation; it may fall into thick, blurred folds; but the least movement smoothes out its creases, or blows it entirely aside.—When all is said, the veil is a medium, and not a barrier. It is a means of communication between inner and external realities. Life cannot be regarded as a collection of hard unchanging facts, with no "visionary gleam" upon them. It is best known when it is most strongly felt—when the outer realities have brooding over them the added grace of human emotion, the traces of a human presence, the fragrance and spirit of a human kinship.

II

ANNE BRONTE, 1820–1849

It is customary to dismiss Anne Bronte in a few sentences, and then pass on to the more arresting work of her sisters Charlotte and Emily. Possibly it is right to do so, because Anne lacked their genius; but it is not right to leave her without a few words of praise. Her books are not great books, yet through both of them are scattered passages and phrases which strike a note of quiet charm. It is probable that these instances could be counted on the fingers of one hand; yet no matter how few they may be, their presence should be noted. For example, in the first chapter of *Agnes Grey* the simple home-life and the simple farewell are described with a sort of plain quaintness. Agnes clearly and lightly indicates the general attitude of the bustling family towards herself.— "It was time enough for me to sit bending over my work like a grave matron, when my favourite pussy was become a steady old cat." There is a pretty little touch set in the midst of the pathos of her farewell; she "kissed the cat, to the great scandal of Sally, the maid." But Anne Bronte could not keep up to even this unpretentious level. After the first chapter of *Agnes Grey* it is hard to find anything with the slightest flavour of distinction.

Again in the first chapter of *The Tenant of Wildfell Hall* we catch gleams of the same quiet humour—for instance, in the flashing picture of Gilbert Markham watching Mrs Graham at church. He describes his sudden shamefaced realisation of his own conspicuous curiosity, and then adds: "I glanced round the church to see if anyone had been observing me; but no—all, who were not attending to their prayer-books, were attending to the strange lady." It is a picture which would have lent itself to the imagination of Mr Hugh Thomson or Mr C. E. Brock. Again, it always seems to me that while the mere story, the central conception of the book, is worthless, there is a freshness of spirit which revives the scenes set in the open air. It may be that hill-lovers have a kindly feeling towards any book which brings a passing oblivion of the loud, hot streets, and stirs memories of the cool, strong breath blowing over high and open places. In reading of the solitary hall, we always seem to feel the companionship of brown hills sloping up before us; sometimes we feel the wind in our faces. We feel it when we stand in the dishevelled garden, with the "goblinish appearance" of its clipped trees grown out of shape; we feel it even more keenly on the evening when Gilbert comes up the hill, and sees the sun crimsoning the windows, while his own heart is shadowed by disillusion. The phrases rise to a sudden distinction—"That spot, teeming with a thousand recollections and glorious dreams—all darkened now, by one disastrous truth."—All the Huntingdon episodes are futile. As Charlotte has told us, Anne's heart was not in them. They are not described with the sharpness which alone might make such squalor tolerable. It is only on that bleak lonely hillside, away from Huntingdon and his sordid story, that we feel any artistic exhilaration. It was in the atmosphere of that wild pure country that Anne wrote her finest passage—a paragraph beautiful in its imagery, its music, and its poetry of conception:

I have a confused remembrance (says Gilbert) of...long hours spent in bitter tears and lamentations and melancholy musings in the long valley, with the west wind rushing through the overshadowing trees, and the brook babbling and gurgling along its stony bed—my eyes for the most part, vacantly fixed on the deep, checkered shades restlessly playing over the bright sunny grass at my feet, where now and then a withered leaf or two would come dancing to share the revelry, but my heart was away up the hill in that dark room where she was weeping desolate and alone—she whom I was not to comfort, not to see again, till years of suffering had overcome us both, and torn our spirits from their perishing abodes of clay.

The freshness of Nature adds poignancy and edge to the intensity of human sorrow. As a rule Charlotte and Emily found in Nature not this contrast of mood, but an affinity and sympathy with their own emotions. Nevertheless in this passage Anne shows the family resemblance more strongly than in any other place. Particularly in the last phrases we catch echoes of the music which flows through *Wuthering Heights*.

This is probably all that can be said in praise of Anne Bronte's work. We are bound to admit that fundamentally she was unsound. She rose to excellence in scattered phrases, but lacked the genius which binds details into an organic harmony. Yet we should not withhold our gratitude for even a few fragments of beauty.

III

CHARLOTTE BRONTE, 1816–1855

IN studying Charlotte Bronte's achievement, it is best to work, as Carlyle would say, "from the skin inwards," considering her, first as a reader and student of other minds; then as a tentative artist; and lastly as the essential personality whose opinions, tastes, and passions determined the external qualities of her work.

Though the Brontes were all great readers, it can hardly be said that they were deep or accurate scholars; certainly they were not bookworms. Like Lucy Snowe, Charlotte had no "contraband appetite for unfeminine knowledge." We hear her speaking through the lips of her own creation: "Alas! I had no such appetite. What I loved, it joyed me by any effort to content; but the noble hunger for science in the abstract, the godlike thirst after discovery—these feelings were known to me but by briefest flashes." To all the sisters knowledge was a means to an end; it would enable them to drink more deeply of experience. When Charlotte wrote so fervently of the projected visit to Brussels, she was not thirsting—as George Eliot might have done—for mere instruction. "I so longed," she wrote, "to increase my attainments—to become something better than I am. A fire was kindled in my heart which I could not quench." George Eliot would not have thought in that way of what she would *become*. Whereas she would have sought to escape from herself into books, Charlotte sought to realise herself more fully through their assistance. To her the intellectual woman was one whose interests were quickened by knowledge; she liked thoughtful, book-loving women, because she expected to find in them a greater vitality. She could not muster up a great enthusiasm for women without intellectual interests. We find, for instance, Jane Eyre surveying Miss Rosamond

Oliver's fascination with an extremely tempered admiration:

She was very charming, in short, even to a cool observer of her own sex like me; but she was not profoundly interesting or thoroughly impressive. A very different sort of mind was hers from that, for instance, of the sisters of St John.

Charlotte went naturally to books of a certain class. Anything outside that—for example, Jane Austen's novels—she read from a sense of duty. Her whole being turned to romance, as a flower seeks the sunlight. She loved the mystery and power of German romances. She told Ellen Nussey that all novels after Scott's were "worthless." (It should be noted, however, that this was said before she had fallen under the spell of Thackeray.) The verses of *Marmion* comforted Jane Eyre as she sat reading by the fire with the "muffled fury of the tempest" beating at her doors:—"I soon forgot storm in music." Charlotte's admiration of Borrow agrees with the same romantic tendency. So is her description of Jane Eyre's childish reading. It was the pictures which she loved:

The words in these introductory pages connected themselves with the succeeding vignettes, and gave significance to the rock standing up alone in a sea of billow and spray; to the broken boat stranded on a desolate coast; to the cold and ghastly moon glancing through bars of cloud at a wreck just sinking.

Later in the book there is an episode where Jane shows her pictures to Rochester; something in their gleaming eeriness and power is reminiscent of Blake. However, it is difficult to say whether Charlotte had ever heard of that strange wild poet and dreamer.—We hear much of her love for the Bible. When a small child she told her father that it was the best book in the world; and M. Héger of Brussels reported on her: "Elle était nourrie de la Bible." One always feels that it was the romance of the Bible that held her affection. The conversation between Mr Brocklehurst and Jane is wonderfully filled with meaning:

"Do you say your prayers night and morning?" continued my interrogator.
"Yes, sir."

"Do you read your Bible?"

"Sometimes."

"With pleasure? Are you fond of it?"

"I like Revelation, and the book of Daniel, and Genesis, and Samuel, and a little bit of Exodus, and some parts of Kings and Chronicles, and Job and Jonah."

"And the Psalms? I hope you like them?"

"No, sir."

"No? Oh, shocking! I have a little boy younger than you, who knows six psalms by heart; and when you ask him which he would rather have, a gingerbread nut to eat or a verse of a psalm to learn, he says: 'Oh! the verse of a psalm! Angels sing psalms,' says he; 'I wish to be a little angel here below'; he then gets two nuts in recompense for his infant piety."

"Psalms are not interesting," I remarked.

They were not interesting to little Jane, because she was thirsting for *stories*. Emotional as Charlotte Bronte might be, she was like Jane in that she was never quite at home with even the most impassioned psychology or reflection. If psychology and reflection were to touch the core of her sympathies, they had to be united to some concrete narrative. This is one case where she was the direct antithesis of George Eliot.

It is true that romance was not the single element of her nature. She possessed a piquancy which brought her at times into the atmosphere of Dickens. *Jane Eyre* was published four years after *Martin Chuzzlewit*, and sometimes we almost hear Mr Pecksniff's voice in the utterances of Mr Brocklehurst.—"Oh, madam," he cried, "when you put bread and cheese instead of burnt porridge into these children's mouths, you may indeed feed their vile bodies, but you little think how you starve their immortal souls!"—Still, this parody of cant is not altogether in the Dickensian manner. It is more malicious, but less sleek and insinuating. It was only occasionally that Charlotte had recourse to this particular kind of irony; Dickens used it as a habitual weapon. She read *David Copperfield*, published two years after *Jane Eyre*, and acknowledged the affinity which had been pointed out to her. The two novelists were brought together by their appreciation of a child's standpoint. Mr Brocklehurst was remembered by the little girl as "the black marble clergy-man"; we call to mind the first impression he made.—"Curt-sying low, I looked up at—a black pillar!—such at least, appeared to me, at first sight, the straight, narrow, sable-clad shape standing erect on the rug; the grim face above the shaft by way of capital."—When Dickens wrote *David Copperfield*, he seemed to look at objects from the same angle. To quote Mr Chesterton, he gives us an impression

of the little Copperfield living in a land of giants. It is at once Gargantuan in its fancy, and grossly vivid in its facts; like Gulliver in the land of Brobdingnag when he describes mountainous hands and faces filling the sky, bristles as big as hedges, or moles as big as molehills....We feel the sombre Murdstone coming upon the house like a tall storm striding through the sky.

Nevertheless, this, which is the prevailing mood in the early chapters of *David Copperfield*, appears quite intermittently, and less vigorously in *Jane Eyre*; and it is impossible to believe that Dickens caught his sustained manner from a few sentences in a previously published book.—In yet another point Charlotte had some affinity to him—and this, in her love of oddness and variety. But her taste was not so much grotesque as grim; it has a note of austerity, quite different from the revelling zest of Dickens. It was Rochester's harshness of manner that appealed to Jane as bizarre, and therefore attractive.—"The eccentricity of the proceeding was piquant. I felt interested to see how he would go on."

There was still another note—in literature as well as in life—which appealed to Charlotte Bronte. That was the note of sincerity. It was this quality which she found most admirable in Carlyle. (Ruskin, whom she praised in the same breath, probably attracted her through the poetic beauty of his style—an element of romance.) Her love of sincerity is most strongly evidenced by her attitude to Thackeray. He seems to have been the only contemporary writer whom she placed on a pedestal. She does not appear to have admired the brilliance and keenness of his satire. She sus-pected anything like a habit of disdain; and it was possibly for this reason that she disliked Jane Austen. It was not Thackeray's satire, but its motive that won her reverence.

She called him a "regenerator," and looked on his work as
a sharp purge and tonic. She admired his direct way of
stating truths, however unpleasant they might be. It is
remarkable that he found in her the characteristic honesty
which she most admired in him. "I remember," he said,
"the trembling little frame, the little hand, the great honest
eyes. An impetuous honesty seemed to me to characterise
the woman."—It is also noteworthy that Charlotte did not
care for Mrs Browning—and because her style was not
straightforward. She absolutely refused to express any raptures over "a certain wordy, intricate, obscure style of
poetry, such as Elizabeth Barrett Browning writes." It was
an essential part of her nature to distrust anything—whether
in life or in style—which did not go directly and simply to
the point. Herein lies much of the steady charm found in
her character and writing.

When we come to consider Charlotte Bronte as an
artist, we are bound to discover the impress left on her
writing by her taste in books. A desultory reader, she constructed plots partaking of the same nature. It has often
been complained that they are too rambling. They curve in
and out, sometimes running, sometimes sauntering. In an
early school report it was set down that Charlotte was
altogether clever, but knew nothing "systematically." It is,
of course, always better to have a good plot than a bad one;
still, as Shakespeare has proved, writers can cover a multitude
of sins in this direction, if only by the presence of stronger
and more inspiring virtues. It is always pleasant to remember
anything about Lamb, and among other matters, his worries
over a projected play—particularly with regard to the plot;
he believed he would have "to omit it altogether." Sometimes Charlotte came perilously close to this daring expedient
of altogether omitting a plot, and nobody can say the result is
entirely satisfactory. Still there is always this to be said; she
was endeavouring to describe life, not a conventional design;
and to the deep relief of most people, life is not a desperately
systematic business. This weakness of plot shows itself very
plainly in her love of digressions. It is strange that Charlotte,

who loved the direct phrase, did not love the direct plot. She lingered by the way to describe each member of the Yorke family with the detailed attention usually found in obituary notices.—It has been complained of *Villette* that she described Lucy's life as if she were writing a diary. The acting of Vashti, for instance, had no connection with the actual story; it made absolutely no difference to the big things in the lives of the chief characters. M. Héger praised Emily's logical power. He could not have paid the same compliment to Charlotte. It is this logical faculty which makes *Wuthering Heights*, in spite of all defects, a more compact story than *Jane Eyre* or *Shirley* or *Villette*. Charlotte had not sufficient logic to omit the inessential.

Although she was a desultory reader, Charlotte had an instinctive perception of the spirit of a book, and she estimated the relative value of her own writings with a tolerably correct insight. She seems to have had more misgivings about her later novels than about *Jane Eyre*. In one place she compared *Shirley* with its predecessor, and said its "dryer" matter might suit the dryer minds of her critics. However, we should never allow ourselves to forget her own justification:

I did not hurry (she wrote), I tried to do my best, and my own impression was that it was not inferior to the former work; indeed I had bestowed on it more time, thought, and anxiety; but great part of it was written under the shadow of impending calamity, and the last volume, I cannot deny, was composed in the eager, restless endeavour to combat mental sufferings that were scarcely tolerable.

Remembering the havoc which death had made in her life, we feel the same shame after carping at *Shirley*, as we should do after criticising *The Fair Maid of Perth* or other novels written in the period of Scott's declining power.—She felt the same want of confidence when she looked at *Villette*:

I can hardly tell you (she wrote to Mr Smith) how I hunger to hear some opinion besides my own, and how I have sometimes desponded and almost despaired, because there was no one to whom to read a line, or of whom to ask a counsel. *Jane Eyre* was not written under such circumstances, nor were two-thirds of *Shirley*.

We find her answering with a touch of weariness criticisms of Lucy's character and of the disjointed plot, or speaking with apprehension of her doubtful success in the study of Paulina. Every reader has experienced a sense of depression, a languid weight settling over some passages of *Shirley* and *Villette*; but there ought to be some consolation in the fact that Charlotte felt the same oppression. By her self-knowledge she commands our respect. She did not give out inferior work believing it was superior. The same cannot always be said of George Eliot.

In yet another respect she stood apart from George Eliot. She inculcated no doctrines. Miss Mary Taylor wrote of *Jane Eyre*, "It is impossible to squeeze a moral out of your production."—Charlotte fully recognised her position. "To teach," she said, "is not my vocation. What I *am*, it is useless to say. Those whom it concerns feel and find it out." In other words, she realised that by the very nature of things, her appeal being emotional, had also to be indefinite. It was not that she despised the novel with a purpose. She said quite humbly that for her it was "of no use trying" to handle topics of the day:

Nor can I write a book (she said) for its moral. Nor can I take up a philanthropic scheme, though I honour philanthropy; and voluntarily and sincerely veil my face before such a mighty subject as that handled in Mrs Beecher Stowe's work, *Uncle Tom's Cabin*. ...I doubt not, Mrs Stowe had felt the iron of slavery enter into her heart, from childhood upwards, long before she ever thought of writing books. The feeling throughout her work is sincere, and not got up.

Charlotte, knowing her resources, accepted her limitations. Jane Austen showed the same self-knowledge when she refused to write a court-novel. This voluntary restriction, although in such different directions, is one of the few instances where the two women stood on common ground.

This recognition of her own weakness and limitation gives nothing new to our estimate; we could easily discover these defects for ourselves. In other points Charlotte's self-knowledge gives valuable assistance to our appreciation of her work. One thing we could not have guessed without a clue from her confessions; this is her deliberate surrender to an overmastering creative impulse. She said that Emily, when under the sway of the power, was unconscious of the effect she had produced. It was, however, of her own experience that she spoke most clearly. Here it should be pardonable to collect a few of her utterances, because nothing else can carry the same weight as her own words, describing a curious and habitual psychological experience. She told Mrs Gaskell, that although she discussed her plots with her sisters as they paced the floor of their room, she hardly ever altered anything she had written, "so possessed was she with the feeling that she had described reality."—To Mr Lewes she spoke more fully:

When authors write best (she said) or at least when they write most fluently, an influence seems to waken in them which becomes their master—which will have its own way—putting out of view all behests but its own, dictating certain words, and insisting on their being used, whether vehement or measured in their nature; new-moulding characters, giving unthought of turns to incidents, rejecting carefully elaborated old ideas, and suddenly creating and adopting new ones.—Is it not so? And should we try to counteract this influence? Can we indeed counteract it?

When the mood departed, she put away her work, and like the Scholar Gypsy, waited "for the spark from heaven to fall."—Perhaps it is this patient waiting for the mood which casts its weight over portions of her later books. This is how she described the pauses in the composition of *Villette*.— "When the mood leaves me (it has left me now, without vouchsafing so much as a word or a message when it will return) I put by the manuscript, and wait till it comes back again. God knows, I sometimes have to wait long—*very* long it seems to me."—In *Villette* we find some most striking instances of this faculty in operation. One is the death of M. Paul. Now, Charlotte was convinced that M. Paul would have to be drowned; her father wished him to live. "But," says Mrs Gaskell, "the idea of M. Paul Emanuel's death at sea was stamped on her imagination till it assumed the distinct force of reality; and she could no more alter her fictitious endings than if they had been facts which she was relating." To please her father she compromised to the extent of veiling his fate "in oracular words."—Sometimes she courted the creative impulse, lured it, and won it. When she wished in a certain part of *Villette*, to describe the effects of opium, she had no experience to guide her; and, as in other cases—unfortunately we do not know which ones—she thought over the matter intently many nights before falling to sleep; till suddenly one morning she woke up "with all clear before her, as if she had in reality gone through the experience, and then could describe it word for word as it had happened."—Most significant of all is her emphatic defence of Emily on the grounds that it was not she who spoke, but some compelling spirit within her. The quotation though long is of such very great importance that it cannot be omitted:

Whether it is right or advisable to create beings like Heathcliff I do not know; I scarcely think it is. But this I know; the writer who possesses the creative gift owns something of which he is not always master—something that, at times, strangely wills and works for itself. He may lay down rules and devise principles, and to wills and principles it will perhaps for years lie in sub-jection, and then, haply without any warning of revolt, there comes a time when it will no longer consent to "harrow the valleys or be bound with a band in the furrow"—when it "laughs at the multitude of the city, and regards not the crying of the driver,"—when, refusing absolutely to make ropes out of sea-sand any longer, it sets to work on statue-hewing, and you have a Pluto or a Jove, a Tisiphone or a Psyche, a Mermaid or a Madonna, as fate or inspiration direct. Be the work grim or glorious, dread or divine, you have little choice left but quiescent adoption. As for you—the nominal artist—your share in it has been to work passively under dictates you neither delivered nor could question, that would not be uttered at your prayer, nor suppressed nor changed at your caprice. If the result be attractive, the World will praise you, who little deserve praise; if it be repulsive, the same World will blame you, who almost as little deserve blame.

From this it would seem that the creative artist is an almost irresponsible tool, held and used by a passion—it may be for good, it may be for evil. It is possible that Charlotte Bronte believed this to be literally the case. It is,

however, undeniable, that she also believed it possible to
guard against the temptations of the creative impulse. She
sought the safeguard, and practised the discipline of a
habitual and unswerving truthfulness. She allowed herself
no technical finish incompatible with reality. It was for this
reason that she transferred the interest in *Villette* from one
set of characters to another. She knew that she was weakening
the construction of her plot; she knew that her action would
be unwelcome to readers who liked the flowery course of
romance; but she averred that the choice made was "com-
pulsory on the writer," for in no other way could she have
been consistent with truth. Between the lines we can read
her admiration of Anne deliberately pursuing an unpleasant
task, because she would not flinch from candour.—"She
hated her work (that is, in *The Tenant of Wildfell Hall*), but
would pursue it. When reasoned with on the subject, she
regarded such reasonings as a temptation to self-indulgence.
She must be honest, she must not varnish, soften, or conceal."
Charlotte admitted that Anne was the last person to tackle
such a topic as Huntingdon's career; but since Anne had
taken up the subject, Charlotte could not help respecting
the courage which faced intolerable facts.—She studied
Thackeray "with reverence" because he appeared to her "as
the first of modern masters, and as the legitimate high priest
of Truth." She felt that he and Dickens had "access to the
shrine and image of Truth," an access denied her by reason
of her limited experience. She accepted these limitations,
and resolved to keep within their boundaries.—"Not one
feeling on any subject, public or private, will I ever affect
that I do not really experience." It was to Mrs Gaskell that
she opened her heart, telling her of the temptation to follow
the line of least resistance, and take the average standpoint,
to write smoothly and plausibly when truth demanded a
severe and solitary candour:

A thought strikes me (she wrote), Do you, who have so many
friends,—so large a circle of acquaintance,—find it easy, when you
sit down to write, to isolate yourself from all these ties, and their
sweet associations, so as to be your *own woman*, uninfluenced or
swayed by the consciousness of how your work may affect other

minds; what blame or what sympathy it may call forth? Does no luminous cloud ever come between you and the severe Truth as you know it in your own secret and clear-seeing soul? In a word, are you never tempted to make your characters more amiable than the Life, by the inclination to assimilate your thoughts to the thoughts of those who always *feel* kindly but sometimes fail to *see* justly?

In this, at least, she and George Eliot had something in common:—they both set before them, as the ultimate principle, an austere and unshrinking fidelity to fact.

What then was the technical result of this deliberate artistry? Of Charlotte's plots we have had much to say by the way. The course of Emily's single novel is like a great fire set alight, and burning its way along till there is nothing left to consume. The fire is in Charlotte's novels also, but it dies down and smoulders, till some new wind of passion rises to fan it again into quickly falling flames. This is less true of *Jane Eyre* than the later books; but even there the narrative does not, like the runner of a race, speed from beginning to end; and we cannot help feeling that Charlotte meant it to rush. The pauses are not what they would be in a Shakespearean play, a cool retreat from tension and heat of episode, but a symptom of flagging energy. It never fits into the plan of Charlotte Bronte's novels that the pilgrim should go to sleep in the arbour half way up the Hill Difficulty; and yet it always happens. Again, particularly in the case of *Villette*, she weakened her construction, not only by deviations of *tempo*, but by a still more radical fault. She used melodrama to link up her plot. Often we feel, for example, in the episode of the grey nun, that these fantastic things are simply pieces of clumsy mechanism brought into action to further the dénouement. They are not allied to the living, breathing fragments of narrative, but connecting links of an extremely garish type.

Apart from plot, there is the technical question of prose style; and here Charlotte stands on somewhat firmer ground. We know from Mrs Gaskell that she never wrote down a sentence till she had completely rehearsed it in her own mind. As to the result of this deliberate care, it must be admitted that many of her paragraphs will not bear a close scrutiny; they do not run smoothly, but (like Jane Eyre's disposition) have a "hitch" about them. It is true also that even her single sentences have flaws in their texture. We find her ending a beautiful description of sunset, with words falling like a blight on its delicacy—"at eight o'clock, p.m." Yet Charlotte Bronte has been compared to De Quincey; and even in him we can find similar descents into the matter-of-fact. We must acknowledge that on every side of her art, Charlotte's touch is not absolutely continuous, but when her fingers are controlled to firmness, she achieves something exquisite and unique. We may get a metaphor sustained through half a paragraph, as where she compares Jane's disillusion to the glories of a shattered summer. Sometimes it comes with a quiet and pervasive imagery—for instance the "gentle hoar-frost" surrounding the "pure fine flame" of Paulina's nature. At other times she treads perilously near to sentimentality, and escapes by sheer virtue of simplicity. "I was full of faults," said Lucy, speaking of her crowning interview with M. Paul; "he took them and me all home." Frequently we find a probing sharpness in her phrases. In one of her fragments we read this sentence: "Hers (Mrs Moore's) was one of those nettle tempers which are very troublesome and stinging if touched lightly, but which squeeze tame as dock-leaves under an undaunted finger and thumb." Surely no other writer—most positively no other woman-writer— ever used fiercer imagery in describing the bitterness of mental agony.—Consider how she describes a young lady's sufferings—unusual sufferings, no doubt; but it is easy to understand how any dense recipients of Jane Austen's apparent meekness would be startled at the strength of this language; they would be shaken out of any realisation of the homeless Lucy's exceptional plight:

Somewhat bare, flat, and treeless was the route along which our journey lay; and slimy canals crept, like half-torpid green snakes, beside the road; and formal pollard willows edged level fields, tilled like kitchen-garden beds. The sky too, was monotonously gray; the atmosphere was stagnant and humid; yet amidst all these deadening influences my fancy budded fresh and my heart basked in sunshine. These feelings, however, were well kept in check by the secret but ceaseless consciousness of anxiety lying in wait on enjoyment like a tiger crouched in a jungle. The breathing of that beast of prey was in my ear always; his fierce heart panted close against mine; he never stirred in his lair, but I felt him. I knew he waited only for sundown to bound ravenous from his ambush.

Bottom, who was not given to many compunctions, felt appalled by the idea of bringing in "a lion among ladies"; but here we have a snake and a tiger, brought into the company of our thoughts, and *by* a lady. It recalls Lockhart's swift comment on Jane Eyre—"rather a brazen Miss."

It is unsatisfactory to cull selections from Charlotte Bronte's writings. Perhaps it is because they are so much alive that they cannot be cut to pieces. It is like pulling petals off a flower, and exhibiting them as representatives of its beauty; while the charm has evaporated, and even the very fragrance is diminished. Charlotte's best phrases are not exquisite when segregated. To appreciate them we must light upon them in the midst of a printed page. She was a homeloving person, never truly herself unless in familiar places; and her phrases are like their creator—we have to find them in their own element before we can love them.

So much has been written about Charlotte Bronte, the woman, that it is a matter of extreme difficulty to avoid a vain repetition of other men's words or ideas. When we speak here of Charlotte's experience, it is with no intention of tabulating in parallel columns the incidents of her life and the episodes of her novels. Nor is it necessary to give a list of all her characters with the names of originals appended to them. These things are valuable, but they have been done more than once, and for all time. They are not like matters of critical judgment which are liable to modification; they are established facts.

From Charlotte Bronte's experience it is advisable to take a few broad characteristics—tendencies and principles rather than episodes; these throw light, not so much on the details of her novels, as on their general spirit and tone. In one point particularly Charlotte seems to have represented the family feelings instead of expressing an original stand-point. All the books written by the Brontes have harsh notes sounding through their melodies. The sisters all liked bluntness. Whereas they could wring some consolation out of gaunt scenes and forbidding people, insipidity held out no solace to them. Charlotte must have agreed even with the objectionable Blanche Ingram, when she made her speak in this way: "'A fig for Rizzio!' cried she..., 'it is my opinion the fiddler David must have been an insipid kind of fellow; I like black Bothwell better.'" Charlotte meant something of the same kind when she wrote the following words: "As well might you look for good fruit and blossom on a rootless and sapless tree, as for charms that will endure in a feeble and relaxed nature." She tells us that Lucy was hurt when M. Paul considered her "as inoffensive as a shadow"; she was hurt, because she knew she could be formidable. She held her head higher after scolding Miss Ginevra Fanshawe—and with what sharpness!—"in language of which the fidelity and homeliness might challenge comparison with the compliments of a John Knox to a Queen Mary." This display of severity made her feel that she had shown herself in her true colours.—We could multiply examples proving that Charlotte was set at ease by roughness. When St John left Jane Eyre with a few cold words of reconciliation, she had only one thought in her mind: "I would much rather he had knocked me down." Jane's antipathy to St John's immobility was intensified by her memories of Rochester's temper. It was, indeed, his rudeness which had at first made her feel at home with him.—"The frown, the roughness of the traveller, set me at my ease."

Now, some of this harshness of tone might be accounted for by the fact that Charlotte lived a bare, almost Spartan life, in a bleak district, and dependent on at least *some* hot-tempered companions; but all this could hardly explain the Brontes' obsession by the brutal elements present in human nature. Jane Eyre, "weary of an existence all passive," welcomed the rough entry of Rochester into her life.—Yet we can hardly say that the mere stagnation and monotony of their lives pushed the Bronte sisters into a reactionary brutality. It cannot account for Emily's Heathcliff, or Anne's Huntingdon. It cannot account for the bullies in Charlotte's novels—Edward Crimsworth or John Reid; or her masterful men like Rochester, St John, Mr Helstone, and Robert Moore—(this latter a combination of "a hard dog" and "a dreamer"). Even where Charlotte wished to paint an attractive portrait, she placed hard dominating lines on the features. M. Paul she compared to "an intelligent tiger." She loved him, not in spite of his sharpness, but because of it. She wrote no book which did not lay emphasis on some masterful characters; and often behind this mastery there is a latent suggestion of something savage. How she reached the idea of rightful authority and mastery, it is difficult to say; but there can be no doubt that the savage side of human nature was revealed to her by her own brother Branwell. The experience of living in the same house with such a man could not fail to change the outlook of any woman It was because she knew Branwell that she wrote to Mr Williams with such a vehement sadness:

"Is there a human being," you ask, "so depraved that an act of kindness will not touch—nay, a word melt him?" There are hundreds of human beings who trample on acts of kindness and mock at words of affection. I know this though I have seen but little of the world. I suppose I have something harsher in my nature than you have, something which every now and then tells me dreary secrets about my race, and I cannot believe the voice of the Optimist, charm he never so wisely.

This reference to Branwell Bronte leads to another and more delicate question—the "purity" of his sister's novels. We can compare the judgment passed on this matter by two gentlemen—both clergymen, and both men of letters. Charles Kingsley wrote to Mrs Gaskell in warm admiration of her *Life of Charlotte Bronte*:

Be sure (he said) that the book will do good....It will shame...the prudery of a not over cleanly though carefully whitewashed age, into believing that purity is now (as in all ages till now) quite compatible with the knowledge of evil.

On the other side we have Sir W. Robertson Nicoll declaring that although Charlotte's knowledge of evil left no stain on her character, it tainted her books.—As Sir Roger de Coverley would have suggested, there is "much to be said on both sides." Purity, as Kingsley reminds us, is not worthy of the name, if it is stupidly ignorant of evil, or so dishonest as to turn its back upon facts. On the other hand Sir W. Robertson Nicoll blames Charlotte, not for facing unpleasant facts, but for becoming accustomed to them. Jane had no right to condone Rochester's evil, or to take it as a matter of course. She should have been horrified by it. Rochester was accurate in describing her "peculiar" and "unique" mind as "one not liable to take infection." He was right also when he admired her self-control—"this young girl who stands so grave and quiet at the mouth of hell." That which was true of Jane Eyre was also true of her creator. It is not good for anybody to stand too long looking into the mouth of hell; but Charlotte had to do it—and her sisters also. They could scarcely help losing their capacity for being shocked. Mr Chesterton has distinguished finely between the standpoint of the pessimist and the optimist.—"The pessimist," says he, "can be enraged at evil. But only the optimist can be surprised at it." He goes on to expound the theory that the surprise of the optimist does more than the rage of the pessimist to alter the face of the world. We do little harm to evil by meeting it with the desperate resignation of the man who expects nothing better. The belief in evil is always something negative—it is the negation of goodness; it must be reinforced with a positive belief in goodness. With Charlotte Bronte this, also, was the case.

There is another fact which leaves a deep impress on the character of Charlotte's writings. This is the fact of her sex. In the most obvious and superficial sense, she felt her sex to be a handicap, because it cut her off from self-knowledge of the masculine character; and yet this apparent handicap probably deepened her faculty of observation. The Rev. Charles Merivale soon guessed Currer Bell to be a woman, because this writer described men's faces "so intensely."—This in itself, is a superficial matter. But the fact of sex went deeper. All through life Charlotte felt it as a check. She realised that a woman always had to be making excuses for writing books. In early life she wrote to Southey, and received a reply, kindly given, no doubt, but containing sentences that must have rankled.—"Literature cannot be the business of a woman's life, and it ought not to be. The more she is engaged in her proper duties, the less leisure will she have for it, even as an accomplishment and recreation." Years later, when she married Mr Nicholls, she found to her cost that her husband held the same opinion. When she wrote to Sydney Dobell of the unselfishness of the truly great man, she must have been thinking of her own self-suppression, of the impediments placed in the way of her genius, primarily because she was a woman:

Do we not all know that true greatness is simple, self-oblivious, prone to unambitious, unselfish attachments?...The truly great man is too sincere in his affections to grudge a sacrifice; too much absorbed in his work to talk loudly about it; too intent on finding the best way to accomplish what he undertakes, to think great things of himself—the instrument. And if God places seeming impediments in his way—if his duties sometimes seem to hamper his powers—he feels keenly, perhaps writhes, under the slow torture of hindrance and delay; but if there be a true man's heart in his breast, he can bear, submit, wait, patiently.

Change the gender of the pronouns from masculine to feminine, and this passage seems to tell the story of Charlotte's life.

It was not that she spurned domesticity. We have much external evidence in support of her efficient housekeeping. Possibly the most convincing evidence is that of her own books. A great restfulness lies over many of her pages. It was her womanly insight which led her like her friend Mrs Gaskell to recognise so quickly the spirit of a room. No man could have described, in her way, the room where Lucy found shelter and solace. Even although there are few, if any, references to things distinctively womanly, we feel that the comfort of this room is the result of a woman's handiwork. (Indeed in a previous passage the references are more specific.) We feel that Charlotte also could have made a room like this, tender and soothing to the spirit. It is hard to refrain from quotation:

My calm little room seemed somehow like a cave in the sea. There

was no colour about it, except that white and pale green suggestive
of foam and deep water; the blanched cornice was adorned with
shell-shaped ornaments, and there were white mouldings like
dolphins in the ceiling angles. Even that one touch of colour
visible in the red satin pincushion bore affinity to coral; even that
dark shining glass might have mirrored a mermaid. When I
closed my eyes, I heard a gale, subsiding at last, bearing upon the
house-front like a settling swell upon a rock-base. I heard it
drawn and withdrawn far, far off, like a tide retarding from a shore
of the upper world,—a world so high above that the rush of its
largest waves, the dash of its fiercest breakers, could sound down
in this submarine home only like murmurs and a lullaby.

We know that Charlotte appreciated womanly refinements,
but she desired other things as well. "Women have so few
things to think about," said Caroline Helstone—"men so
many."—Like Rose Yorke, Charlotte had no objection to the
mending of stockings and the darning of sheets; but she
would have exclaimed with Rose: "Am I to do nothing but
that? I will do that, and then I will do more."—St John told
Jane that she was a woman "formed for labour, not for love."
This was a distinction constantly present in Charlotte's
scheme of thinking. With regard to the second alternative,
it is rather significant that she did not marry till late in life,
and also that most of the husbands portrayed in her novels
have a touch of arrogance. Sometimes this appears quite
naïvely, as in the reflections of William Crimsworth—
"Frances was then a good and dear wife to me, because I was
to her a good, just, and faithful husband." At the other
extreme is the arrogance which is another word for brutality.
Mr Moore—a character in an unfinished novel—took away
his wife's letters, and scoffed at her accusation of robbery.—
"Robbed?" he said, "a man rob his wife? What's yours is
mine."—This idea found its way to Emily Bronte's mind
when she described even young Edgar Linton assuming the
airs of the married man, who possesses his wife's house, her
books, her birds, and her pony.—"I told her she had nothing
to give, they were all, all mine." Somewhere in the minds
of both Charlotte and Emily there seemed to lurk a suspicion
of matrimony. They may have come across men who de-

spised women. It is remarkable that Charlotte should have placed in a single book two such confirmed misogynists as Mr Helstone and Joe Scott.

This tendency led her to constant reflections on the relative status of men and women. These things are hackneyed to us now, but they were new then. Caroline Helstone and Shirley Keeldar debated on this topic. In fact the keynote of *Shirley* is this question of woman's rights. The heroine—"Captain Shirley Keeldar"—was a woman successfully performing a man's functions. She bitterly resented her uncle's attempts to deprive her, as a woman, of free speech. Charlotte's whole attitude to the question finds expression in a sharply-turned sentence taken from her letters, and describing the distinction made between a brother and his sisters.—"He is expected to act a part in life; to *do*, while they are only to *be*."

This leads us to the first of St John's alternatives— labour. Charlotte Bronte felt that a woman could not keep her soul alive without one of these alternatives—labour or love. In *Shirley* she had many things to say about old maids; most emphatically she believed that no old maid could afford to be idle. George Eliot records Mr Lewes' impressions of Charlotte: "Lewes," she wrote, "was describing Currer Bell to me yesterday, as a little, plain, provincial, sickly-looking old maid, yet what passion, what fire in her!" That passion and fire would have died if she had been a sickly old maid without a vocation; but Charlotte had her art. She championed the cause of the woman-worker. As she wrote to Mr Williams, "One great curse of a single female life is its dependence." In the same letter she revealed more fully the solace which had come from her work, and the place it held in her life:

Lonely as I am, how should I be if Providence had never given me courage to adopt a career—perseverance to plead through two long weary years with publishers till they admitted me? How should I be with youth past, sisters lost, a resident in a moorland parish where there is not a single educated family? In that case I should have no world at all; the raven, weary of surveying the deluge, and without an ark to return to, would be my type. As

it is, something like a hope and motive sustains me still. I wish
all your daughters—I wish every woman in England, had also
a hope and motive. Alas! there are many old maids who have
neither.

All her arguments may seem trite to us, who have travelled
so much further; but they serve to prove that Charlotte was
characteristically a pioneer—a pioneer, among other things,
of the "feminist" movement.

Only one more reference can be made to the nature of
Charlotte Bronte's experience; and this is not so much her
experience as the way in which she faced it. It does not take
many words to say that Charlotte was courageous; yet this
fact left no slight trace on her life or her books. In her
Biographical Notice of Ellis and Acton Bell she wrote: "Ill-
success failed to crush us; the mere effort to succeed had
given a wonderful zest to existence; it must be pursued."
Fortitude like Charlotte's lends a moral dignity to anything
it touches. Everybody remembers how she began her greatest
book. With her first book rejected and still going the round
of the publishers; with her father suffering from cataract, and
herself as his only companion in a strange town: "In those
grey, weary, uniform streets," wrote Mrs Gaskell, "where
all faces save that of her kind doctor were strange and un-
touched with sunlight to her—there and then did the brave
genius begin *Jane Eyre*." In some ways it seems incomprehensible that she could have written anything fine under
such a weight of depression. In other ways it would seem
incomprehensible and unjust, that one running so bravely,
should fail to win a prize.

Charlotte Bronte was not a woman of many "opinions."
While she had experience and emotion, she did not possess
much in the half-way house between them. Sometimes her
opinions travelled on further, and became emotions. This
is seen in her attitude to certain wholesome traditions.
Charlotte was not a conventionalist like her own Hortense
Moore, who ever disapproved what was unintelligible.
Rather she believed that a belief might grow quietly in the
heart, without any stir of criticism to hinder its development:

in the course of years it would take the form of a tradition always accepted without protest; till suddenly, at a moment of crisis, the folded colourless bud would break into flashing colour. It was so in Jane Eyre's case. "Who in the world cares for you?" asked the tempter. "Or who will be injured by what you do?"—Every reader must remember Jane's indomitable reply, as she feels her traditions closing round her like a wall of defence. I quote a few sentences:

I will hold to the principles received by me when I was sane and not mad—as I am now. Laws and principles are not for the times when there is no temptation; they are for such moments as this when body and soul rise in mutiny against their rigour; stringent are they; inviolate they shall be....They have a worth—so I have always believed; and if I cannot believe it now, it is because I am insane—quite insane; with my veins running fire, and my heart beating faster than I can count its throbs. Preconceived opinions, foregone determinations, are all I have at this hour to stand by; there I plant my foot.

In other cases the opinion remained unwarmed by passion. This is true of her attitude to democracy. We get the impression that Charlotte had never made up her mind on this subject. She had a few ideas, but they did not cling well together. In general her tendency was not strongly democratic. She recognised the necessity for philanthropy, but she had a lurking respect for men like Mr Helstone or Mr Moore, who opposed "the people." True, in the end she made Moore a beneficent employer; but she was quite as sympathetic to him before his conversion as after it. She admitted the sterling qualities of a working man like Farren. She remarked also on the natural politeness of Caroline's Sunday School scholars, with their instinctive feeling for her shyness. Yet she never seemed to mention these things as Mrs Gaskell would have done, out of a full heart.—Jane was attracted to the Rivers sisters because they were "ladies in every point." They received her more generously than did their servant, Hannah. "Prejudices," commented Jane, "it is well known are most difficult to eradicate from the heart whose soul has never been loosened or fertilized by education; they grow there, firm as weeds among stones."—

It is well known, that Charlotte was a Tory, and the Duke of Wellington her hero. It is one case in which she was not a pioneer of new ideas.

There was one other direction in which Charlotte's opinions lacked fire. She was a sincerely devout woman. In the days of her greatest solitude she rested quietly and firmly upon faith. Yet her faith was deficient in passion. It did not possess that piercing quality of all vital truth, penetrating the heart like swords. It was a consolation and a support, but not an exhilaration. Different manifestations of the religious spirit awakened in her mind no corresponding note of sympathy. "I consider," she wrote, "Methodism, Quakerism, and the extremes of High and Low Churchmen foolish, but Roman Catholicism beats them all." She believed in dogmas and forms of religion, holding that they are a support to the finite human intellect. Still these opinions of hers seemed to count for very little. She who could write so fervently on other matters, expressed religious ideas with a surprising coolness. It is true that throughout her letters we find references to religious consolation; there can be no doubt about their sincerity; but they do not carry with them an intense and infectious conviction.

Her portrait of St John is her nearest approach to the study of religious psychology; and we feel that he repelled her. Jane found no healing in his preaching. His prayers elevated, but did not change his nature. In short, his religion had about it no transfiguring quality; it did not alter his natural hardness of temperament. While George Eliot would have comprehended his love of great causes, she would not have exaggerated the potency of such influences; she would have made him less single-minded, and more human. However, Charlotte loved individuals better than movements. She had the same objection to Mme Beck—a far less estimable person than St John. In her she found the same tendency to public charity, the same incapacity for private compassion. To return to St John: we always catch in Charlotte's delineation the hint that he was not so noble as he seemed. His devotion to a great cause was a form of selfish absorption. In renouncing Miss Oliver, he sought a higher reward.—"He would not give one chance of heaven, nor relinquish, for the elysium of her love, one hope of the true, eternal Paradise." While Charlotte tepidly admitted his cause to be right, she hotly insisted that his motives were wrong. The faint appeal made to Charlotte by St John's cause is possibly the most significant instance of her limitations in religious sympathy.

"Charlotte Bronte is great in clouds," writes Mr Frederic Harrison, "like a prose Shelley." It was not only in her love of stormy skies that she resembled Shelley; she was like him in the dominant passion of her nature—its craving for liberty. Sometimes she wrote of the free spirit struggling under oppression. As little Jane Eyre said of herself, "The mood of the revolted slave was bracing me with its bitter vigour." Later in her story we find Jane wrestling to preserve her own identity of soul. Rochester had never claimed what St John took for granted—the mastery of her spirit. Rochester so loved her individuality that he never sought to merge it in his. Jane felt that she was fighting St John with her own soul at stake. She rejected his offers of marriage because she realised what such a marriage would involve: "As his wife—at his side always, and always restrained, and always checked—forced to keep the fire of my mind continually low, to compel it to burn inwardly, and never utter a cry, though the imprisoned flame consumed vital after vital—*this* would be unendurable."

Nevertheless this was not the most constant aspect of her yearnings after liberty. She was not a woman ground down by oppression, but a woman confined in a narrow place. As Sir W. Robertson Nicoll has remarked with a wise sympathy, she gave to her heroines the freedom from which she had been debarred.—"She liberated her heroines that they might win their way to that world of perfect happiness whose doors were closed to her." Jane Eyre looked wistfully across fields and hills to the dim sky-line, and after much stress her cravings found satisfaction. It was never so with her creator. Charlotte's school friend Mary Taylor once told her that she and her little sisters were "like potatoes growing in a cellar." —"She said sadly, 'Yes! I know we are!'" When Mary wrote to her from Belgium, her news was more than Charlotte could bear:

I hardly know (she confided to Ellen Nussey) what swelled to my throat as I read her letter; such a vehement impatience of restraint and steady work; such a strong wish for wings—wings such as wealth can furnish; such an urgent thirst to see, to know, to learn; something internal seemed to expand bodily for a minute. I was tantalised by the consciousness of faculties unexercised,— then all collapsed, and I despaired. My dear, I would hardly make that confession to any one but yourself,—to you rather in a letter than *viva voce*. These rebellious and absurd emotions were only momentary; I quelled them in five minutes. I hope they will not revive, for they were acutely painful.

Rochester's entry revived the stagnant atmosphere of Thornfield Hall—"a rill from the outer world was flowing through it."—Charlotte also felt her life flowing outwards to the world beyond the confining Yorkshire hills. Like her own Lucy, she escaped. She felt what she made Lucy feel on first seeing the dome of St Paul's.—"While I looked, my inner self moved; my spirit shook its always-fettered wings half loose; I had a sudden feeling as if I, who never yet truly lived, were at last about to taste life. In that morning my soul grew as fast as Jonah's gourd."—Like Lucy she went to Brussels; but unlike Lucy, she had to return; and this is what she felt.—"Something in me which used to be enthusiasm, is tamed down and broken. I have fewer illusions; what I wish for now is active exertion—a stake in life. Haworth seems such a lonely quiet spot, buried away from the world." By her own account Mary Taylor again stepped in, and made Charlotte restless, by urging her not to stay at home.—"Such a dark shadow came over her face when I said, 'Think of what you'll be five years hence!' that I stopped and said, 'Don't cry, Charlotte!' She did not cry, but went on walking up and down the room, and said in a little while, 'But I intend to stay, Polly.'"—This was said in 1845; before the five years were out, Charlotte had so mastered fate as to publish *Jane Eyre* and *Shirley*.—But she never escaped from her prison. When Jane took up her obscure duties in the village school, she laid aside her highest faculties.—"What," asked St John, "will you do with your accomplishments? What with the largest portion of your mind, sentiments, tastes?" Jane's reply was significant: "Save them till they are wanted. They will keep."—Charlotte also saved her gifts for the days of fuller opportunity; but they never came. "It is better," she wrote, "to be worn out with work in a thronged community than to perish of inaction in a stagnant solitude." What that solitude must have been we can best imagine from a sentence in one of her letters, describing "the dead silence of a village parsonage— in which the tick of the clock is heard all day long." We should also quote the last sentence of the same letter: "The prisoner in solitary confinement, the toad in the block of marble, all in time shape themselves to their lot." She shaped herself to her lot. She brought her widow's mite to the treasury of literature. We cannot help comparing her with George Eliot in this respect. George Eliot travelled, and met many people. She had all the experience that would have counted for so much to Charlotte, and which seemed in some ways wasted upon herself. Charlotte's receptive, sensitive nature vibrated under new impressions; and how few she received! George Eliot, who was constantly receiving new impressions, had not the same *experiencing* nature; she could not make of her experience what Charlotte Bronte would have done. Such an isolation of outlook could not fail to cast a shade of remoteness on her art. She often described things as if she were looking at them from a distance. When Jane Eyre was a little girl, she looked up to Miss Temple through the idealising mists of childhood. Even when she was a grown woman, she surveyed human beings of a certain type with a curious and uncomprehending detachment. She described the fashionable ladies who visited Thornfield as if they had been nothing more than beautiful and interesting specimens. Take, for example, this sentence.—"All talked in a low but clear tone, which seemed habitual to them." Rochester was right when he told her that she had no eyes to see Thornfield in its true light.—"'The glamour of in- experience is over your eyes,' he answered, 'and you see it through a charmed medium.'"—Charlotte had the same medium between her and much of reality. Even when the medium was dispersed, she retained the habitual pose of the spectator. She liked watching excitement. Most of the piquancy of *Villette* is contained in Lucy's quiet scrutiny of M. Paul's hurricane moods. "I liked," she said, "to see M. Emanuel jealous; it lit up his nature, and woke his spirit; it threw all sorts of queer lights and shadows over his dun face, and into his violet-azure eyes."

This limitation of experience also led Charlotte to a constant questioning of the imagination. Like her own Jane, she could have said, "All sorts of fancies bright and dark tenanted my mind." How far was she to make use of them? She debated this problem in a letter to Mr Lewes who had told her that experience, and not fancy, is of permanent human interest:

I feel (she replied) that this also is true; but dear Sir, is not the real experience of each individual very limited? And if a writer dwells upon that solely or principally, is he not in danger of repeating himself, and also of becoming an egoist? Then, too, imagination is a strong, restless faculty, which claims to be heard and exercised; are we to be quite deaf to her cry, and insensate to her struggles? When she shows us bright pictures, are we never to look at them, and try to reproduce them? And when she is eloquent, and speaks rapidly and urgently in our ears, are we not to write to her dictation?

Years afterwards, she tried the experiment of drawing a character entirely from the imagination. This was Paulina, "old and unearthly" as a child; playing in a sickroom "as noiselessly and as cheerful as light"; carrying with her always a delicate fragrance of personality,—"It was the perfume which gave this white violet distinction, and made it superior to the broadest camellia, the fullest dahlia that ever bloomed." Very characteristic was her childlike attitude to Graham's love of marmalade. She coaxed it out of his mother, carried it to him, and stood over his breakfast, sharing everything with him, except the marmalade: for she did not wish it to appear that she had procured it for herself. " She constantly evinced," added the narrator, "these nice perceptions and delicate instincts." Charlotte set out to make the character the most beautiful in the book; and to a certain extent she succeeded. Paulina's character *is* beautiful; and if we had known nothing else of her creator, we could have been sure of this—that her nature also was beautiful, to have formed such a conception. But the beauty is not convincing or moving. Charlotte herself was not satisfied. She suspected that the defect of the conception lay in its purely fanciful origin—it lacked "the germ of the real." "I felt," she wrote, "that this character lacked substance; I fear that the reader will feel the same. Union with it resembles too much the fate of Ixion, who was mated with a cloud."

Again another outcome of Charlotte Bronte's restricted experience was her dependence upon intuitions. It will be remembered how Jane Eyre's anticipations of marriage were marred and haunted by vague foreboding dreams; at another moment of crisis she heard ringing in her ears a supernatural summons. George Eliot praised the "preternatural" quality of Charlotte's novels. Frequently indeed we get the impression of something almost clairvoyante in her perception of character. She often seemed to walk by faith, not sight. Lucy, for instance, had an instinctive fondness for Mrs Bretton, and an instinctive distrust of Mme Beck. She learnt to understand the inscrutable *directrice*, but could not explain the process.—"Deep into some of Madame's secrets I had entered, I know not how—by an intuition or an inspiration, which came to me, I know not whence."— We feel throughout that Charlotte's psychology was not acquired, but instinctive. She realised the mystery of mental processes, and tried in that most interesting fragment, *The Moores*, to give, not an explanation, but a report, of a certain psychological experience. She vividly described William Moore's intuitive judgments of character:

He had at times a second sight which showed him his acquaintance at once in the spirit and in the flesh....He saw the fine forms of the two ladies in his presence, and he saw something else—a nameless entity accompanying each material shape. This abstraction was honest and healthy, if vulgar, in Sarah Julia's case; in Alicia's it was wrinkled, frigid, and sordid. Her young figure cast on the wall for him an old and ghostly shadow. Critics, if you ever read this, do not misunderstand me, do not say I am writing about figments, or giving you a hero possessed of the Highland second sight. That is not what I mean. Perhaps some of you have the power yourselves; if so, you will seize my intent at once; otherwise I had better not force it on you.

She does not force this on her readers, as it is not a matter for demonstration. It is deeply characteristic of her that she should have rejected logical, scientific inferences in favour of her primitive, human instincts.

All this goes to prove that Charlotte possessed an intensely emotional temperament. We have yet to consider the extraordinary vitality which flowed from her personality into her books. They glow and quiver with life. Nature, the furniture of houses, the expressions on faces—everything seems to throb and beat to the rhythm of the story. In nature she felt the thrill of storm and darkness, the physical sensation of rain and cold. We can take a few scattered instances from *Jane Eyre*.—At Gateshead we have brought before us the chilly depressing walks, the rain-swept garden, the storm beating outside the red room, or the wet dawn of Jane's departure. We see her on her night journey, with "the wild wind rushing amongst trees." Her first sleep at Lowood was broken by the cry of the wind raving "in furious gusts." On a night of windy moonlight she saw Miss Temple approaching her.—She arrived at Thornfield by night—saw the narrow galaxy of lights in the village, the outline of the church tower, and heard the chimes of its clock. When Rochester saw her pictures, he asked her how she had learnt "to paint wind." The scene of confusion after Mason's injury took place in glimmering moonlight. Jane's presentiments of catastrophe were intensified by the restless winds which whirled about the house on the eve of her marriage.— Again, one of the best chapters in *Shirley* is that describing the still night suddenly broken with tumult, as the rioters attacked the mill.—In *Villette*, we see Lucy watching by Miss Marchmont's sick-bed, and listening to the "strange accents in the storm." In the next chapter we find her tracing a dim path, with no light save that of the stars, and the "moving mystery" of the Aurora. Later on she was rowed down the Thames in the night, with the river black "as a torrent of ink." When she arrived at the foreign port, glimmering lights confronted her "like unnumbered threatening eyes." On her first night in Villette, she had to find her way through a dark, wet, and deserted boulevard. She escaped from the class-rooms to watch a thunderstorm, to stay with "the wild hour, black and full of thunder, pealing out such an ode as language never delivered to man—too terribly glorious, the spectacle of clouds split and pierced by white and blinding bolts." Later on there comes a description of a still Continental night.—"Heaven was cloudless and grand with the quiver of its living fires." When Lucy fell ill, she was haunted by the voices of tempest: "Sleep went quite away. I used to rise in the night, look round for her, beseech her earnestly to return. A rattle of the window, a cry of the blast, only replied. Sleep never came." The grey nun swept past her and M. Paul with the wind and rain in her company: "She looked tall and fierce of gesture. As she went, the wind rose sobbing, and the rain poured wild and cold; the whole night seemed to feel her." Most impressive of all is the final chapter, with its description of the passionate storm casting its mysterious shadow over the fate of M. Paul.

This note of storm or darkness was constantly repeated in the music of Charlotte Bronte's moods; but there were other tones in her chords. She was not "all unhappy." In *Villette* she described the "sweet, soft, exalted sound" of pealing chimes. In *Shirley* we find Caroline in love with the beauty of the woods. But it is chiefly in *Jane Eyre* that we feel around us the exquisite and tender companionship of Nature. It does not appear so much in the earlier chapters—not until the winter breaks at Lowood, and spring deepens into that beautiful yet dreary summer, tainted with disease. It is at Thornfield that we find Nature taking on warmth, depth, and sympathy. We feel it first in the "utter solitude and leafless repose" of the still lane where Jane lingered through sunset into the dusky moonlight; till into this hush and wonder there came the resonant clatter of Rochester's arrival. Later in the same evening Jane came out into the exaltation of the night, with her mind uplifted in response to its appeal. She watched the "solemn march" of the moon through the sky: "and for those trembling stars that followed her course, they made my heart tremble, my veins glow when I viewed them." Further on we see Mason going away in the freshness of the dawn—with no sound save the twittering of birds, no stronger colours than the flush of fruit blossoms. Then with the rising of the sun there comes a deepening fragrance from the flowers, a radiant light flashing on the "quiet walks"; and as Rochester talks in the garden with Jane, she is aware of the sweet, inarticulate voice of birds, singing in the tree-tops, high above the human crisis. Through the tension of his words, she feels wonder that the birds should sing and the leaves should whisper while her own heart is hushed "to catch the suspended revelation." The murmurs and movements in the garden, the silence and tension of Jane's heart— these things seem to cling together, to glow, and melt, and fade, like mists. The human passion lends a new dignity to the garden; and the garden sheds its own "tender grace" over the minds of the human actors.—It was in the same garden that Jane talked with Rochester in the warm, scented twilight—till the storm crashed upon them in their new-found bliss.—A few moments before the great catastrophe Jane looked up at the "ruddy morning sky," and a rook wheeling round the grey church-tower; then she passed out of the fresh sunlight into the shadows of the church, and on her way to disaster. After that we come to the moor, with its lonely roads cut through the deep, wild heather. We feel the appeal and shelter of that solitude, its touch upon that elemental passion for the good, strong Earth that bore us; we seem to lie with Jane through the kindly summer day, and into the mystery of the grave star-lit night; till the dawn rises, hard and golden, on the desolation of her spirit.

It is not always Nature which lends its mood to the story. Very often it is something inanimate which casts a shadow over the episodes, or some chance human sound awakes wild echoes falling strangely and weirdly through the ordinary music. Again we must go to *Jane Eyre* for the best illustrations. We do not read far in the story before we find this weirdness of mood reflected back from the dark mirror in

the red room. Jane looked fearfully at the "strange little
figure" there gazing at her, "with a white face and arms
specking the gloom, and glittering eyes of fear moving where
all else was still." A swift darting light on the wall came
from an ordinary lantern, but in her nervous frenzy she took
it to be the "herald of some coming vision from another world."
—When Jane was left alone to tend the wounded Mason, her
terror was intensified by the flickering shadows cast by a
waning candle on the ancient tapestries, the hangings of the
bed, the panels of the cabinet grimly carved with the heads,
of the apostles, and above it the dark, stern crucifix. These
inanimate objects had the power of piercing her emotions;
still more so the weird human noises in that uncanny house.
She could not shake off the repulsion of that strange, mirth-
less laugh, harshly echoing through the still, empty rooms.
On the night when Rochester's bed was set alight, Jane
heard vague murmurs through the house, the sound of fingers
groping at her door, and then a low, grim laugh.—Even the
faces of people—particularly their eyes—are deepened with
a peculiar intensity. Mrs Reed had a "Cairngorm eye";
St John fixed his "blue pictorial-looking eyes" on Jane. Even
the tame-looking Mr Mason had in his eyes a hint of something fateful: "His eye wandered, and had no meaning in
its wandering; this gave him an odd look, such as I never
remembered to have seen....There was...no command in that
blank, brown eye." In *Shirley* also there is a casual reference
to "a pair of blue eyes, that were usually thought sleepy,
secretly on the alert."—"I knew by their expression," con-
tinues the writer, "—an expression which chilled by blood,
it was in that quarter so wondrously unexpected—that for
years they had been accustomed to silent soul-reading."
These things may seem details which can be mentioned in a
few words; but they have the wonderful potency of creating
an atmosphere which pervades the story. They are like a
slight touch, setting an electric current in motion.

Nevertheless these things are moods, wrapped round
the story, and lying on its surface. Further down there are
restless, central fires of passion. The fire is at different tem-
peratures in Charlotte's three chief novels. In *Jane Eyre* it

is hottest; in *Shirley* it smoulders; in *Villette* it leaps and flickers.

In *Jane Eyre* we watch the gradual awakening of an un-quickened life. "You are cold," says Rochester to Jane, "because you are alone; no contact strikes the fire from you that is in you." He tells her that happiness is close beside her; all she has to do is to stretch out her hand and take it. But she is of the kind to reject external opportunities. The flame within her is something isolated, secret, and self-dependent. In her face Rochester reads aloud the witness of her thoughts: "I need not sell my soul to buy bliss. I have an inward treasure born within me, which can keep me alive if all extraneous delights should be withheld, or offered only at a price I cannot afford to give." It is this "hitch" in Jane's character which stirs Rochester to persistence. He fans her fire till her heart trembles and glows in the exalta-tion of dawn breaking over the garden; the red glow bursts later into flaming words, terse, scorching, invincible: "I am not talking to you now through the medium of custom, conventionalities, nor even of mortal flesh; it is my spirit that addresses your spirit; just as if both had passed through the grave, and we stood at God's feet equal—as we are!"— The fierce tearing flames died down to the sullen burning of disillusion. This is one of the exceptional places in Charlotte Bronte, where the thought of religious consolation comes— but only for a moment—with the simplicity and exaltation of a fresh and vital passion:

One idea only still throbbed lifelike within me—a remembrance of God. It begot an unuttered prayer; these words went wandering up and down in my rayless mind, as something that should be whispered, but no energy was found to express them,—"Be not far from me, for trouble is near; there is none to help."

The trouble came: "In full heavy swing the torrent poured over me." And Jane found what she deemed a fit reason for this suffering: she had been overwhelmed just because she had been incapable of articulate prayer. This is literally the meaning of the last paragraph of the twenty-sixth chapter. There is something astounding in the harshness—no, the

brutality—of the motives so unhesitatingly imputed to God.
It is after such words as these that we begin to understand
more clearly the inadequacy of Charlotte's religious utterances.
The passion then fades to a great quietness as Jane forgives
Rochester—"yet not in words, not outwardly; only at (the)
heart's core."—She goes out to face the "awful blank" of
the future—"something like the world when the deluge was
gone by." After that the savage flames die down to a more
temperate warmth. Never for a moment is the story cold;
but we pass out of the Torrid Zone.

With *Shirley* the case is different. It is not a great work of
art. Its greatest fault is the want of that invigorating passion
which kept *Jane Eyre* on the high grounds of poetry. Much
of the emotion in *Shirley* is weak or over-strained; but there
is an occasional hectic beauty of fancy, as where Caroline
saw Shirley and Moore standing together in the moonlight
like two great happy spirits: "Yonder silvered pavement
reminds me of that white shore we believe to be beyond the
death-flood; they have reached it, they walk there united."
However, no fair-minded person stops to cast blame on
Shirley, for it was written under a strain of calamities that
subdue hostile criticism.

The emotional temperature of *Villette* varies from page
to page. As a story it is more diffuse, less concentrated than
Jane Eyre. The fire burns over a larger area, and involves
more people; but the extension of its province tends to the
dissipation of its energy. The emotion here is not so zealous
as in *Jane Eyre*, but it is more delicate. While in *Jane Eyre*
we find a magnificent sweep, zest and daring, many pages of
Villette are written with a cool, clear grace. It is hard to
understand Professor Jack when he finds no solace in this
novel. It is true of course that the book is unequal; yet how
good it is at its best! It is more lovable, more restful than
Jane Eyre.—Most of the story is very quiet. Paulina's light
gestures and her elfin pathos stir the first quiet melodies. To
the very end her presence seems to bring with it a kind of
hush and simplicity. When Dr John's letter lies unopened
in her hand, and she stands at the entry of womanhood, her
mind is as clear and direct as a child's. "Then," she said,

"I remembered all at once that I had not said my prayers that morning....I put the letter down, and said my prayers." Lucy's wistful and yet generous appreciation of Dr John's temperament has elements of the same placid charm. We like her best, I think, when she is out of love with him, and her strained emotions sink to the surer and more tranquil levels of friendship. "The frail frost-work of reserve" has felt the dissolving breath of anger; and Lucy develops her instinctive, heart-taught comprehension of his character. It may be that many of the conversations between her and Dr John are dull or unnatural; but this does not take anything away from the happy, kindly grace of his nature; and it is through Lucy's eyes that we see these qualities. After all, it is not Paulina, but Lucy, who provides the key-note of all the music; and whatever the other tones of the melodies may be, the key-note is always quietly sounded. *Villette* is a long book, full of words; but hardly a quarter of these words found their way into open speech. Most of them form Lucy's unspoken reflections. From her silence the story gains in atmosphere and suggestion. "As gold and silver are weighed in pure water," says Maeterlinck, "so does the soul test its weight in silence, and the words that we let fall have no meaning apart from the silence that wraps them round[1]." It is in this way that Lucy's silences give point and meaning to the episodes. Charlotte realised she could not use words to explain her heroine's psychology; it had to be felt:

If however (she wrote) the book does not express all this (that is, Lucy's mixture of strength and weakness), there must be a fault somewhere. I might explain away a few other points, but it would be too much like drawing a picture, and then writing underneath the name of the object intended to be represented. We know what sort of a pencil that is which needs an ally in the pen.

Nevertheless, the story is not faint in spite of its quiet notes; for M. Paul is in it. His presence obliterates all traces of languor; and yet the life which he brings into the story is not of the same order as that passionate energy which beats

[1] "Les âmes se pèsent dans le silence, comme l'or et l'argent se pèsent dans l'eau pure, et les paroles que nous prononçons n'ont de sens que grâce au silence où elles baignent."

through *Jane Eyre*. The emotion in the hearts of Jane and
Rochester is something hot and intense; M. Paul's emotions
may be hot, but that is not their specific quality; they are
superlatively swift. His feelings are elusive, like quicksilver;
they seem to have acquired the secret of perpetual motion.
He is, as Lucy said, an odd "mixture of the touching and the
absurd." The impression made by him is not so much a
permanent mixture of the two qualities as a constant zig-
zagging between them; and we are never quite sure with
which point—humour or pathos—he is going to prick us.
He comes on the scene at the very times when the story is
slipping heavily over precipices into deep gulfs of sentiment
or dullness; and in a moment, "in the twinkling of an eye,"
the narrative is rescued—it is hard to say how. It is set on
its feet again, and goes forward, treading the firm wholesome
ground. His crowning triumph is the occasion of the *fête*,
and this fourteenth chapter of *Villette* equals, if it does not
surpass, the glowing heights of *Jane Eyre*. The garden scenes
there seem almost commonplace in comparison with this
rapid, dashing originality. We see the dark little man,
"pungent and austere," his irritability covering his human
visage "with the mask of an intelligent tiger." We see his
sudden descent upon Lucy, his insistence that she shall act
a part upon a few hours' notice. We stay with her in the
attic, as with uplifted skirts, she rehearses her part to the
beetles. We hear the sounds of the bustling household below,
we feel the gathering shadows, and almost share Lucy's
pangs of hunger, till M. Paul arrives, and we go "down—
down—down to the very kitchen." Then comes the final
preparation for public exhibition under the vibrating stars.
M. Paul recommends each performer to "penetrate herself
with a sense of her personal insignificance"; and he whispers
a last word of encouragement to Lucy: "Do not look at the
crowd, nor think of it....Imagine yourself in the garret, acting
to the rats."—Here there is no attempt at symbolism or
allegory; but as a picture, a memory, and a joy for ever, the
whole scene could stand beside that of Don Quixote tilting
with the windmills.

The consideration of *Villette* brings home to any reader

the pervading essence of Charlotte Bronte's emotions: they are tinged with irony. In certain senses she is not humorous; decidedly she is not witty. Her humour emerges only in moments of stress; and then it usually plays the part of a saving common sense, preserving the story in a perilous land of passions and excitement. Jane drops her cool sedative of irony into the heat of Rochester's love-making. She keeps her head sufficiently to know that he is quite wrong in praising her "radiant, hazel eyes."—"I had green eyes, reader," she explains by way of aside; "but you must excuse the mistake; for him they were new-dyed, I suppose." She resolves to keep him from the gulf of sentiment with "a needle of repartee"; and this method becomes an established habit of their intercourse. When she has anything pungent to say, she falls back upon the scheme of an almost naked plainness of speech, containing a suggestion of unexpressed satire. On her return to Rochester, she restores his mental equilibrium by such means, interrupting his fancies with direct, invincible sense:

"Have you a pocket-comb about you, sir?"

"What for, Jane?"

"Just to comb out this shaggy black mane. I find you rather alarming when I examine you close at hand. You talk of my being a fairy, but I am sure you are more like a brownie."

"Am I hideous, Jane?"

"Very, sir; you always were, you know."

By such devices she resolves to fret him out of his melancholy; and she cannot fail to succeed.

This piquancy is constantly peeping out from the pages of *Villette*. Even Ginevra has the preserving "salt" of honesty. In this book, indeed, the saving sense is not so much ironic as piquant. It always seems to be lurking somewhere in Lucy's mind, and springs out into the open whenever she describes M. Paul. We see him, for instance, closely resembling "a black and sallow tiger" as he gives a stormy lesson in arithmetic, a subject which "invariably disagreed with him"; or we stand by Lucy as she lies in wait for the "brownie" who ransacks her desk, corrects her exercises, and leaves refreshing books between the "sallow dictionary"

and "worn-out grammar." In some ways it seems strange
that Lucy should be conceived to write like this, laughing at
M. Paul long after he was dead; and yet it is entirely wholesome. Hers was the loving laughter which rivets intimacies.
Lucy could recall M. Paul's spirit through this medium more
vividly than by any other means. This piquant laughter had
been the very breath of their intercourse. In no other way
could she have kept her memories healthy, sane, and true.
It is a great mastery to remember the dead as if they were
still vividly alive; and those who have attained to this power
usually display no false shame in the matter of humour. The
unforgotten laughter counts to them for as much as the unforgotten tears. Often, indeed, the tears are forgotten, while
the laughter is remembered. It was so with Lucy in her
memories of M. Paul. So fresh are they, and so lifelike, that
as we read them, the possibility of his death never crosses
our minds. It almost appears as if Lucy had forgotten that
he was dead. For death has made no difference to her
reminiscences. She writes just as she would have done if
M. Paul had stood looking over her shoulder.

When we think of this achievement, it seems impertinent
to add any comment on this which is the most subtle, the
most perfect, and the most unstudied of Charlotte's triumphs.
"He goes furthest," said Cromwell, "who knows not where
he is going." Like Abraham, Charlotte set out with no
certain destination before her. Perhaps she never realised
where she had gone, and what she had done. We ourselves
do not always understand how far, how bravely, and how
high she travelled.

*   *   *   *   *   *

Immaturity and growth—these are the predominant
characteristics of Charlotte Bronte's art. The term "growth"
must be taken with certain reservations; it does not imply
that Charlotte grew older or better; it simply means that
she went on growing. Perhaps her art was of the kind that
could never grow up. It seems impossible to associate her
with any matured result. For maturity involves a standing
still; and Charlotte's art was always moving.

Immaturity appears in every gesture and characteristic. Her outspoken courage is very young in its rashness; the same can be said of her eager preoccupation with life.—Her personal standpoint meant a great deal to her; and so does a child's. Like a child, she loved stories and pictures, but disregarded the commentary. She reported on life, but did not try to explain it. There is always an allurement about anything which we cannot fully understand; and Charlotte seems to have regarded life with the child's sense of awe and mystery. Her love of honesty had about it a suggestion of youth; she liked things to be *real*. "Did it really happen?" is a characteristically childlike query. Charlotte sometimes— but not invariably—altered one word.—"Could it really happen?" she asked herself as she wrote. Often indeed, she was content to record what had actually happened, not what might have happened.

Like a child, she made up her mind about people quickly; and she shared in the child's delighted observation of "exciting" personalities. She never quite grew out of the juvenile taste for melodrama. There was something spasmodic in her plot construction—like the gusts of episode in a child's narrative. Her very excellences of phrase seemed to come and go; she was like a young untrained athlete, whose style is erratic.—She was very young too, in her reliance upon emotion and intuition. It is only when we grow up that we establish altars to the Goddess of Reason; and then, we are often sorry for what we have done.—Charlotte had, moreover, something of a child's sturdy common sense. Every young person is overjoyed when a serious matter suddenly becomes amusing; and as we have seen, Charlotte's irony had this effect. She introduced commonplace facts to save herself from exaggeration of feeling. It is true that on one side of her nature Charlotte Bronte grew to middle age, suffered disappointment, bereavement, and a great solitude; but there was in her temperament another side which preserved the frankness and vehemence of youth. She kept her bloom to the end.

With regard to her position in the sequence of literature, it is evident that Charlotte imparted no doctrine for the guidance of future artists. If she possessed any philosophy at all it was of the kind which goes to work "teaching by examples." And even these examples were faulty. No book written by Charlotte Bronte could be a model for young and undisciplined writers. Technically—in plot-construction, and equality of treatment—her books are full of errors. Still, we persist that Charlotte Bronte taught by her examples. She taught nothing definite—no rules of technique, no theories of the artistic function.—She gave no "tips" to succeeding writers. But she bestowed something infinitely better—the stimulus of a great enthusiasm. She brought passion into the novel. Nobody before her wrote with such intimacy and fervour; and nobody since has been able entirely to forget what she did. The work of Romantic Revival was hastened by the daring and impetuous emotion glowing through the poetry of Burns. Romanticism was kept alive by the daring and impetuosity of Charlotte Bronte's novels. No doubt there were other preservative tendencies at work; but none were stronger than Charlotte's. The Victorians were growing up; the time for "dizzy raptures" was swiftly passing away. Charlotte helped to retard the inevitable process towards middle age. She quickened the pulse of her generation.

IV

EMILY BRONTE, 1818–1848

EMILY BRONTE was a woman singular in the midst of a singular family. Few women can have resembled her, and her writings are as unique as her personality. Charlotte said of her that " an interpreter ought always to have stood between her and the world." Perhaps it was with something of this object that she painted the portrait of Shirley. She tries to dazzle us with Shirley's brilliance. We hear that she was wistful and careless, fond of animals, childlike and queenly, with " odd points and grand points " about her. We know that her charms were able to soothe even the Rev. Peter Augustus Malone, and we are told that she had dreams and fancies of a unique quality.—" Indolent she is, reckless she is, and most ignorant, for she does not know her dreams are rare—her feelings peculiar; she does not know, has never known, and will die without knowing, the full value of that spring whose bright fresh bubbling in her heart keeps it green." Still, with the possible exception of her dreams, this bright Shirley Keeldar does not seem like the forbidding Emily Bronte whose personality stands gaunt behind her writings. Shirley cannot represent Emily as she was, but as she might have been. We feel there is something else which has never been fully told. Attempts have been made, but competent critics and scholars have condemned them as exaggerated or fantastic. Mr Clement Shorter, who probably knows more about Emily than any living man, has called her " the sphinx of our modern literature." There is nothing for it but to resign ourselves to the certainty that we shall never know the whole truth concerning Emily Bronte.

We know this much—she was an entirely different being from her sister Charlotte. As children they played their game of " The Islanders," each choosing a real island, and real inhabitants, and then setting their imaginations loose to work out the unguessed future. Charlotte went south, and selected the Isle of Wight; but Emily chose the rugged island of Arran. The choice was characteristic. Emily was always the sterner sister; in fact Charlotte admitted that she was harsh.—The same distinction came out in their love of animals. "The helplessness of an animal," says Mrs Gaskell, "was its passport to Charlotte's heart, the fierce wild intractability of its nature was what often recommended it to Emily." From their books, too, we feel that they were attracted or obsessed by different aspects of Nature; they looked at it from different angles. An idea constantly recurring to Charlotte's mind was the whirling and beating of winds against the solid walls of houses. She was not often out in these storms, but usually watched or heard them from a place of shelter. On the other hand Emily walked through tempests. Lockwood came in "benumbed to the very heart," and we feel that Emily had tasted the same experience. It is significant also that there was much reference to snow in Emily's descriptions, whereas Charlotte spoke more of rain. Emily's world was in all points sharper and more bleak than Charlotte's. She did not describe anything like the gardens at Thornfield. She struck the rock to obtain the living waters of beauty; from the rugged moors she extracted a solace which she could not find—and would not seek—in any gentler place.

Wuthering Heights is what attracts most readers to the personality and problem of Emily Bronte. Most people read the poems for the sake of the novel; and yet, after reading the poems it would not be at all strange to go back and re-read the novel—this time for the sake of the poems. Novel and poems make a similar appeal with marked differences. It is difficult to say which brings us closer to the actual woman. Professor Jack places his finger on the novel, and tells us that there we shall find her—"the girl, who all her life, and except when she was writing *Wuthering Heights*, controlled the utterances of her heart." Still the poems were not all written with the same definite prospect of publication as *Wuthering Heights*; and we find in them some private revelations which never escaped Emily in her impersonal narrative. We can

hardly understand Charlotte's devotion to Emily until we
have read the poems; and then it is not so incomprehensible.
This does not mean that in *Wuthering Heights* we find
no traces of a personality which could inspire affection.
People watched the living woman uneasily, and her book is
uncomfortable reading. Yet we know that her sister Charlotte
loved her; and as we read the weird passionate story, we feel
stirring in it something wistful, and pitiful, and worthy of
love. It is a book which has to be taken, like Emily herself,
with apologies. The plot is a dishevelled tangle of episodes,
each in its turn so overpowering that it seems to blot out all
that came before. The reader is incapable of "looking before
and after." It is as much as he can do to take one thing at
a time, and maintain his mental poise under the tremendous
pressure of single, isolated incidents. Everywhere there is
the terror and confusion of nightmare. If it be true that
life is incoherent, this story expresses its incoherence. Though
the plot is shapeless and tangled, it is not loose-jointed.
When we read the book constantly, we find it less confused.
It is the darkness of the story that blurs its outlines; the
incidents themselves are quite sharply defined, but our eyes
have to get accustomed to the unfamiliar gloom. There may
be no unity in the episodes; there is unity, however, in the
spirit of the book. As Swinburne has said of it, "There is
no monotony, but there is no discord." Everything there is
in its proper element—in keeping with the darkness.

Notwithstanding, many people who can tolerate a much
slacker plot cannot endure *Wuthering Heights*. They do not
dislike the arrangement of the episodes, but the episodes themselves. The book repels them as a meaningless
exhibition of brutality. "The action is laid in hell," said
Dante Gabriel Rossetti, "only it seems places and people
have English names there." Many tranquil people read
Paradise Lost without any compunction. They knew from
the beginning where they would have to go in Milton's
company.—It is the same also, with Dante's *Inferno*.—But
Emily raises no fingerposts along her road. She takes her
readers, if not to hell, at least within sight of its portals; and
she has said nothing by way of warning. The surprise shocks

many readers far more than the actual revelation. *Wuthering Heights* repels them chiefly because they did not know "what they were being let in for." In fact, Emily did not realise that she was doing anything unusual. She was so accustomed to her own singularity, that in all probability she never considered the singular impression which her book was bound to make. As Charlotte wrote of the book after Emily's death:

Its power fills me with renewed admiration; but yet I am oppressed; the reader is scarcely ever permitted a taste of unalloyed pleasure; every beam of sunshine is poured down through thick bars of threatening cloud; every page is surcharged with a sort of moral electricity; and the writer was unconscious of all this—nothing could make her conscious of it.

What matters most for us is the question whether Emily was trying to tell the truth, or to make a sensation. A person speaking faithfully cannot be neglected; and it should be remembered, it is often easier to make a sensation. If Emily had been studying effects, surely she would have tried to display more artifice in her plot. She would hardly have left us to discover, after many readings, that there is some slight method in her wildness. The very artlessness of the story impels conviction. It does not seem "made-up." Emily Bronte was a strange woman, but sincere; and in her strange book there is the mark of sincerity. In this story so bleak of spirit, so unkempt in appearance, there is something which, as it were, *smells* of reality. We can discern its truthfulness, though we cannot prove it; it is—

Felt in the blood, and felt along the heart.

Emily wrote of life as she saw it, but there were defects in her eyesight, and she was ever "a stranger in this world." She lived at a great distance from life. In her outlook there was a curious twist, and much that recalls the nameless terror of a child groping along a dark passage. She was afraid of life because she knew it so slightly. But she had the amazing intensity which brings with it flickerings of vision. Her fierce revelation was far from the art of "sweetness and light." She made no attempt to smooth out the shapeless chaos of human thinking, but she pierced it through with fire.

Nobody has understood better the passionate contrasts at the root of sullen, sensitive natures. Shakespeare has shown us Macbeth, crying at the height of his temptation,

> I dare do all that may become a man,
> Who dares do more, is none.

In him we can perceive the extremes to which human nature may stretch—the nobility which transcends, and the brutality which falls below average manhood. In something of the same way Heathcliff touched the outer limits of human possibility. Usually less than man—"pitiless, wolfish"—he also approached a level more gigantic than that of common men. In one direction alone his nature shot upwards, and even there a savage taint clung to him in the wildness of superstition. As the Pantheist beholds God in all creation so Heathcliff saw everywhere the reflection of Catherine's face.

"I cannot look down to the floor," he cried, "but her features are shaped in the flags! In every cloud, in every tree—filling the air at night, and caught by glimpses in every object by day—I am surrounded with her image! The most ordinary faces of men and women,—my own features, mock me with a resemblance. The entire world is a dreadful collection of memoranda that she did exist, and that I have lost her!"

Inferior writers have transformed evil men into monsters. Emily saw more deeply when she included in Heathcliff's mind both the monster and the poet.

We should be unfair to her if we thought that she understood only one abnormal type of character. When she tells us of Heathcliff's quietness under suffering, she adds: "Hardness, not gentleness, made him give little trouble." Such words make us feel that Emily searched and probed to the core of his nature. But these penetrating revelations do not surprise us; somehow we expect her to understand Heathcliff. She never understood anybody else in her book to the same degree; but she could feel for them wonderful subtleties of compassion—which implies no mean intelligence. She did not exhibit an entire sympathy with Catherine in the full tide of her living; but when Death cast over her his persistent deepening shadows, Emily's whole nature went out to her with an instinctive, passionate comprehension. As she wrote she almost ceased to be herself. Everything else was swallowed up; she forgot all things save Catherine dying. From her own inner life she must have constructed Heathcliff's temperamental defiance; but there she looked back to the past. Can it be that in her comprehension of Catherine's dying emotions, she looked forward to her own future? It is impossible not to feel that she wrote with some premonition, some brooding anticipation of her own destiny. How characteristic of her it was that Catherine's mind should have groped outwards to objects filled with suggestion of the wild, fresh moorland. In her delirium she plucked the feathers from her pillow, and fingered them wistfully; the mere touch of them opened her mind to the "cold blowing airs" outside her sick-room. Then the reflection in the mirror seemed to close her mind with a snap. Stifled and confused, she pled, and struggled for one breath of the air sweeping down from the heights. She looked out through the dense cold darkness and saw what nobody else could see—the comforting lights of home.—Emily wrote this passage with her whole heart illumined.

She had flickerings of vision. Occasionally it broke into flames of pure, clear radiance, but normally it was a vision of terror. There is a terror which cleanses, and a terror which shatters. It is the destructive power which dominates the entire book. The very imagery suggests forces palpitating beneath the surface. Of Catherine's temper we read: "For the space of half a year the gunpowder lay as harmless as sand, because no fire came near to explode it"; and over the story there spreads the tension of approaching catastrophe. In the same way we hear of the subdued "black fire" in Heathcliff's eyes; and we wait in the positive certainty that sooner or later it will break out of bounds. Before long anything placid jars on the nerves with a sense of unreality. The mere sight of Linton's tranquillity stirred Catherine to recklessness.— "Your cold blood," she cried, "cannot be worked into a fever; your veins are full of ice-water; but mine are boiling, and the sight of such chilliness makes them dance." In this dancing of her blood there is something hot and strained. The whole story is strung up almost to the breaking point. It is like a person, tense and irritable, with nerves set on edge.

This brings us to the standpoint of another class of conscientious objectors to *Wuthering Heights*. The first class we have already mentioned; after a few pages they are repelled by the sudden and unexpected plunge into ferocity. There are other readers who endure the story to the bitter end, waiting to see what it all means, and whether the book can produce something to justify its existence. They are on the look-out for a brave philosophy wrung from terror, and at first sight it does not seem forthcoming. Throughout the book the capacity of brute force seems magnified beyond all endurance. Nowhere is there any respite or escape. There is neither moral triumph nor moral retribution. Heathcliff is not vanquished by anybody nobler than himself. He dies of exhaustion. Even after death his memory cannot be entirely obliterated, for his spirit haunts the moors. There is in the story little of the eternal antagonism of goodness and evil. In Heathcliff's mind we discover goodness and evil contrasted—but not conflicting. Everywhere else the antagonism stands between evil and mediocrity. All the solid fighting is done by the forces of evil. The "good" people are too harmless to destroy evil, or indeed to leave the faintest impression upon it. Their part is protest, and disapproval, and suffering. They are hardly worth fighting. We seek the exhilaration of a close, honest conflict, and find in the record of Heathcliff's easy triumphs only an outrage to the moral sense. His death makes no difference. It simply means that evil has unexpectedly worn itself out. It may be rather consoling to know that the "good" people are happy in the end; but they have done little enough to make us proud of them or of goodness.—And yet I am not sure that this is the last word about the matter. We shall not find anything better in the first or the second or even the third reading of the book. We must dig deep and patiently before we find any encouragement. Dimly in Emily's mind we may discern a faint glimmer of hope. Heathcliff it is true, was not defeated by goodness; he wore himself out. Yet—and here is the stimulus—he did not *need* to be defeated by goodness. Ultimately it did not matter if the champions of goodness were feeble or non-existent; for the evil within him was self-doomed and self-destructive. Its extinction required no blow from an external antagonist. He realised at the end that he had been beaten. His power of resistance was broken, not by opposition, but by the new affection rising in the hearts of Hareton and young Catherine. "It is a poor conclusion," he observed, as he watched love springing where he had sown the seeds of hatred.

In speaking thus of the moral effect of the story, surely little need be added with regard to its purity. The narrative may be fierce, but it is never unclean; and how easily it might have become so! Emily passes through the churning rivers of passion with no stain upon her raiment. She goes across a land of pestilence, where ten thousand—including, possibly, her sister Charlotte—would have fallen by her side; but the plague does not come nigh her. Unlike Charlotte, her sense of wickedness never became blunted; evil horrified her to the very end. If we need anything to quicken our sense of wonder and reverence, we have it in our power to take to our hearts some matchless words of praise. We can go to Swinburne, and learn from him of this purity and sweetness set at the very core of "living storm."

When all is said, this is a wonderful book, full of an un-tamed beauty. If the people are morbid, their environment is fresh. The moors act as tonic and antidote to the heat and strain of human actions. About this turmoil there is set a world austere, full of sharp movement and shadow, yet touched with a delicate sweetness. These men and women live surrounded by snow, and sunlight and restless clouds; by the brightness of solitary flowers, the sounds of trees and water, the invisible life of the winds. In the moors there is no permanence of peace or gloom. They know the weirdness of black tempest, the living joy of summer, the stillness of twilight; and in all these things there is health. The wild, clean air seems to blow through every page of the book, disinfecting the mind of the reader.

Throughout the story, in the hearts of the people, and in the breath from open country, there is the pulsation of life. It appears in the figure of Zillah with "fire-flushed cheeks," brandishing a frying-pan over the turbulent dogs, till the storm subsides and she remains "heaving like a sea after a high wind." The same energy clings about her as she urges "flakes of flame up the chimney with a colossal bellows." —It will be remembered how the younger Catherine described to Linton her idea of heaven's happiness:

Mine was rocking in a rustling green tree, with a west wind blowing, and bright clouds flitting rapidly above; and not only larks, but throstles, and blackbirds, and linnets and cuckoos pouring out music on every side, and the moors seen at a distance, broken into cool, dusky dells; but close by great swells of long grass undulating in waves to the breeze; and woods and sounding water and the whole world awake and wild with joy. He wanted all to lie in an ecstasy of peace; I wanted all to sparkle and dance in a glorious jubilee. I said his heaven would be only half alive; and he said mine would be drunk.

This sense of verve and intoxication penetrates to the very rooms and furniture of houses. From the moment that the door opens to show us the glowing, uneasy kitchen at Wuthering Heights, we are swept into the rush and tension of the narrative. Often we shudder, and are left out of breath; but then it may be that we find a moment's rest in the beautiful and unexpected tenderness which slips into the grimmest places of the story. It brings a simple grace to Catherine's reconciliation with Hareton. Or we find it perhaps in a casual reference to the weather.—"The snow is quite gone down here," said Edgar, "and I only see two white spots on the whole range of the moors; the sky is blue, and the larks are singing, and the becks and brooks are all brimfull."—The moors are unlike the human figures, for their tranquillity never frets us; there is nothing insipid in their grave sweetness:

I turned away (said Lockwood) and made my exit, rambling leisurely along with the glow of a sinking sun behind, and the mild glory of a rising moon in front—one fading, and the other brightening—as I quitted the park, and climbed the stony by-road, branching off to Mr Heathcliff's dwelling. Before I arrived in sight of it, all that remained of day was a beamless amber light along the west; but I could see every pebble on the path, and every blade of grass by that splendid moon.

Even through Mrs Dean's unstudied words we can catch tones of the same quiet charm:

We deferred our excursion till the afternoon; a golden afternoon of August; every breath from the hills so full of life that it seemed whoever respired it, though dying, might revive. Catherine's face was just like the landscape—shadows and sunshine flitting across it in rapid succession; but the shadows rested longer, and the sunshine was more transient.

Even when Heathcliff is savagely dying, we hear the music of Gimmerton beck, flowing over its pebbles; Catherine also had been soothed by its "full mellow flow," as she caught above its murmurs, the ringing of Gimmerton bells.—Sometimes the passion is pulled up with a rough jerk as a sudden pathos breaks its way into words. Almost by accident Emily seems to stumble upon beauty, to release from within her a reticent sweetness and grandeur. The thought of death sweeps away that harsh unbalanced quality which tears and disfigures her narrative. Her heart seems to flow out to Catherine in her poignant hunger for death:

"And," added she musingly, "the thing that irks me most is this shattered prison after all. I'm wearying to escape into that glorious world, and to be always there; not dimly seeing it through tears, and yearning for it through the walls of an aching heart; but really with it and in it."

This yearning lies buried at the heart of the wild story. Joy—earthly, human joy—entered very slightly into the compass of Emily's thinking. In all her vitality there was a gasp and a struggle. It is an exhausting process to enter into her book. Still more exhausting must it have been for such a woman to live among her thoughts. To her life was a delirium. In one of her poems she declared it an agony for

The soul to feel the flesh, and the flesh to feel the chain.

In her own way Christina Rossetti felt the same constraint, and welcomed death for its very negations, as

Silence more musical than any song.

It appeared to both women as an escape from heat and stir into the freedom of perfect stillness. When Emily Bronte came to the end of her book, she passed aside from the fitful destinies of the living to stand by the graves of the dead:

I lingered round them, under that benign sky; watched the moths fluttering among the heath and harebells, listened to the soft wind breathing through the grass, and wondered how any one could ever imagine unquiet slumber for the sleepers in that quiet earth.

With these words she closes her story; and we, who are so glad to live, feel curiously apart from a woman so glad to die. Again we halt before the enigma of her temperament. We remember that she never desired death with the feeble longing of those more dead than alive. In Emily there was no faintness of spirit. She was not overwhelmed with thoughts of Death and nothing else. She lived close by the frontiers of Eternity, within sight and sound of its mystery; and looking wistfully across she felt the solace of fleeting visions:

> Yet ever and anon a trumpet sounds
> From the hid battlements of Eternity;
> Those shaken mists a space unsettle, then
> Round the half-glimpsèd turrets slowly wash again.

The reader of Emily Bronte's poems should not lay himself out for a period of uninterrupted enjoyment. If he reads straight ahead he will often feel dulled and blunted. If, however, he perseveres, he will find the reward of a few rare and beautiful treasures. Shylock would not have given his turquoise ring for "a wilderness of monkeys." The happy discoverer of Emily's great lines would not give them up for a wilderness of ordinary poems; more than that, he would search a wilderness of bad poems, if there should be any hope of finding in it a few more priceless lines of Emily's quality, to add to his collection.

Emily's poems are best studied, not for their style, but simply as an illumination of her personality. In those few passages or phrases where we see her face to face, the style comes right of its own accord. It is best also, to begin the study from the standpoint of those external objects which

laid the firmest touch on her inner life; in other words, from
the aspect of Nature. This passion for external Nature awoke
in her mind an intense spiritual yearning. She escaped from
herself into the glimmering visions of the imagination, but
had to return again to her own identity, with its inner
struggles. Finally she stayed herself upon the expectation
of Death with its ultimate solace.

Emily Bronte lived in the same century as Wordsworth.
Unlike him she had never beheld the "bleak and visionary
sides" of mountains; but she had extracted visions from the
slopes of moors quite as bleak, and never as majestic. She
was, however, far removed from the Wordsworth who made
theories about Nature. She was nearer the youthful Wordsworth; like him she had felt the tall rock and cataract
haunting her "like a passion."—She could have appreciated
all that was inarticulate in him—

> Thoughts that do often lie too deep for tears.

Her own feeling for Nature was largely inarticulate. She
could find words to describe hills and clouds and running
water, but gave the scantiest explanation of her own psychology under these impressions. Her passion for such
things was almost as dumb as the homing instinct of some
wild creatures. For this reason it will be found that the
impersonal descriptions of Nature in *Wuthering Heights* are
usually more beautiful than her nature-poems with a superadded personal note. She tells us, for instance, that she
found in Nature an escape from self; it recalled the past,
and dimmed the anxious future:

> Is it not that the sunshine and the wind
> Lure from itself the woe-worn mind,
> And all the joyous music breathing by,
> And all the splendours of that cloudless sky,
> Regive him shadowy gleams of infancy,
> And draw his tired gaze from futurity.

But this is not supreme poetry, especially to anyone who has
loved Wordsworth. She speaks in another place of the human
spirit touched by the grace of summer—

> With heart as summer sunshine light,
> And warm as summer sky.

Again we say, paradoxically, that there is better poetry to be found in the prose of *Wuthering Heights*.—She tells us— what we could have guessed from the novel—that wind had an extraordinary stimulus for her imagination:

> All hushed and still within the house;
> Without, all wind and driving rain;
> But something whispers to my mind,
> Wrought up in rain and wailing wind.

Elsewhere she explains clearly what the wind does to a sensitive mind:

> Yes,—I could swear that glorious wind
> Has swept the world aside,
> Has dashed its memory from thy mind
> Like foam-bells from the tide.

In another place she says still more definitely that the winds are the home of visions; a spirit speaks thus:

> This is my home where whirlwinds blow,
> Where snowdrifts round my path are swelling.

After selecting many similar fragments an inevitable question confronts us.—These things have an element of interest for us who have read *Wuthering Heights*; but is this all that Emily Bronte has to give us in the way of poetry? Would we have ever given these lines a second thought, if not for the sake of her novel? The only answer is that we must have patience. We are as yet treading but the blurred circumference of Emily's magic circle. Her alchemy was the mysterious solitude of darkness. Something weird in the air communicated itself to her spirit, as she looked out over the cold moors and heard the solemn sound of moving waters:

> Streams and waterfalls and fountains
> Down the darkness stole away.

In one of her early poems she laments the passing of the night's cool radiance, and the approach of scorching sunlight; the stars have

> Departed, every one
> And left a desert sky.

She sighs for the inspiration which has faded with the dawn, for the glamour and stimulus of the dark hours, when

> Thought followed thought, star followed star,
> Through boundless regions on.

She calls on night with its dreams, for salvation from the "blinding reign" of day:

> Oh, stars, and dreams, and gentle night,
> Oh, night and stars, return!

It was under such influences that Emily awoke to the infinite mystery of life. It might be the mystery of her own spirit—

> This hidden ghost that has its home in me;

or she felt, like Blake, the uncanny contrasts of beauty and terror in the world without her—

> All nature's million mysteries,
> The fearful and the fair.

She could not yield a happy admiration to the "godlike faculty" of the human mind. She could have understood Milton's Belial when he spoke of thoughts which "wander through Eternity"; but with the glory of his conception she mingled some elements of terror. She was afraid to release her questing imagination:

> So stood I, in Heaven's glorious sun,
>   And in the glare of Hell;
> My spirit drank a mingled tone
> Of seraph's song and demon's moan;
> What my soul bore, my soul alone
>   Within itself may tell!

Yet she was so made that she could not resist the lure of the imagination. She had to go out in spirit, and follow its leading. More than that, she had to purge her soul, till it was fit to receive the glory of passing visions. If we wish to appreciate the vitality of Emily's spiritual experience, we must place her poem *The Visionary* beside Tennyson's *Sir Galahad*. Tennyson's knight is for ever pursuing an elusive echo or gleam; we see him riding through an enchanted region, his eyes dim with dreams. How bare in comparison seems the narrow room where Emily's visionary awaits the coming bliss! Here there are no sombre forests stretching out to dark, mystic waters. We hear no fragments of unearthly melody, we catch no gleams of supernatural light. We are in a plain room, with matted floor; the light comes from a small well-trimmed lamp, and the night-storm whistles without. But the bare little room is vibrating with expectancy. If we could see the eyes of the visionary, what glow and what passion should we find! The visionary waiting for visions thrills with the rapture of a lover keeping his tryst:

> He for whom I wait, thus ever comes to me.

She knows that though the vision may tarry, assuredly it will not fail. As it has always come in the past, so it will come again.—Sir Galahad presses on in hope—

> And so I ride, whate'er betide,
> Until I find the Holy Grail.

So far he has never found it; he has not tasted his cup of bliss. Beside Emily's visionary, he is merely a wistful novice in the spiritual life.

Place even Christina Rossetti's visionary poems side by side with this one, and we find Emily Bronte no whit behind her in intensity. In Christina we are always conscious of a certain cultivation of atmosphere. She seems to move about in a dim, religious light, and the vision strikes upon a prepared surface. With Emily Bronte there is a naked and Puritan simplicity; she brings with her no suggestion of stained glass, ecclesiastical symbolism, or Pre-Raphaelite art. Her only preparation is the trimming of the lamp, and the discipline of the expectant heart. The vision is never described to us—and this not from ignorance; for the vision is a familiar experience to the solitary watcher. She can find no words to describe her experience, and stops short with an infinitely suggestive silence. She stands within the bare room, confidently awaiting the coming illumination. This is—

> All (we) know, and all (we) need to know.

We must be careful not to interpret the word "visions" in a specifically religious sense. For Emily the word was synonymous with imagination. Her visions were loopholes through which her spirit could escape from sordid or depressing actuality. She bowed before the mystery of her imagination, and yet sought to rule it. In one of her greatest poems she invoked the "God of visions," beseeching Him to plead for her, to justify her in quitting the worldly paths of common sense and pleasure to follow the beckoning of the imagination:

> (I) gave my spirit to adore
> Thee, ever-present, phantom thing—
> My slave, my comrade, and my king.
>
> A slave, because I rule thee still;
> Incline thee to my changeful will,
> And make thy influence good or ill;
> A comrade, for by day and night
> Thou art my intimate delight—
> My darling pain that wounds and sears,
> And wrings a blessing out from tears
> By deadening me to earthly cares;
> And yet, a king, though Prudence well
> Have taught thy subject to rebel.

Why, it may be asked, should it be imprudent to follow the beckoning Imagination? Emily knew the reason. She said—

> I'm happiest now when most away
> I can tear my soul from its mould of clay.

She escaped through the "magic casements" of which Keats sang, into a sort of Nirvana—a No Man's Land where all identity and all matter fade like mist:

> (Where) I am not, and none beside,
> Nor earth, nor sea, nor cloudless sky,
> But only spirit wandering wide
> Through infinite immensity.

And then, like Keats, she had to come back to her "sole self." That was the peril of the imagination. Like the enchanted knight, she had to awake from dreams

> On the cold hill-side.

Emily Bronte was afraid of her soul, with all its capacity for visionary escape, and its certainty of re-capture in the

web of material things. She was afraid of the consuming
passions within her. In one of her poems she made an exile
cry aloud to her oppressors that her soul was free of their
bonds—

> My mortal flesh you might debar,
> But not the eternal fire within.

If the "eternal fire" is an exaltation, it is also an agony.
Emily probed down to the recesses of her soul, and tried to
understand its fiery mystery. She seemed in touch with no
Power to whom she could appeal—"Thou knowest my
down-sitting and mine up-rising; thou knowest my thoughts
afar off." She does not seem to have wondered whether
God understood her; nobody else did; she could not understand herself. A few things about herself she did know. She
expressed her solitude in words of bitter desolation:

> I am the only being whose doom
>   No tongue would ask, no tongue would mourn;
> I've never caused a thought of gloom,
>   A smile of joy, since I was born.

> In secret pleasure, secret tears,
>   This changeful life has slipped away,
> As friendless after eighteen years,
>   As lone as on my natal day.

She looked into her heart, and found there the most cruel
sting of despair. Discerning falsehood in the outside world
she turned inwards:

> But worse to trust to my own mind,
> And find the same Corruption there.

This discovery is, indeed, the supreme Vanity of vanities.
Under the pain of her own shortcomings, she cried aloud—

> Shall my young sins, my sins alone,
>   Be everlasting here?

Though she struggled to shake off her weakness, she could
not escape from self. She described herself as one

> Often rebuked, yet always back returning
> To those first feelings that were born in me.

She had to follow her own nature. There was no other clue
to the problem. But even that clue was defective. How was

she to understand her temperament? Thus we find her
puzzling over her own identity. In *The Philosopher* she
speaks of the constant warfare within her spirit:

> Three gods, within this little frame
> Are warring, night and day;
> Heaven could not hold them all, and yet
> They all are held in me;
> And must be mine till I forget
> My present entity!

She dreams of a unifying Spirit, blending all these conflicting
elements into harmony. If she could have believed in this
dream, she would never have—

> Raised this coward cry
> To cease to think, and cease to be.

As it is, she can find no relief. She longs for death to end
with its oblivion the strife of

> Conquered good and conquering ill.—

At other times she cannot bear to die, knowing that life is
still unconquered. How can she go out with her task unfinished, her lesson in endurance unlearnt?—In *Self-Interrogation* she gropes towards satisfaction. Not till the
moment of death can she learn this, her ultimate lesson. The
highest fortitude is that which can bear even humiliation
with a tranquil spirit. Death will call upon her for the supreme
test of courage—the courage which renounces conflict at the
very moment of defeat, when the zest for struggle grips the
heart most tightly:

> The long war closing in defeat—
> Defeat serenely borne—
> Thy midnight rest may still be sweet,
> And break in glorious morn!

Emily Bronte looked inwards and found a desperate moral
conflict. She found something else, which, though no less
poignant, was much less complex. In remembrance of
lost joys she found her "sorrow's crown of sorrows." It is
very important to remember that Emily was not constitu-
tionally gloomy. She could not have been capable of deep
sorrow unless she had also possessed the high faculty of joy.

It is impossible to explain the facts which called forth all her regret. These things were her secret, and she never told it fully. We only know that from her lips there fell a dim story, echoing in tones of wild, sad music. Nobody could wish for anything better than silence in the presence of the wonderful lines from *Death*:

> Death! that struck when I was most confiding
> In my certain faith of joy to be—
> Strike again, Time's withered branch dividing
> From the fresh root of Eternity!

Every reader lingers unbidden over the beautiful poem *Remembrance*. There is no weakness in this tenderness; its fibres are tough, although they look so slender:

> Then did I learn how existence could be cherish'd,
> Strengthened and fed without the aid of joy.

These lines strike the firmest chord of Emily's music. The result of her introspection was a resolution to endure to the end:

> I saw my fate without its mask,
> And met it too without a tear.

The springs of her life were withered. She walked forward, grimly perhaps, but always bravely, through the parched valley of stones. By the time she wrote *The Old Stoic*, she had learned to despise many things, but she never disdained the hunger for liberty. That kept her soul alive; it nourished the self-respect which was content with a single boon—

> In life and death a chainless soul
> With courage to endure.

She always endured with reference to the end. As we have seen, life had in some way been robbed of its splendour; all that remained was a bleak, songless waste. Occasionally she felt some reluctance at quitting the conflict, but she could experience no pangs on relinquishing earthly joys. She had no joys to lose. Because life held so little for her, any claim to a final justice had to look beyond the grave for satisfaction. With this hope burning in her heart, she was strong to anticipate "rewarding destiny." As we infer from

The Prisoner, she had passed through a phase when the very terror of life held fascination—

> When Joy grew mad with awe at counting future tears.

But that stage was soon over. That youthful awe was transmuted into something more solemn and austere—the expectation of Death as the strong liberator of the soul:

> Its wings are almost free,—its home, its harbour found;
> Measuring the gulf, it stoops and dares the final bound.

In her last poem she was prepared to admit even the comfortless doctrine of personal extinction. Life seemed to have drained her of that passion which dies so hard—the clinging to personal identity:

> Though earth and man were gone,
> And suns and universes cease to be,
> And Thou wert left alone,
> Every existence would exist in Thee.

Whether this was a habitual attitude, it is difficult to say. Would she, who sought Death as the entrance into liberty, have been content, at the very moment of her release to lose the personal consciousness of joy? We know at all events, that she believed passionately in some form of immortality. There is a positive conception of Death—as a liberating force; this conception formed the basis of her life. There is also a negative conception of Death—as the extinguisher of Life; but of this negative Death she had no fears, for he was pitted against the Ultimate Sources of Life:

> There is not room for Death,
> Nor atom that his might could render void;
> Thou—Thou art Being and Breath,
> And what Thou art may never be destroyed.

Thackeray recognised in Charlotte Bronte's writings an indefinable quality which almost impelled a conviction of her immortality. This does not mean the immortality of her art—of that there is no question. It means the personal immortality of the artist. He felt that she was not used up; somewhere she must be still going on—

> On the earth the broken arcs; in the heaven a perfect round.

It seems fitting to close any consideration of the Brontes
with that quotation. Much of it, of course, can apply to
nobody but Charlotte. It was written solely with reference
to her, and in regret for the unfinished fragments she left
behind. Yet, as Charlotte would have joyfully admitted,
Thackeray's climax touches a point common to both sisters.
Of Emily we feel, even more than Charlotte, that however
much her life may have been withered, her art was not finished.
The actual achievement is like a tentative experiment; we
have never seen the mature and perfected result. Thus we read
into the lines of the quotation a new and extended meaning:

As one thinks of that life so noble, so lonely—of that passion for
truth—of those nights and nights of eager study, swarming fancies,
invention, depression, elation, prayer; as one reads the necessarily
incomplete, though most touching and admirable history of the
heart that throbbed in this little frame—of this one among the
myriads of souls that have lived and died in the great earth—this
great earth?—this little speck in the infinite universe of God,—
with what wonder do we think of to-day, with what awe wait for
to-morrow, when that which is now but darkly seen shall be clear!
As I read this little fragmentary sketch, I think of the rest. Is it?
And where is it? Will not the leaf be turned some day, and the
story be told?

Surely this is the supreme victory of supreme art;—that in
the very moment when it awes us with the immensity of the
Universe, it does not show us humanity shrunk into insignificance; it convinces us of the eternal life of those myriad
atoms which we call human souls.

*   *   *   *   *   *

We have said that Charlotte Bronte's value to her age took
the form of a gift—a great enthusiasm. Emily Bronte's gift
was a great intensity. There is a distinction; for the first gift
carries with it a suggestion of joy, and the second a suggestion
of sorrow. This does not mean that Charlotte's mood was
one of sustained joy; nothing could be further from the
truth. But she tasted more common happiness than Emily;
and she felt life to be full of zest. Emily may have risen to
rare heights of overwhelming bliss, but it was death and not
life for which she hungered.

Emily indeed was like Charlotte, but she had greater heights and depths. What was winning in the one sister became appalling in the other. Yet, there is usually an element of grandeur in anything which appals us. And Emily had a majesty of her own.

Charlotte's unsystematic tendencies stopped short at her plots; Emily saw all life as a wild and hopeless confusion. We feel that she was struggling for a philosophy—a pattern instead of a tangle; and she only got it in glimpses. Charlotte groped for no interpreting clues; she was far younger at heart. Charlotte felt life to be mysterious and alluring; Emily felt it to be mysterious and terrible. She looked inwards as well as outwards, and was appalled by her discoveries. Charlotte wrote of her own experiences, but hardly ever diagnosed her own spirit. She was not afraid of her soul, like Emily; for she knew much less about it. Both sisters found in the imaginative impulse an escape from sordid reality; but Charlotte escaped into an external narrative where she herself—or somebody like her—was playing a part. Lucy and Jane are, in some degree, reflections of herself. Emily, on the other hand, escaped into a more impersonal narrative; or she tasted moments of ecstasy, when the essence of bliss consisted in a temporary oblivion of identity. In several senses Emily was more detached from life than Charlotte; yet where she touched it at all she probed much further below the surface. Charlotte watched fierce brusque characters from without; Emily seemed to enter the very being of Heathcliff. Nature was to Charlotte a sympathetic background, an atmosphere, a solace. To Emily it was an indispensable medicine. She could not live without it.

There was a warming fire in Charlotte's spirit; Emily's fire was a tremendous conflagration. It burnt her plot into a wild unity of mood. It touched her glaring melodrama, and almost always made it glow with the rich hues of tragedy. It purged her world of grossness; it cleansed the inmost recesses of her spirit.

That was Emily Bronte—a terrible woman, but wonderful. Do we ask after this what she did for English literature? She gave it the marvel of her own personality. It is futile to talk of *Wuthering Heights* as a literary model. Books like that are miracles incapable of repetition. It is a queer book—quite unlike anything we have ever seen or imagined. It is more than odd; it is entirely abnormal. Nobody wishes for an exact reproduction of abnormality; nothing could be more unwholesome. But an exceptional book like this, coming upon us unasked, stirs up our easy conventions. It seems to reveal new worlds in human nature; it strikes us dumb before the wonder and mystery of living. The writer who can achieve this has no call to justify her position in literature.

MRS E. C. GASKELL[1]
1810-1865

I

INTRODUCTORY

BORN September 29, 1810; married August 30, 1832; died November 12, 1865; Mrs Gaskell's life fits naturally into the record of "Domestic Occurrences." All human records are suggestive; but this one does not suggest anything at all uncommon. Put aside the fact that Mrs Gaskell wrote books, and there is hardly anything left to place her apart from thousands of ordinary women. If—and it is a big "if"—eccentricity is the mark of genius, she could not have been a genius; for nobody was less peculiar. Neither in herself nor in her circumstances did she achieve the least strain of singularity. Perhaps that is why she is often forgotten. Some people are so apt to consider literary women as psychological curiosities, that they never pause before any cases which present no enigmas. Writers who conduct themselves in a normal fashion make no more appeal to such readers than hale and hearty people to the professional instincts of a doctor. Mrs Gaskell will never have much standing among those who hanker for sensations or problems; but she deserves the love of everybody who takes delight in the ordinary business of living.

We need not expand that brief record of birth, marriage and death. Mrs Gaskell wished that no formal biography should be written; and we can get to know her without such a medium. Sir A. W. Ward has told us all that we really need to be told. She seems to have had a temperament which

---

[1] Mrs Gaskell, though an older woman than Charlotte Bronte, commenced her definite literary career slightly later, and continued it to a much later date. For this reason she is placed chronologically after the Brontes.

expressed itself through many ordinary channels; but without ostentation she utilised one extraordinary means of self-expression. This was her literary instinct. The rare and wonderful thing about Mrs Gaskell was her mastery of this instinct. Many writers have been the tools of their own genius; it has moulded them and lifted them into a strange isolation. But Mrs Gaskell never allowed her genius to dominate her whole nature. She was not only a writer of books, but a wife, a mother, a friend and succourer of many. All these experiences contributed, no doubt, to her art; but she does not appear to have valued them solely "for art's sake." Probably this was the secret power which guarded her, in art and life, from artificial thinking. Yet we should not dogmatise. The ways of genius are dark. To some it comes with an overwhelming impulse which sweeps them out of the common current; it speaks through others, quietly and without affectation, in places of general resort. Who shall decide which is the higher type of inspiration? It is surely wiser to reverence the power blowing where (and how) it listeth.

How are we to approach Mrs Gaskell's art—that part of her which was moved by the winds of the spirit? Her work is so full—chiefly of priceless little things—that we hardly know where to turn. Her attitude to life is best summed up in the well-worn couplet from Stevenson,

> The world is so full of a number of things,
> I'm sure we should all be as happy as kings.

From our point of view it is pleasant, but not exactly easy, to move about in such a full place as Mrs Gaskell's world. We have so little time, and there is so much laid before us, that we cannot see everything properly. "Goodly pearls" can only be acquired by the sacrifice of less costly jewels. If we know Mrs Gaskell at all, we have a sure clue to her richest treasures. Men and women and children—these were her absorbing interests. She rated all things in terms of their human significance; the less they were related to men, the less did she esteem them.

We shall proceed then in something of this fashion: first, to study the background and setting of Mrs Gaskell's stories; secondly, to come into touch with the human figures; and, thirdly, to enter through them into contact with Mrs Gaskell's own ideas and emotions. We shall then make our way out to the wider world beyond, and see where she stands in the company of other writers.

II

ATMOSPHERE AND SETTING

IT has been said of Mrs Gaskell that she rarely walked into the country merely for the sake of the landscape, but more often with the object of arriving at some human habitation. This custom reflected itself in her writings. Though they are full of out-door Nature, they are rarely set in solitary places. Most of the incidents take place within sight or sound of a house.

Nevertheless, mere considerations of place make no difference to the value of Mrs Gaskell's pictures. Wherever she may take us, we cannot help using our eyes. She tells us that Charlotte Bronte had at one time wished to express her ideas by drawing.—"After she had tried to *draw* stories, and not succeeded, she took the better mode of writing." This pictorial impulse was equally strong in Mrs Gaskell. Her words formed themselves into pictures without any semblance of effort.

Unlike Wordsworth or the Brontes, she appears to have sought no enduring consolation from the hills, which in her stories are usually connected with human suffering. Ruth was different from Jane Eyre, for she found no peace in the wild, harsh moorland, but only a weary, intolerable solitude. There was no solace for Philip Hepburn in "the wild fells" which faced him as he tramped on "heedless of the startled plovers' cry, goaded by the furies." It is true that little Maggie Browne felt soothed and uplifted by the high open moors; but Mrs Gaskell implied that this reliance upon the consolations of Nature was token of her spiritual immaturity. Mrs Buxton had tried to teach her that it is possible to commune with God in crowded populous places. It was because Maggie's soul was "a young disciple" that she found it easier to speak to Him with "wild moors swelling and darkening around her."

Mrs Gaskell often seems to imply that the beauty of Nature

leaves no permanent impression on the spirit. Passing through
the "green gloom" of the forest, Ruth and Bellingham came
upon a still pool, and caught the gleam of water-lilies.
Mrs Gaskell felt the sensuous peace of that place almost as
Keats would have felt it. Notwithstanding—and here is the
difference—we know all the time that the peace will not last;
it lies on the road to trial. Margaret Hale loved the New
Forest, and for a time she was sustained by the memory of
its beauty, "the very thought of which was an echo of
distant gladness in her heart." Yet she was vaguely disappointed when she returned to the Forest, and found change
in its human associations. We cannot help feeling that when
she went to ugly, smoky Milton as John Thornton's bride,
the loveliness of the woods would rise to her memory without
arousing any pang of regret.

Mrs Gaskell never claimed too much for the influences of
Nature. The whole of *Sylvia's Lovers* seems freshened by the
sea-winds; the story has woven into its texture the lights and
colours, the music and mystery of great waters. This flawless
beauty of the sea is set against the records of imperfect,
struggling men. It was on a day of unstained loveliness that
Philip fell before his great temptation; the beauty of the
external world had no power to tranquillise his spirit. It was
the same many days later when he went out into the exquisite
serenity of a spring evening: "All spoke of brooding peace;
but Philip's heart was not at peace." It is right to add that
Sylvia sought consolation from the sea and "the peaceful
heavens."—"It's my only comfort," said she to herself....
"I'll go and cry my fill out under yon great quiet sky."—
Occasionally also, Mrs Gaskell yielded to "the pathetic
fallacy." When Mary Barton was rowed down the Mersey,
her grief was in subtle harmony with the dreary colourless
day; and weeks after she felt those waters to be haunted
with the memory of suffering. As an example of narrative
the whole passage is almost unsurpassed; it shows the extraordinary power with which Mrs Gaskell portrayed human
emotions growing out of an external environment.

Mrs Gaskell liked a domesticated Nature. Flowers were
to her what hills were to the Brontes. Though she mentioned

wild flowers with a peculiar note of affection, it was in gardens, cherished by human beings, that she felt most intimately at ease. She would not have shared in the antipathy of Miss Pole's cook to "dumb flowers" (*The Cage at Cranford*). How tenderly she spoke of the deserted garden at Milham Grange! Even more beautiful is the description, in the same book, of a mountain-shadowed Welsh garden awakening to the song of birds, the stir and glory of dawn. At once we remember the wonderful garden-scene in *Jane Eyre*, where the glowing fragrant beauty added exaltation to the minds of Jane and Rochester. But here, in Mrs Gaskell's story, Ruth turned back from the window "faint and sick with anxiety."

Passing from gardens to the actual houses of men, we are impressed by the deep poignancy with which Mrs Gaskell described old deserted places revisited by those who had loved them. Ruth stood looking into the "uninhabited desolation" of her mother's room, "seeing nothing of what was present," but "a vision of former days."—"It was gone —all gone into the land of shadows." When Sylvia returned to her deserted home, every detail added its pang to the aching sense of desolation; each object sharpened the edge of regret. The pathos culminated at the point where she actually touched the doorway of her home.—"She paused softly before the house-door, and entered the porch, and kissed the senseless wood."

Mrs Gaskell was no less sensitive in her apprehension of the atmosphere clinging about houses filled with a living human presence. Sometimes she described a home like the Hope Farm with its pervasive spirit of peace. Again, in *The Old Nurse's Story* she told of a house with a vaguely sinister "feeling." At other times the sense of mysterious terror became more sharply defined. She told us of many things which made the solemn winter "strange and haunted and terrific" to Lois: "The long, dark evenings; the dimly-lighted rooms; the creaking passages;...the white mist coming nearer and nearer to the windows every evening in strange shapes, like phantoms."

In the history of every home there are certain days and hours when an unusual mood pervades every corner of the house; this is particularly evident at times of fatal sickness or death. Nobody ever felt these things more keenly than Mrs Gaskell. The hushed house at Milton where Mrs Hale lay dying—the frozen stillness of Hamley Hall where Osborne lay dead—such matters are too intimate and overwhelming for the rudeness of speech.

We have no space to praise at all adequately the charm of Mrs Gaskell's rooms. True, she described Mrs Thornton's drawing-room, with its "painfully spotted, spangled, speckled look." She was woman enough to feel that a room could be antagonistic in its atmosphere; and she was also woman enough to love making a room comfortable. She seems to have felt that no room was quite right without flowers, or at least a glimpse of garden. Ruth's little room was un-adorned with actual flowers, but it possessed the com-pensating quality of being like a snowdrop.

At this point we must call a halt; not because the material is exhausted, but for the plain reason that we must stop sometime. We are seized with temptation to follow Mrs Gas-kell back into the open air; to wrestle with Philip Hepburn through the blinding snow, or to stand beside Phillis Holman in the golden evening light. The best way of escaping from such temptations is to remember that good as these things may be, there are better things to follow. So far we have not looked beyond the framework of the picture.

III

HUMOUR

Up to this point we have been considering the physical setting of Mrs Gaskell's stories. We next proceed to their spiritual setting—those moods and emotions wrapped about the human figures, and communicated to the mind of the readers. We must restrict ourselves to the two predominating moods—laughter and pity. We take the word "laughter" because it includes more than "humour." A delicate sense of humour is a living quality which grows towards maturity. In Mrs Gaskell's earlier stories the things which make us smile are not so much humorous as infectiously exuberant. Of this nature is the rather Dickensian description in *Christmas Storms and Sunshine* of the rival households— Jenkins *v.* Hodgson, the cat versus the baby. The same unconventional buoyancy springs up through much of *Company Manners.* Surely we all hanker after those teas in "the superannuated schoolroom." How consoling it is to discover that Mrs Gaskell fidgetted in "rational" company, and even felt inclined to relieve her feelings by bursting out "with some interminable nonsensical word" like "Aballibogibouganorribo"! Further on she tells us of a highly serious company rejuvenated by a game of "blow-feather"; "Making fools of ourselves was better than making owls, as we had been doing." After so much advice on how to be happy though at parties, it is delightful to consider Mrs Gaskell in another light. From *French Life* we can see how dearly she loved a journey. She revelled like a child in the excitement of the crowded *Place* at Chartres. Like a child also, she was particularly drawn to the wild beast shows. It would be possible to go on and on selecting passages like these, with every phrase dipped in the waters of happiness. We can turn for our final example to the first paragraph of her last book; it was written in the style of a nursery rhyme—"the old rigmarole of childhood." We may be sure that Mrs Gaskell never grew old.

A joyous attitude to life is sometimes the possession of those moderately well-to-do people who are not rich, like Mrs Gaskell, in the faculty of humour. As this faculty in its most beautiful and exquisite manifestation is something which mellows and matures, it is best to glance over the whole course of Mrs Gaskell's work and watch the ripening process. It can only be a glance, not an examination.

At first Mrs Gaskell's sense of humour was happy, but crude. This applies in a great degree to *Mary Barton*, her first ambitious work.

Satire made its first appearance in *The Moorland Cottage*. The affectations of Mrs Browne are interesting, not only from this point of view, but also as a promise of something better to follow. In many respects her portrait is a first sketch of a great masterpiece—the figure of Mrs Gibson. Mrs Gaskell's art was never stationary; her second draughts were always incomparably finer than her first.

Mr Harrison's Confessions was an exercise which prepared Mrs Gaskell for the full technique of *Cranford*—an exercise almost as pretty as the more elaborate "piece." The satire which glanced out here and there in *The Moorland Cottage* had a tinge of bitterness; here it was more pervasive, and absolutely without malice. We bear no ill-will to anybody in the book—excepting perhaps Miss Horsman. Even Mr Harrison felt remarkably little annoyance, considering his uncomfortable position in the centre of an equilateral triangle, with a lady at each angle. He made his humorous "confessions" after all perils were safely past; but we wonder, if even at the worst moments of catastrophe he ever lost all sense of the ridiculous—not even on that morning when he woke up and could not remember whether he was engaged or not.—"If I was engaged, who was the lady?"—He stood before the mirror weighing epithets to fit his personal appearance—plain, fascinating, handsome, agreeable, and so forth; but in the midst of this grave investigation he seemed to have a sudden realisation that he actually looked rather comic. This good-tempered humour is not in the least obtuse. We see through all these people who give us so much amusement. Although Mr Harrison was rather "dense,"

Mrs Gaskell lets us understand the point of Mrs Rose's elegant hints.—"She said she wished she had the power to sweeten my life as she could my tea." Mrs Gaskell may have been tolerant, but she was not blind. She was happy, just because she saw so much and so keenly.

Then we come to *Cranford* itself. We know that Mrs Gaskell delighted in this book.

I am so much pleased you like it (she wrote to Ruskin). It is the only one of my books that I can read again; but sometimes, when I am ailing or ill, I take "Cranford," and, I was going to say *enjoy* it (but that would not be pretty), laugh over it afresh. And it is true, too, for I have seen the cow that wore the gray-flannel jacket—and I know the cat that swallowed the lace that belonged to the lady that sent for the doctor that gave the...."

This lets us into one source of Mrs Gaskell's charm; she was not too far removed from her subject. She selected Mary Smith as the narrator, and the whole tale runs through in the first person. Mary belonged to Drumble, but she was so well known at Cranford that she could hardly rank as an outsider. "I had vibrated all my life," she said, "between Drumble and Cranford." She was sufficiently detached from Cranford to see it in true perspective, and yet sufficiently near to enter into its life. If she stood at a distance where she could see the irony of its affairs, she was not too far away to appreciate its pathos—or even to share in its epidemics of panic. She felt the burglar-scare as keenly as anybody who owned property in Cranford. "I...had proposed to Miss Matty that we should cover up our faces under the bed-clothes, so that there should be no danger of the robbers thinking we could identify them."

Cranford is so generally loved that it is scarcely necessary to praise it. We shall have to put aside most of the stock passages which everybody quotes—the scares about burglars and ghosts, the refined way of eating oranges, and so on. Even if we leave these out, the book is full of delicate beauties, like small twinkling points of light which flash out swiftly, and then fade away. Take the culminating detail in the comparison of the two Miss Browns.—"Any female observer might detect a slight difference in the attire of the two sisters

—that of Miss Jessie being about two pounds per annum more expensive than Miss Brown's." When Martha refused to leave Miss Matty, she unwittingly came out with a *bon mot*.— "I'll not listen to reason. Reason always means what some one else has got to say."

These glimpses of humour are like gleaming threads closely woven into the material of the story. If we examine the general effect of that material, we see that it is very largely a species of social satire. The question of social precedence is kept well to the front. The narrative never soars beyond the rank of Lady Glenmire, and rarely drops below that of Miss Betty Barker, the milliner; and she, we are told, felt herself

justified in shutting up shop, and retiring from business. She also...set up her cow; a mark of respectability in Cranford almost as decided as setting up a gig is among some people.

Everybody remembers the story of that cow. We are more apt to pass over the suggestive question placed at the end of the episode.—"Do you ever see cows dressed in grey flannel in London?" The same kind of question is repeated in almost identical words, after we have been told of the newspapers laid on Miss Jenkyns' carpets.—"Do you make paper paths for every guest to walk upon in London?" This suggests that Cranford, having a social etiquette of its own, was well worth being studied by outsiders of a more conventional type. Yet "conventional" is hardly the word. If Cranford did not follow all the London conventions, it established others of its own. It had a rigid, though unusual code, with binding articles prohibiting certain topics, such as poverty, in refined society.—"It was a word not to be mentioned to ears polite." The general passion for keeping up appearances led Miss Matty to extraordinary contrivances with her candles. This, no doubt, was an instance of the "shabby gentility" which pinches in private, and keeps up a brave show in public. Usually we taste the irony of such things with a distinctly bitter flavour. But there is no bitterness in *Cranford*. We have already noticed the shrewdness behind Mrs Gaskell's good-nature. In our hasty way, we are prone to condemn all affectation as despicable. Mrs Gaskell

saw further when she realised that there are some innocent
affectations which endear themselves to us by their very
quaintness.

It is hard to leave *Cranford* without speaking a very little
about the Jenkyns sisters. It would be interesting to speculate
on the influences of heredity as they affected the two sisters,
Miss Deborah taking after her father, and Miss Matty after
her mother. But for this we have no space. The sisters themselves are significantly contrasted. Miss Matty was far less
odd than her elder sister, and in a sense less amusing. But
it was comparatively easy to make Miss Deborah "funny";
she lent herself to caricature. It is a higher type of humour
which surrounds Miss Matty's figure, and reveals its gentle
pathos. This poor faded little woman had an instinctive
sympathy for her dare-devil brother. Miss Deborah would
never have repeated Peter's pranks with so much zest. "No!
my dear, I won't tell you of them, because they might not
shock you as they ought to do; and they were very shocking."
But with a delightful inconsistency she went straight on to
tell how Peter dressed up as a lady. That phrase about
Peter's "shocking" deeds seems to be an echo of her own
tragedy. When she visited Mr Holbrook, she slipped out a
little remark of the same kind. "'It is very pleasant dining
with a bachelor,' said Miss Matty softly, 'I only hope it is
not improper; so many pleasant things are!'" Yet we know
that Miss Matty should have married Mr Holbrook long ago;
that hope had been abandoned as pleasant, but "improper."
Marriage seemed to dwindle and fade out of her scheme of
life. It startled her to find it coming back to her immediate
circle. This is how she received the news of Lady Glenmire's
engagement to Mr Hoggins.—"'Marry!' said Miss Matty
once again. 'Well! I never thought of it. Two people that
we know going to be married! It's coming very near!'"
Jane Austen's Mr Woodhouse might have used the same
words; but in his case we feel no impulse of pity; our laughter
remains stationary, without passing into compassion. Miss
Matty spoke of marriage, almost as if it were an epidemic
disease to be shunned; but she ought to have been married.
Her whole life was emptied because the thing which ought

to have been never came to pass. This left its colouring of pathos on every side of her nature.

Mrs Gaskell never attempted anything else quite in the *Cranford* manner. Her tendency in later books—with the possible exception of *My Lady Ludlow*—was to concentrate her humour into a few figures, set in a somewhat contrasted environment.

In *Ruth* we have the characters of Sally and Mr Bradshaw. The former, though less subtle, is very distinctly portrayed. Her brusqueness never takes us in, and we put little faith in her protests against babies.—"I never could abide them things. I'd sooner have rats in the house." Still Mrs Gaskell never leaves us under the impression that Sally's temper was not just a trifle inconvenient. It cannot have been comfortable to hear "low mutterings of thunder in the distance, in the shape of Sally's soliloquies, which like the asides at a theatre, were intended to be heard." Moreover, in her cavalier treatment of Ruth's hair, she went beyond the stage of hard words, which are reputed to break no bones. But for all that, on a memorable occasion she proved herself less severe than gentle Mr Benson; she reminded him that Solomon's belief in the rod had produced a lamentable result.—"It were King Solomon's son that were King Rehoboam, and no great shakes either." For all her roughness of speech Sally was by no means sour; she could rise to great acts of devotion. She also provided the alleviation of her general conversation. The record of her sweethearts is so flagrantly and delightfully humorous that it hardly fits into the highly-strung, and somewhat strained tragedy of the whole story. But that is nothing to the discredit of the humour; it is truer than the tragedy. She read Ruth a lecture on the duty of cheerfulness, and enforced her point with personal reminiscences regarding the connection between penitence and puddings; and we feel that humour like this makes life sane and wholesome.

Mr Bradshaw, unlike Sally, is surveyed from the standpoint of satire. He stands apart from figures such as Mr Pecksniff or Mr Brocklehurst, because he was self-righteous without being an absolute humbug. It has been urged with some justice that Mrs Gaskell was too lenient to him, and too hard on Ruth. But she was hard on him at the beginning. When the Bradshaws entertained Ruth and the Bensons, "two well-behaved but unnaturally quiet children were sent to bed early in the evening, in an authoritative voice by their father, because one of them had spoken too loud while he was enlarging on an alteration in the tariff." He is represented as an intolerable egotist, who never lost an opportunity of taking credit to himself. "Your mother," he said to Jemima, "is in the habit of repeating accurately to me what takes place in my absence....I have trained her to habits of accuracy very unusual in a woman." Yet he had a kind of honour which manifested itself in unlovely forms. Though he left Mr Benson's church, he resolved, from a hard sense of duty, to keep up his pew-rents. Towards the end of the story he became humbled. His repentance struck a more genuine note than similar cases in Dickens—for instance, that of Mr Dombey. Mr Chesterton has remarked upon Dickens' tendency to confound softening of the heart with softening of the brain. Mrs Gaskell escaped this peril of false sentiment, possibly because she never made Mr Bradshaw quite so bad as Mr Dombey. He was bad enough, but not absolutely beyond redemption.

Taking *North and South*, Mrs Gaskell's next long story, we find an even greater diminution of humour. It contains neither satiric portraits nor definitely humorous situations. In the reconciliation between Mr Thornton and Higgins there are dashes of humour, but very little else.

My Lady Ludlow marks a return to the humorous standpoint. Sir Roger de Coverley might have behaved like Lady Ludlow, if his clergyman had resembled Mr Gray in having a strong mind. As for Lady Ludlow, she was like the Cranford ladies in possessing many amiable crotchets, though hers were of a more aristocratic type. She approved, for instance, of no man who wore his hair unpowdered— "which was to insult the proprieties of life by being undressed. It was English sansculottism." A capacity to detect the odour of decaying strawberry leaves was her supreme test of gentility. We can never forget how anxiously and vainly she tried this experiment on Margaret Dawson. Such crotchets were quite harmless. Lady Ludlow's whims became more inconvenient when they extended to a prohibition of popular education. The crowning episode of the whole book is the description of her terrible discovery that Harry Gregson could read. It would be a pleasure to quote from it, but it is a compensation to remember that nobody who has read the book requires to have his memory of that passage stimulated by quotation.

Lady Ludlow is not the only humorous figure in this story, steeped as it is in an atmosphere of comedy. We get many flashing pictures, full of humorous verve. We catch, for example, a glimpse of Harry Gregson's lawless father being rebuked by Mr Gray.—"He had...listened to the parson's bold words with an approving smile, much as Mr Gulliver might have hearkened to a lecture from a Lilliputian." Captain James again, is a person who always calls up a sort of benevolent amusement. We hear much of his agricultural experiments and the "uproar" they created; much also of his frankness.—"I cannot fancy," said the narrator, "his ever lowering his strong, loud, clear voice, or having a confidential conversation with anyone."

Then we have Miss Galindo, who was an avowed humorist —a "scold," as she termed herself, in a world of saints, scolds, and sinners. She gave a most delightful account of her methods of turning the tables on Sally, the servant, who in an access of devotion roasted the meat to a cinder, and then justified herself by quoting Martha and Mary; Miss Galindo decided to take her turn of acting the part of Mary—with most edifying results. She was "nearly being an authoress once";—and how?

I got paper and half-a-hundred good pens, and a bottle of ink all ready....It ended in my having nothing to say, when I sat down to write. But sometimes, when I get hold of a book, I wonder why I let such a poor reason stop me. It does not others.

We have no space to quote her views on education, matrimony, or machinery. We can simply remind ourselves that it is worth while going back to the book to relish them again.

We pass over *The Manchester Marriage*, with its fleeting glimpses of humour—particularly in relation to Mr Openshaw's proposal.—A small sketch, *Curious if True* showed Mrs Gaskell's humour in a new vein. It was her only attempt at parody; but with what a fantastic and dainty result! Sir A. W. Ward has pointed out the reference to Bluebeard, so we shall not quote this which is the crowning touch of the phantasy. We must content ourselves with a passing comment on Mrs Gaskell's peculiar leaning towards cats. She often referred to them, but in no place with greater gusto. We could instance her description of the chasseur—Puss-in-Boots, of course; or the account of his affinity to Madame de Mioumiou, betrayed, be it observed, by the unusual state of their nerves when they heard "a commonplace sound" like the scuttling of rats behind the tapestry.—Four years later, in the middle of *French Life*, Mrs Gaskell suddenly "came out with" a tale of the last Manx fairy. It was quite irrelevant, and altogether entrancing. It is easily missed; but anybody who finds it once, will surely never mislay it. It occurs on page 663 of the Knutsford Edition, vol. VII. This and the sketch we have just been considering prove to us that Mrs Gaskell could, if she liked, have risen to an easy, unaffected mastery of a literary "kind" in which mediocrity is so common, and absolute perfection so rare. She could have written literature to please children, and at the same time taken all "grown-ups" by storm.

Returning to the chronological course, our next book is *Sylvia's Lovers*. Here, as in the case of *Ruth*, the humour is comparatively rare, and chiefly confined to a few portraits. In fact there is only one. There are a few humorous situations, such as that where Sylvia learnt her lessons. But the real humour of the narrative was bound up with Daniel Robson; and it died out when his troubles came upon him. His opinions of "the Frenchies," or King George's share in the laws, may not have been at all logical or well-informed, but it is most pleasant to hear any opinions so vigorously stated. He always claimed the superiority of his sex, and was most indignant when Bell suggested he was wearying for company.

That's all t'women know about it. Wi' them it's "coompany, coompany, coompany," and they think a man's no better than theirsels. A'd have yo' to know a've a vast o' thoughts in mysel' as I'm noane willing to lay out for t' benefit o' every man. A've niver gotten time for meditation sin' a were married.

Nevertheless, when the travelling tailor arrived, Daniel broke forth into an ecstasy of welcome:

Come in, Harry, come in, and talk a bit o' sense to me, for a've been shut up wi' women these four days, and a'm a'most a nateral by this time....A reckon it's th' being wi' nought but women as tires me so; they talk so foolish, it gets int' t' bones like.

We cannot linger over Daniel's faculty for narrative, either when relating his astounding adventures on a whale's back, or when recounting his exploits at the "Randyvowse." Neither can we discuss the delicate irony with which Mrs Gaskell portrayed his relations with his women-folk. There is something strangely attractive about his simple egotism, his incorrigible youthfulness, his hearty, impetuous kindness. But we cannot linger. As we have remarked already, all humour faded from him as he passed into the shadow of calamity. When he became a tragic figure, there was nothing else in the story to retain the flavour of comedy.

Mrs Gaskell's happy grace of manner returned to her while she wrote large portions of *Cousin Phillis*. Yet this beautiful story displays no deliberate attempts after wit. It contains no characters whose chief justification would appear to be their faculty of affording amusement. The light humour which gleams out here and there is entirely spontaneous. There is something peculiarly engaging in Paul's frankness and youth. He was so afraid—doubtless, with reason—of Independent ministers and their inconvenient tendency to catechise him. No sooner had he escaped this hazard than he fell into the still more desperate predicament of having to keep up conversations with a girl taller than himself, and alarmingly fond of Latin.—We can look past him to the minister, who surely had no intentions of being "funny" when pleading for a removal to the grey bedroom, where he could not see lazy Timothy Cooper:

It would save me from a daily temptation to anger....Some day,

I am afraid, I shall go down and send him about his business—let alone the way in which he makes me cut myself while I am shaving —and then his wife and children will starve. I wish we could move to the grey room.

Cousin Holman also, had her moments of unconsciously affording amusement. When Paul's father in his zeal for demonstration used a charred stick to draw diagrams on her clean white dresser, Paul was the only person to notice her housewifely dismay:

Cousin Holman had, in the meantime, taken a duster out of a drawer, and under pretence of being as much interested as her husband in the drawing, was secretly trying on an outside mark, how easily it would come off, and whether it would leave her dresser as white as before.

This sort of humorous aside comes up at intervals as if to remind us that there is an amusing side to most ordinary matters. We never feel as if Mrs Gaskell were laying herself out to make mirth for us; and for this very reason our enjoyment is easily awakened.

When we come to *Wives and Daughters*, we feel that in respect of humour and all other features, everything is exactly "right." The unforced and inevitable humour grows out of the story instead of being placed here and there in patches. It appears at all sorts of odd moments, just as in everyday life. Stray allusions to little Molly's preparations for the great fête make us feel very tenderly to her innocent agitation. We smile at her, but in a protective manner.— "Her gloves were far too large for the little dimpled fingers, but, as Betty had told her they were to last her for years, it was all very well." At other times we are casually informed of certain people's mannerisms—Mr Gibson's trick of whistling, or Lord Cumnor's interrogative mode of conversation. Sometimes again, humour asserts itself for a brief moment in the midst of disturbing factors with an incongruity true to the facts of ordinary experience. Miss Browning had declared her intention of confronting Mrs Dawes with her slanderous lies against Molly; and Miss Phoebe burst out piteously: "Oh, don't call them 'lies,' sister; it's such a strong, ugly word. Please call them 'tarradiddles,' for I don't believe she meant any harm."

The people in this book often appeal to us by their utter simplicity. They seem so entirely unaware of an opposite point of view, and make questionable statements with a serene confidence that nobody could call them in question. Squire Hamley would hear nothing of his wife's opinions on love and marriage:

Pooh! away with love! Nay, my dear, we loved each other so dearly we should never have been happy with anyone else; but that's a different thing. People aren't like what they were when we were young. All the love now-a-days is just silly fancy, and sentimental romance, as far as I can see.

Lady Cumnor, though aware of her own excellence, was quite unconscious of her own vanity. Only once did she evince the least sign of misgiving, and that after she had been explaining by a logical process that independent and open-minded people could not fail to be convinced by her judgment. "I am not a despot, I hope?" she enquired by way of anxious after-thought. Possibly it was the only time that she suspected the truth about herself.

The humour of *Wives and Daughters* is so many-sided that we must turn it about to catch the light on its different facets. For instance, we might consider how far Mr Gibson is a benevolent reproduction of Jane Austen's Mr Bennet. Or we could trace throughout the story any elements which seem reminiscent of *Cranford*;—Mrs Goodenough's method of hiding a stained gown, for example, though Mrs Goodenough herself was not quite "genteel" enough for Cranford society; or we might play a sort of guessing-game, shuffling up little speeches of Miss Deborah Jenkyns and Miss Clarinda Browning (also those of Miss Matty Jenkyns and Miss Phoebe Browning), and then trying to guess who was the actual speaker; it would be a somewhat "tricky" game.

Take another facet—and this the presence of humorous "situations." The supreme excellence of these passages lies in the fact that they are never solely humorous; they are closely related to matters of serious import, and often form strong links in the plot. The description of the Charity Ball

began in an atmosphere of comedy; but the ball itself, with
its general effect of bringing together a good many people,
had a direct impetus on the course of the story. Mr Gibson's
prescription for "Master Coxe" may have been exceedingly
witty, but Mr Coxe's love-malady was the "first cause"
of the doctor's second marriage. Mrs Gaskell never lets us
feel that by yielding to her humour we are idly relaxing our
powers. We cannot afford to pass lightly over her lightest
scenes. "Hoc semper humile," said Quintilian of laughter.
But modern readers are not quite so supercilious. They have
come to realise that trifling laughable things may have far-
reaching consequences over the lives of men and women.

We can hardly leave *Wives and Daughters* without some
allusion to its single sustained topic of satire—and this the
question of aristocratic convention. Though not the central
motive of the story, it recurs constantly as a part of the
general environment. Molly grew up in a community where
everybody felt an awed admiration for the Cumnors. When
she was a little girl, Lord Cumnor appealed to her fancy as
"a cross between an archangel and a king." Her first experience of high life was the school function at the Towers,
where everybody was expected to talk "on stilts." We
remember how she and her friends drove through the lodge
gates, and "silence fell upon the carriageful of ladies." When
Mrs Goodenough's niece—"a stranger to the town"—ventured on a casual remark, the only answer she obtained was
a simultaneous "Hush!" No wonder that Molly thought it
"very awful," and almost wished herself back at home.—The
Miss Brownings had another glimpse into "the best society"
when Lady Harriet paid them a call. "'O Molly,' exclaimed
Miss Phoebe, 'I thought you'd never come back! Such a
piece of news! Sister has gone to bed; she's had a headache
—with the excitement, I think; but she says it's new bread.'"
We recall the gossips at the Charity Ball, and how they were
buoyed up with the expectation of seeing a real duchess in
her diamonds; Mrs Goodenough had kept on her glasses
for an hour and a half to lose nothing of the imposing spectacle.
How mortified they were when the great lady arrived—
minus her diamonds! And how joyfully Mrs Gaskell set

herself to describe their disappointment!—We have spoken
so far of the Cumnors; but they were by no means the only
representatives of the nobility. The Hamleys indeed were
of a far more ancient stock. The passage where Miss Browning,
the vicar, and Mrs Goodenough discuss their reputed origin
reads very like Jane Austen—particularly the emphatic
conclusion.—"At any rate the Hamleys were a very old
family, if not aborigines."

We must mention two casual phrases which afford a clue
to much of this excellence. They give us an inkling of the
foundations on which true laughter is established. Molly
said of her father—"Papa enjoys a joke at everything, you
know. It is a relief after all the sorrow he sees." Mrs Gaskell,
however, relied on humour, not only for this function of
effective or soothing contrast, but as a part of the truth.
Roger Hamley looked at people as she would have done.—
"Though he had a strong sense of humour, it never appeared
to diminish his respect for the people who amused him."
This humour, allied to respect, is an element of interpre-
tative insight.

*   *   *   *   *   *

What then, are our general conclusions as to the development of Mrs Gaskell's humour?—We see that she started
with a natural endowment of happiness, and preserved it to
the end. Quite early in *Mr Harrison's Confessions* and *Cranford*, she developed a peculiar type of pervasive humour,
which, in the second case, merged almost imperceptibly into
pathos. This particular kind of humour never again formed
the complete substance of her stories; but it survived into
her latest work as part of a larger scheme. We next observe
the emergence of humorous portraits, such as Sally's in *Ruth*.
But in that book the humorous passages seem somewhat
roughly patched into the texture of the narrative. *My Lady
Ludlow* marks a partial return to the method of pervasive
humour clinging round subjects of a type slightly different
from those handled in *Cranford*. *Curious if True* and the
little fairy-tale from *French Life* give us Mrs Gaskell's sole
excursions into the realm of nursery humour. In *Sylvia's
Lovers* we have a single humorous portrait which undergoes

transformation, and becomes a figure of tragedy; the humour is not of a kind to survive the shock of calamity. Then comes *Cousin Phillis* with its spontaneous, unaffected humour, growing naturally like an exquisite blossom among other flowers. Finally we have the tenderness and grace which crown *Wives and Daughters*. In this book Mrs Gaskell seemed to gather together all her resources of humour. She retained to the end her natural buoyancy of mood; she retained also her faculty for suggesting that humour is constantly stirring just below the surface; she mingled humour of the pervasive *Cranford* type with matters of deeper import, this humour being blended into the narrative not as a patchwork, but as something inherent in its nature; she preserved her old knack for turning out satiric portraits—such as Mrs Gibson's; but these satiric figures were more closely bound up with the lives and happiness of their fellows. In her earlier books Mrs Gaskell practised many varieties of humour; in her latest book she wove these different chords and phrases of music into a perfect harmony. Or, to change the metaphor, the humour of this novel shows different lights and colours, like those of a running stream. There are many causes for these variations—the depth and rush of the water, the objects seen through its transparent medium, its contact with slanting rays of sunlight. Yet the water is all the same water, and not a series of variegated patterns. The humour of *Wives and Daughters* has the same living unity. It varies according to the emotional pitch of the story; it catches lights and reflections from different themes; it fades from sunshine into the dim shadows of pathos; it flows through eddies and currents and still, deep pools. But in all these wanderings it obeys the law of its own being; it is never diverted from its natural course.

IV

PATHOS

IT is interesting to consider which faculty came first to Mrs Gaskell—compassion or humour. It will probably be acknowledged that her compassion was at first more evident, though it needed to grow side by side with humour before it could attain to its perfection of delicacy and insight.

Mary Barton shows us Mrs Gaskell's pathos as yet undisciplined by humour. It is genuine, no doubt, but how dreadfully overpowering! When Ruskin wrote to congratulate her on *Cranford*, he said, "You're fond of killing nice people"; but here it is not only the "nice people" who are killed off. Death comes back and back to the story. It is like an overhanging scourge.—Mrs Gaskell's treatment of bereavement is often singularly beautiful. John Barton's "groping hand fell on the piled-up tea things" which his wife had left aside, and this simple action "touched the source of tears."—"He was reminded of one of the daily little actions which acquire such power when they have been performed for the last time by one we love."—Further on in the story we have to stand by death-beds. We notice how gently Mrs Gaskell handles the superstition of those watching over the dying twins, and trying not to "wish" them; she looks on with a mind free from disdain or impertinent curiosity.—The passing of Davenport is infinitely more heart-rending. We see more of the physical aspect of death, and for a moment we are reminded of Tolstoi's resolute mind to shirk nothing of the grim truth. But Mrs Gaskell never remains shrinking over the physical horror; she follows it up with some spiritual beauty or tenderness:

The flesh was sunk, the features prominent, bony and rigid. The fearful clay-colour of death was over all. But the eyes were open and sensitive, though the films of the grave were setting upon them.

It is that one word "sensitive" which transmutes terror into

beauty. And so the story goes on, with physical details here
and there, invariably purified by their contact with the
spiritual—the love of husband and wife, the brotherly kindness of neighbours, the brooding mystery of the end.—"The
face grew beautiful as the soul neared God."

In the case of Alice Wilson's death we seem to forget
everything physical and earthly. She herself never thought
of such matters. Nearly blind and deaf, she knew the end
was coming; and so great was the spiritual refinement of
this "uneducated" woman, that her words took on an unconscious poetry:

I'm as happy as a child. I sometimes think I am a child whom the
Lord is hush-a-bying to my long sleep. For when I were a nurse-
girl, my missis always told me to speak very soft and low, and
to darken the room that her little one might go to sleep; and
now all noises are hushed and still to me, and the bonny earth
seems dim and dark, and I know it's my Father lulling me away
to my long sleep.

It was not only death that stirred Mrs Gaskell to sympathy.
She had an instinctive reverence for all ties of human
affection. Of John Barton and Mary she wrote: "Between
the father and the daughter there existed in full that mysterious
bond which unites those who have been loved by one who
is now dead and gone." Or we hear of Mrs Wilson's pride
in her son, Jim—"He'd always speak as kind and soft to me
as if he were courting me like."

Mrs Gaskell went even further into the heart of sympathy.
Not only did she reverence deep feeling from without; her
imagination travelled far into the spirits of her men and
women. She knew—what personal experience could not have
taught her—how Mary felt when placed before the judge.
Sometimes also, she condoned human failings with sudden
flashes of insight. John Barton was a hard man; but, she
adds, "Real meekness of character is called out by experience
of kindness. And few had been kind to him." At every stage
of the story we feel that she must have been one of those
"understanding" people who have an intuitive power of
consolation. When Margaret spoke out her secret dread of
blindness, "Mary knelt by her, striving to soothe and com-

fort her; but, like an inexperienced person, striving rather
to deny the correctness of Margaret's fear, than helping her
to meet and overcome the evil." We feel at once that
Mrs Gaskell was not "raw," like Mary, at giving comfort.
The sympathy which George Eliot achieved by discipline
seems to have come to her by nature.

It is impossible, in a short paragraph, to do anything like
justice to the wonderful concentrated passion which beats
through *The Heart of John Middleton*. There is something
peculiarly searching in its stern candour, and the compressed
energy which strains through its plain, curt phrases. Yet
John remembered little things, almost irrelevant, in the
midst of so much fierceness; all through we feel this contrast
between gentleness and violence—particularly in the trifling
domestic details which give a strange reality to the record of
turbulent passion. John's language ranged from an utter
homeliness of statement to an austere, almost Scriptural
grandeur; and every word rang true. We cannot abstain
from quotations. Indeed this story is worthy of quotation.
On the culminating night of storm John's enemy stumbled
over the threshold:

Had he been a stranger, I might not have welcomed him; but as
he was mine enemy I gave him welcome in a lordly dish....I pro-
mised him a bed on the floor, and I thought of Jael and Sisera.

All the pent-up egotism of his nature burst free as he looked
down on the sleeping, helpless figure.—"I looked again. His
face was old, and worn, and miserable. So should mine enemy
look." Then all things moved towards the end.—"In the
storm of the night mine enemy came to me; in the calm of
the grey morning, I led him forth, and bade him 'God
speed.'" There may be a slight overbalancing of the emotion
in the account of little Grace and her message. We cannot
pause to discuss this point. If it is a flaw, it is the only one.
The most wonderful thing of all is the fact that a gentle
woman like Mrs Gaskell should have understood wild John
Middleton. Yet we feel that she read him through and
through. She had eyes which sometimes looked

Right through the deeds of men.

We cannot pause to consider the brief entry of mystical pathos into the light-hearted comedy of *Mr Harrison's Confession*. We simply quote and pass on. Mr Harrison left the house where little Walter lay dead.—"The street was as quiet as ever; not a shadow was changed; for it was not yet four o'clock. But during the night a soul had departed."

The pathos of *Cranford* finds its centre in the person of Miss Matty. It is not usual to find so much patience for colourless, inefficient people, wanting in "push." Jane Austen never showed such daring. Her central figures were all of them young, and most of them sprightly. Charlotte Bronte thought she was running great risks when she chose a plain heroine; but Jane Eyre was young, and as well she was clever. Miss Matty was old and diffident. "I knew I was good for little," she said, "and that my best work in the world was to do odd jobs quietly to set others at liberty." Some people would have despised her as ineffective; but not Mrs Gaskell.

No! there was nothing she could teach to the rising generation of Cranford; unless they had been quick learners and ready imitators of her patience, her humility, her sweetness, her quiet contentment with all that she could not do.

Mrs Gaskell always showed a very tender reserve in speaking of her tragedy. As Miss Matty herself kept silence, her creator seems to have felt that any outspoken comments would be jarring. We know perfectly well, why, after Mr Holbrook's death, Miss Matty ordered caps like the Honourable Mrs Jamieson's; for Mrs Jamieson was a widow. We do not require any further explanation. On a night of unaccustomed revelation Miss Matty opened her heart more fully, and showed its emptiness. She was telling Mary about her yearning love for children, and the little noiseless child who came to her in dreams:

She never grows older, though I have dreamt about her for many years....I have wakened with the clasp of her dear little arms around my neck. Only last night...my little darling came in my dream and put up her mouth to be kissed, just as I have seen real babies do to real mothers before going to bed.

There was another story buried in Miss Matty's heart, and this the tragedy which broke her mother's spirit. How wistfully she turned over the old faded love letters! Mrs Gaskell has been compared to Lamb, and some of her phrases echo the very tones of *Dream Children*. But it was not the love letters that called out Miss Matty's reminiscences. Her memory unfolded as she turned over "poor" Peter's schoolboy effusions. It was there that her mother's sorrows had their beginning. When Miss Matty was deeply moved, she had a wonderful gift for narrative. The very scents and atmosphere of the old emotions seemed to revive as she told the story of Peter's final escapade.—"I was in the storeroom, helping my mother to make cowslip wine. I cannot abide the wine now, nor the scent of the flowers; they turn me sick and faint as they did that day." She went on with her story, very quietly, and without any flutter; but this "emotion recollected in tranquillity" had lost nothing of its sting. Her simple words, spoken, we may be sure, without any gesture, seem to bring before our eyes her mother's unceasing movements:

The afternoon went on, my mother never resting....My mother kept passing from room to room, in and out of the house, moving noiselessly, but never ceasing....My father and mother walked on and on; it was more than an hour since he had joined her.

Again, as she lived back in the past, the old atmosphere revived.—"Oh, it was an awful time; coming down like a thunderbolt on the still sunny day, when the lilacs were all in bloom." She spoke of that day in her early youth, and then remembered with a flash that she was old. Who can calculate all the pathos which is suggested in these simple words, following the account of her mother's fading life?— "Well, my dear, it's very foolish of me, I know, when in all likelihood, I am so near seeing her again."—The story came to a ragged end. How could it be otherwise? Nothing had happened to smooth out the edges of the sad old tale. Miss Matty could not say whether Peter was dead or alive:

I believe he is dead myself; and it sometimes fidgets me that we have never put on mourning for him. And then, again, when I sit by myself, and all the house is still, I think I hear his step coming up the street, and my heart begins to flutter and beat; but the sound always goes past, and Peter never comes.

We are glad, somehow, that Mary did not follow her friend out to the open door; and we can only guess from Martha's startled remarks what happened there in the darkness. It was right that Miss Matty should have had that moment of sacred privacy.

One more word may be forgiven. Miss Matty rose to her greatest occasion that day in Mr Johnson's shop when she exchanged her sovereigns for the discredited bank-note. By this stage of the story we know her worth so well that her self-possession amazes us, without arousing our scepticism. We have never seen her like this before. We could never have foretold such behaviour from her. Yet, when we have heard the whole story, we do not for a single moment doubt its probability. Somehow, we know that this surprising thing was just what Miss Matty would have done.

Published the same year as *Cranford*, *My French Master* exhibited something of the same gentle pathos applied to a different subject; but *Ruth*, also belonging to that year, attempted larger matters with far less success. George Eliot admired this book, but wished that Mrs Gaskell had been "content with the half-truths of real life." We are glad now that Mrs Gaskell was not content with half, but pushed on to obtain the whole. In *Ruth* she was struggling to find her way. It was an ambitious attempt, which gave her exercise; though imperfect itself, it was her only way of winning through to something better. It is hard to say exactly what is wrong with this book. We always feel that the emotion is laboured, and often that it is forced. Mrs Gaskell seems to have been overwhelmed by her own earnestness. She felt it necessary to explain so much that would have been better left for granted. There is too much soliloquy, and too little silence. We should never have been told every word of Ruth's confession to Leonard. We sometimes wonder whether a real mother would have used such words—and so many of them— to a real child; but in any case it seems a breach of privacy for anybody else to hear them. This passage typifies the emotional defects of the novel as a whole.

North and South, published two years later, marks a distinct advance. We no longer feel that we are being artificially prompted to emotion. As in *Ruth*, Mrs Gaskell was tackling a big subject, but with a surer control. In *Mary Barton* she treated the sorrows of the poor with a noble sympathy. Here the impression is deepened by the greater justice with which she adds the sorrows of those who are not actually destitute. We feel Boucher's wretched misery all the more acutely for knowing that his class does not possess the monopoly of suffering. Moreover in *Mary Barton*, Mrs Gaskell showed pity for the "deserving" poor; its characters were people whom we could heartily respect. In the later book her pity was broader and more tolerant. Though she could not respect Boucher, she recognised the fact that even weak and foolish men are worthy of pity:

"Yo see," said Bessy, "all folks isn't wise, yet God lets 'em live —ay, an' gives 'em some one to love, and be loved by, just as good as Solomon. An' if sorrow comes to them they love, it hurts 'em as sore as e'er it did Solomon. I can't make it out."

Nevertheless the real interest of the story is centred on middle-class people—Margaret Hale and her family. What comes nearest to our hearts is the story of Mrs Hale's sickness and death. The strain was long protracted, and utterly unrelieved by humour. Frederick's home-coming gave the household a kind of uneasy pleasure. But—"It was a joy snatched in the house of mourning, and the zest of it was all the more pungent, because they knew in the depths of their hearts what irremediable sorrow awaited them." Death came at last, and Margaret's heart "ached within her," as she sat silently watching her father's unspoken grief:

He sat by the bed quite quietly; only, from time to time, he uncovered the face and stroked it gently, making a kind of soft, inarticulate noise, like that of some mother-animal caressing her young.

The tension would have become unbearable, if towards the grey dawn, Margaret's clear voice had not broken the death-like stillness.—"'Let not your heart be troubled,' it said; and she went steadily on through all that chapter of unspeakable consolation."

We pass on to *Half a Lifetime Ago*, a shorter story written with sustained dignity. One of its most poignant moments is that where, Susan, having rejected Michael, receives old Peggy's sympathy.

"Lass!" said Peggy solemnly, "thou hast done well. It is not long to bide, and then the end will come."

"But you are very old, Peggy," said Susan quivering.

"It is but a day sin' I were young," replied Peggy.

This theme of voluntary renunciation, which would have appealed strongly to George Eliot's type of sympathy, was rare in Mrs Gaskell. Yet she wrote in the unaccustomed strain, heart-taught, and with a stateliness quite equal to George Eliot's. We need only refer to the beautiful searching passage where Susan in "a fever of the mind" almost regretted that she had not chosen the luxurious life "haunted by no stern sense of duty." It catches the very tones of George Eliot's utterances. Yet there is this difference, that the emotion rings out more clearly and freely. It "comes through" without any impediment.

We can afford only a single reference to *The Poor Clare*. In many places Mrs Gaskell brings before us the pity of Bridget's solitude; but nothing goes home more surely than two simple sentences. Bridget, her heart "gnawed by anxiety," wrote to obtain news of her child.—"But no answer came. It was like crying into the awful stillness of night."

So far we have referred little to *The Life of Charlotte Bronte*. We do not always realise how greatly the success of that book was derived from Mrs Gaskell's previous experience. Her dealings in *Cranford* with timid old maids must have quickened her feeling for the flurried Bronte sisters, finding their way in London, and "taking nearly an hour in walking the half-mile they had to go." The whole book is steeped in pathos. All through we feel that Mrs Gaskell was "very sorry for" Charlotte Bronte. Certain things she tells us seem to haunt the memory, particularly any reference to Charlotte's loneliness. Take, as an example, her habit of pacing the parlour floor.

Three sisters had done this—then two, the other sister dropping off from the walk—and now one was left desolate, to listen for echoing steps that never came, and to hear the wind sobbing at the windows with an almost articulate sound.

For *My Lady Ludlow* we can take but one reference. It is an instance of that intermediate state between pathos and humour in which Mrs Gaskell approached so closely to Charles Lamb. Margaret Dawson told of the family pride in her mother's exquisite lace ruffles.

Not but what my dear father often told us that pride was a great sin; we were never allowed to be proud of anything but my mother's ruffles; and she was so innocently happy when she put them on— often, poor dear creature, to a very worn and threadbare gown— that I still think, even after all my experience of life, they were a blessing to the family.

The luxury of innocent pride received from Mrs Gaskell almost the same type of apology as that which Lamb put forward in *Old China* for the luxury of a rare and unselfish extravagance. Everybody must remember how he made "Bridget" justify an occasional indulgence in early strawberries or peas.—"I see no harm in people making much of themselves in that sense of the word. It may give them a hint how to make much of others." This is the sort of attitude where Mrs Gaskell most closely resembled Lamb; not in her actual humour, which was not nearly so obstreperous; not in her deliberate pathos, for this, though present in Lamb, was extremely rare; but in the recognition of things which are at once laughable and pitiful, without being contradictory.

We must pass over the pathos of *Lois the Witch*—especially remarkable in that scene of terrible accusation, or the touching passage where Lois comforts her fellow-prisoner. Nor can we say much about *The Crooked Branch*, which is one of the most appealing of Mrs Gaskell's short stories. As this narrative works to its pitiful conclusion, we feel more and more strongly her instinctive compassion for age and frailty. We noticed it before in the case of lonely Miss Matty. Here we see the clinging affection of two old "done" creatures, broken down by sorrow. It is quite common to find novelists extending sympathy to youth. It is far more unusual to find a type of mind stirred by the pathos of faded, feeble lives, without losing for itself the bloom and colour of youth.

We turn to *Sylvia's Lovers*, a book so rich in pathos that
selection is a difficult matter. We must put on one side
that wider sympathy which apprehended the background of
sorrow in Monkshaven village overshadowed by the fear of
the press gang. We can merely refer to the passing note of
pathos in Bell's story of poor forsaken Nancy Hartley, with
her constant cry—"He once was here." Neither can we
analyse the extraordinary tact with which Mrs Gaskell makes
us pity Philip without blinding us to his unlovable qualities.
He stood on the border-line of priggishness; yet she makes
us feel that even into such lives there can enter a redeeming
and refining tragedy. All this beautifully finished work is
placed at the side of her picture. The central emotion is
concerned with Daniel's arrest and trial. Mrs Gaskell surpassed herself in those scenes following in rapid succession:
Daniel led a prisoner from his own home; the ride through
driving rain to Monkshaven, and Bell's half-dazed anxiety
for trifling services of love. She wished to send her husband
his red comforter—"He'll get his rheumatiz again"—and a
bit of peppermint cake—"He's main and fond on it." Most
moving and searching of all is that wonderful twenty-seventh
chapter where we live through the long, last day of suspense.
Bell was astir long before it was light; but Sylvia, with some
premonition of the weary, empty hours, wished to lie longer.—
"'It's very early, mother,' said weary, sleepy Sylvia, dreading
returning consciousness."—Little domestic details fill our
hearts with the reality of that never-ending morning. It was
"just gone ten" when Bell thought it time to put on the
potatoes. Then came the hopeless half hour of gazing down
the empty road; and after that Sylvia's last resource—the
making of "clap-bread" to while away the time. "'Ay do!'
replied the mother, 'He'll like it fresh—he'll like it fresh.'"—
Finally Philip arrived with the dreadful tidings, and Bell rose
—how magnificently!—to the occasion.

Lass, bear up! We mun bear up, and be agait on our way to him;
he'll be needing us now. Bear up my lass! the Lord will give us
strength. We mun go to him; ay, time's precious; thou mun
cry thy cry out after!

It shows us Mrs Gaskell's own growth in reticence and

delicacy, that she told us so little more. We know that Sylvia
and her mother went to York, and we are vaguely informed
what happened there; but we are not taken along with them.
In her earlier novels Mrs Gaskell might have led us every
step of the agonising journey. Here she was stronger and
wiser. She showed us Bell and Sylvia growing towards their
ordeal; and she let us see them when they returned, changed
for life. She felt—and so do we—that it would hardly be
decent to pry further into their tragedy.

It has been observed that this tale of plain working people
is as instinct with genuine refinement as any story of high
life. A stray sentence from another book—*My Lady Ludlow*—
may give us some inkling into the methods of Mrs Gaskell's
success.—"The thoughts of illness and death seem to turn
many of us into gentlemen and gentlewomen, as long as
such thoughts are in our minds." Yet this gives the clue to
only a part of Mrs Gaskell's secret. Even in her happy days
Bell had the instincts of a gentlewoman. It was not necessary
for her to come into contact with deep sorrow before she
could achieve culture. Her nature was refined by its strong
faculty for love. It was that capacity which made even Daniel
something of a gentleman. Putting aside his dialect and his
clothes, he would have appeared no less refined than Squire
Hamley of Hamley. Mrs Gaskell realised that the essential
element of fine feeling was a power for strong affection. She
saw this power working through the lives of very "plain"
people; and this is how she managed to find gentlefolks in
dingy slums and upland farms.

The pathos of *Cousin Phillis* shows the same matured and
beautiful reticence. Phillis could not speak of her secret
happiness; still less of her secret grief. Even when Paul
gave her the letter which broke her dream, for a long time
"she did not move or say a word, or even sigh." Paul sat
in the still deep silence of the house, hearing no sound save
the "tick-tack" of the unseen clock, and—once only—the
rustling of the thin letter paper. When at last Phillis found
words, they were very few, and very simple. That period
of silence in which her sorrow began seemed to set the tone
for all that followed. It was not long before the minister

guessed the truth, but he also fell into Paul's method of helping Phillis by silence. He tactfully changed the conversation when his wife probed him with the innocent query, "Has anything gone wrong?" The direct explanation had to be given, but not before it was required. Silence brooded over the house while Phillis lay ill. When Brother Robinson and his colleague called, the minister could not bear the thought of wordy consolations;—"They will want me to lay bare my heart. I cannot do it. Paul, stay with me!" When Phillis was out of danger, he knelt down for household prayers, but no words came to his lips; and old John had to come to his rescue.

Minister, I reckon we have blessed the Lord wi' all our souls, though we've never talked about it; and maybe He'll not need spoken words this night. God bless us all, and keep our Phillis safe from harm! Amen.

This reserve is maintained to the very end. Paul feared "that she would never be what she had been before; no more she has, in some ways." We know nothing more beyond what we can guess from Phillis' own resolution for the future. "We will go back to the peace of the old days. I know we shall; I can and I will!"

Finally we come to *Wives and Daughters*. We can never neglect this book if we are looking for examples of Mrs Gaskell's finest achievement. Here again mere words of pity were very much reduced. When Roger comforted Molly, he ended up with a kind of apology. "My sermons aren't long, are they? Have they given you an appetite for lunch? Sermons always make me hungry, I know." Mrs Gaskell must have felt, with Molly, that few words of consolation are thoroughly satisfactory. It is always possible for a person to argue himself out of comfort.

I daresay it seems foolish (said Molly to Roger on a later occasion), perhaps all our earthly trials will appear foolish to us after a while; perhaps they seem so now to angels. But we are ourselves, you know, and this is *now*, not some time to come, a long, long way off. And we are not angels, to be comforted by seeing the ends for which everything is sent.

All through comfort was administered with the very minimum of words. When Roger sat and smoked with his father, very little actual reference was made to the sorrow which both men felt to be in the background; and when the Squire was stricken with grief for Osborne, Molly soothed him absolutely without speech.

Molly came up to him with the softest steps, the most hushed breath that ever she could. She did not speak, for she did not know what to say. After a moment's pause, standing by the old man's side, she slipped down to the floor, and sat at his feet. Possibly her presence might have some balm in it; but uttering of words was as a vain thing....Time had never seemed so without measure, silence had never seemed so noiseless, as it did to Molly sitting there.

This reduction of words applies also to the actual records of death. There are few death-bed details. Those things which mourners remember but never mention are kept back from the printed page. Mrs Hamley's death is announced in two sentences.—"Mrs Hamley had sunk out of life, as gradually as she sunk out of consciousness and her place in this world. The quiet waves closed over her, and her place knew her no more."

The mourners also had little to say; but their words pierce the soul. "I don't know what's come over me to speak of 'we'—'we' in this way," said the Squire; "I ought to say 'I'; it will be 'I' for evermore in this world." As he sat over his ledgers, dazed with grief, he spoke more fully to himself.—"I was never much to boast on; but she thought a deal of me—bless her! She'd never let me call myself stupid; but for all that, I am stupid." If he spoke aloud from his heart, it was with a strange oblivion of other listeners.— "I used to write to her when she was away in London, and tell her the home news. But no letter will reach her now! Nothing reaches her." Months afterwards, when he and Mr Gibson were discussing Roger's successes, the Squire again broke off as if he had been alone.—"'I wish I could tell his mother,' said the Squire in an undertone." When Osborne died, it was almost the same. The Squire could not speak. Molly silently gave him a spoonful of soup, and his speech was released in a jerk. But he made no set "book" speech, only six startling words; "He will never eat again—never."

It is not seemly to make comments on such utterances. It is enough to say that they were made, and then leave them in their sacred poignancy. Mrs Gaskell's was the method of silence, and if we are to be worthy of understanding her "deep things," we must follow in her ways.

Summing up the general development of her pathos, we need say only this: It began in freedom of speech; it matured into deliberate reticence which suggested whole worlds of emotion outside the province of human utterance. A few ideas are brought captive across the frontiers of speech simply to represent that multitude of passions and emotions lying beyond in the wild, dark, voiceless spaces of the human spirit.

V

THE WOMAN'S POINT OF VIEW

WE pass now to consider the obvious manifestations of "sex" in Mrs Gaskell's writings. Even if she had written under a masculine *nom-de-plume*, nobody would have been deceived. She was not able, and did not try, to hide the fact of her womanhood.

She was never a pronounced theorist. We could search her works without finding much in the way of an articulated sex philosophy. Yet her opinions, though scarcely defined, are very strongly implied.

The contrast between man and woman gave her little anxiety. Without being in the least masculine she was quite able to understand certain men—and not necessarily those of an effeminate type. In fact men like Osborne Hamley are the exception in her books. From John Barton in her first story to Mr Gibson in her last, she portrayed men of a virile, masculine type. She was on sufficiently familiar terms with men to appreciate their manliness. Probably it was due to this familiarity that she rarely, if ever, seemed to feel that her sex should stand in an attitude of defence. We get an occasional reference to the relative positions of men and women. Ned Browne in *The Moorland Cottage* believed in the subjection of women; but neither his character nor his opinions counted for very much. On the other side, Miss Jenkyns "would have despised the modern idea of women being equal to men. Equal indeed! she knew they were superior." —Still, in the very same book, Mrs Gaskell took no shame in making fun of ladies' committees; they reminded Mary's father of a passage in Dickens,

which spoke of a chorus in which every man took the tune he knew best, and sung it to his own satisfaction. So, at this charitable committee, every lady took the subject uppermost in her mind, and talked about it to her own great contentment, but not much to the advancement of the subject they had met to discuss.

In *French Life* also, Mrs Gaskell casually remarked that all the ladies' committees she had ever seen were "the better for having one or two men amongst them." Nevertheless it would be rash to take such utterances gravely, without making allowance for Mrs Gaskell's tendency to caprice. It is perfectly easy to find conflicting statements. Mary Smith thought men's letters "dull"; Margaret Hale applied the same adjective to women's conversation; again Miss Galindo thought that the best way to emulate a man was by being "abominably dull." It would be a difficult matter to deduce a theory from such contradictory statements. The real truth is this: Mrs Gaskell found dullness in neither men nor women.

She recognised the existence of a question which agitated her contemporaries;—Should a woman be learned? Paul, it will be remembered, objected to marrying Phillis on the grounds of her superior knowledge. His father thought this "more her misfortune than her fault," and prophesied that she would forget all her embarrassing learning when once safely married. Mr Gibson also had some misgiving lest Molly should be over-educated, but in deference to "the prejudices of society," he allowed Miss Eyre to teach her reading. However, we should not be so credulous as to take him over-seriously. He certainly showed no disappointment when Molly grew up remarkably intelligent. Nevertheless she very much resented being called a blue-stocking, which implied, she thought, that she was interested in things which were not really interesting. She protested that the book lent her by Roger was "not at all deep. It was very interesting." Molly's mental exercises were by no means confined to books; she was a shrewd judge of character. She told her father that she loved Cynthia dearly without completely understanding her. "Umph," replied Mr Gibson; "I like to understand people thoroughly, but I know it's not necessary to women. D'ye really think she's worthy of him (*i.e.* Roger)?"—The query at the end proves that he respected Molly's judgment even though she formed it after a non-masculine fashion.

Although Molly was very specially loved by her creator, it is by no means certain that Mrs Gaskell "took to" anybody just because he (or she) was clever. Phillis Holman was a student; Margaret Hale delighted in Dante. But Mrs Gaskell never pushed these things into the foreground. She certainly liked Sylvia Robson very much indeed; and some more "superior" people might have considered this charming heroine a dunce. On the other hand we have Mrs Gaskell's testimony that she disliked Lucy Snowe in *Villette*; but to Charlotte Bronte Lucy's cleverness made a most emphatic appeal. Mere intellectuality in either man or woman was a quality which Mrs Gaskell never set out to seek. If she found it, she rejoiced in it; if not, she could do without it.

When dealing with Charlotte Bronte she fully recognised and stated the exceptional problem set before the exceptional woman of genius. There is always a "something else" in the woman's sphere of responsibility, some human tie which she dare not sacrifice to any other claims. At the same time she dare not renounce her genius; she has to keep the balance between both obligations.

This brings us to domesticity as another aspect of the woman's question. Libbie Marsh took a "woman's natural work" to be the care of home, husband and children. As this was denied her, she decided to look around for "the odd jobs God leaves in the world for such as old maids to do." "As I have neither husband nor child," said Margaret Hale, "to give me natural duties, I must make myself some." Margaret recognised the fundamental restrictions placed on all women, married or single.—"She tried to settle that most difficult problem for women, how much was to be utterly merged in obedience to authority, and how much might be set apart for freedom in working." But Mrs Gaskell never seemed to feel any confinement within these natural bonds; she would not have liked to be without ties. The woman's joy in "home-making" was taken by her for granted. *Bessy's Troubles at Home* tells of a girl's failure to make her home happy; but Bessy was told where she had been wrong.—"You wanted to make us all happy your way —as you liked." Though references to the theory of home-making are extremely rare, every book is full of allusions to simple domestic matters. This applies even to the records of

a woman of genius; for we are told a great deal about Charlotte Bronte's housework, even to her methods of circum-
venting Tabby in the peeling of potatoes. Mrs Gaskell told
how she and Charlotte talked over some proposed alterations
in Haworth Parsonage "with the same unwearying happiness
which I suppose all women feel in such discussions." This,
like many domestic references in *French Life*, gives us a
glimpse into Mrs Gaskell's own tastes. We could learn as
much from her pictures of women taking on a sort of poetry
from their domestic backgrounds—Miss Benson shredding
beans, Sylvia lifting milk-pails, Phillis mending stockings,
cutting bread, or stooping among the peas. The mere mention
of such commonplace details gives no conception of the grace
with which they are pictured. We have to read the passages
again to feel for ourselves the exquisite "rightness" of such
living. Most of Mrs Gaskell's young girls moved about a
house with a soothing efficiency. She specially referred to
Sylvia's "pretty household briskness," and the "deft and
quiet speed" with which Phillis attended to Mr Holdsworth.
Once, indeed, Mrs Gaskell suggested that the domestic
woman might be narrow-minded. Theresa of *Crowley Castle*
disdained Bessy's incapacity for entering into her husband's
larger interests. "You drag him down," she said, "to your
level of woman's cares." Still we can never feel that Mrs
Gaskell despised Bessy. She evidently believed that it would
have been better for Theresa if she had been able to pity this
ordinary, affectionate woman.

Nearly all Mrs Gaskell's women found their true life in
the atmosphere of family affection. Although she herself had
been motherless, she laid an extraordinary emphasis on the
power of mother love. Mary Barton used to dream of her
dead mother. Sylvia also remembered her mother's strong
undemonstrative love; she never forgot—neither can we—
"the straight, upright figure of her mother, fronting the
setting sun, but searching through its blinding rays for a
sight of her child."—Again and again we find the picture
viewed not from the child's but the mother's standpoint.
We do not need the references in Charlotte Bronte's letters
to convince us that Mrs Gaskell loved her own children. Her

books are sufficient testimony that she wrote from her own personal experience of motherhood. One of the saddest things in *Mary Barton* is the story of the "babby," who having lost its mother, received kindness from a mother who —like Mrs Gaskell—had lost her child. Ruth was comforted by the touch of the "little soft warm babe, nestled up against her breast, rocked by her heart." Mrs Gaskell often fell back upon a baby's touch as an unfailing source of consolation. When Mrs Boucher was distracted with sorrow, the kindly neighbour thought of this remedy;—"Best comfort now would be the feel of a child at her heart." This also was the method by which shrewd Mr Gibson saved Aimée Hamley's life. It is doubtful whether Sylvia would have lived on, had it not been for her child.

Sometimes in the nights she would waken, crying, with a terrible sense of desolation; everyone who had loved her, or whom she had loved, had vanished out of her life; everyone but her child, who lay in her arms, warm and soft.

We cannot dwell fully on Mrs Gaskell's treatment of child life—the delightful episode of the broken pitcher in *Cousin Phillis*, the fleeting pictures of Aimée's child, or the particular gentleness with which she described a sudden attack of shyness, such as that befalling Molly on her first visit to the Towers. We cannot leave the children, however, without saying something of their relations with their fathers. This comes out most strongly in the case of only daughters like Sylvia or Phillis or Molly.—There was always something a little protective in Sylvia's relation to her father. She wanted to tease him about his domestic instructions, because she knew, better than he, what she was about. On the day of his arrest he left her, shaken to the depths, with an apology for his crossness. In many ways he was a child compared to his daughter, who, for all her immaturity, had a greater capacity for development.—Phillis Holman shared her father's joys, but looked up to him with an unbroken respect. She relied on her father more than Sylvia could have done; she was at once less familiar, and more intimate.—We have no space to speak at all adequately of the "most delightful inter-

course" enjoyed by Molly and her father. As a little girl
she wished that she might be fastened to him with "a chain
like Ponto's."—"When I wanted you, I could pull; and if
you didn't want to come, you could pull back again; but
I should know you knew I wanted you, and we could never
lose each other." The friendship between father and daughter
was secured by firmer bonds than Ponto's iron chain. Their
affection was so enduring that it survived even the constant,
estranging influences of Mrs Gibson's presence. For a time
they saw less of each other; they had less opportunity for
spoken confidences, and to the very end, they never lost
consciousness of one excluded subject. They both refrained
from any criticism of the wife and step-mother who had
proved such a ludicrous—but for them, a pathetic—failure.
Yet they grew towards each other across the cleft of Mr Gibson's unfortunate second marriage. They came to live in a
sort of undemonstrative comradeship, welcoming chances of
open intercourse, but able to do without them. At times of
real emergency, such as Osborne Hamley's death, they came
very close together—nearer than in the old free days before
their friendship had been tested. They had achieved an
intimacy which could grow on in comparative isolation,
independent of jarring, outward circumstances.

We cannot pause to consider the relationship between
children in the same family—such as the steady, brotherly
friendship of Osborne and Roger Hamley.—The love of
husband and wife was often implied rather than described.
Mrs Gaskell seemed to have more to say when she was dealing
with couples, like Squire and Mrs Hamley, who—on the
surface at least—appeared unequally matched. Minister
Holman had a wife utterly incapable of entering into his
hearty, wholesome love of knowledge; but he had his own
remedy for a situation which might easily have become
pathetic. With "delicate tact" he habitually brought back
the conversation to "such subjects as those on which his
wife, with her practical experience of everyday life, was an
authority." Like Miss Matty, his wife became content with
all she could not do; and this because her husband showed
himself so amply satisfied with everything she could do to

perfection. She felt no loss of self-respect, when she could not completely follow the meaning of the passages he read aloud from Virgil.—"Go on, minister," she said, "it is very interesting what you are reading about; and, when I don't quite understand it, I like the sound of your voice."

We have dealt at some length with this background of family affection, not in any sense that it is exclusively a woman's affair, but because Mrs Gaskell felt so strongly that no woman could find her true self apart from the life of the home. In conclusion we shall consider, very briefly, Mrs Gaskell's implications of the womanly ideal. She had a great range of types and a large compass of sympathy. She chose young, growing things like Sylvia or Phillis or Molly, and placed them in an atmosphere of wild, fresh grace; or she could turn with equal zest to the appeal of something more disciplined and austere. From the very beginning Margaret Hale had a touch of severity; quite early in the book we read that "her keen enjoyment of every sensuous pleasure was balanced finely, if not overbalanced, by her conscious pride in being able to do without them all, if need were." As a whole Mrs Gaskell portrayed winsome, gentle women; yet in real life she felt the fascination of grim Emily Bronte. Though she liked many different kinds of women, there were certain qualities which she would have wished common to all women. She was just as scrupulous as Jane Austen or Charlotte Bronte in demanding a delicate neatness. This was part, though by no means the whole, of Molly's appeal to the Squire. When considering Cynthia as a prospective daughter-in-law, he asked Mr Gibson;

Is she—well, is she like your Molly—sweet-tempered and sensible —with her gloves always mended, and neat about the feet, and ready to do anything one asks her, just as if doing it was the very thing she liked best in the world?

Again, Mrs Gaskell always took kindly to young girls who had just a touch of bashfulness. She admired the shy charm of Sylvia's manner at the Corney's party all the more because she was so full of wild grace and piquancy at home.—But for Mrs Gaskell these things lay on the surface of womanly

charm. Nearly all the womanly qualities most prized by her
were bound together in the conception of her last heroine,
Molly. And what were they? We could draw up a list of
adjectives; she was loyal, buoyant, honest, wholehearted,
affectionate, modest, unselfish. All these epithets are correct;
yet they do not tell us the one quality to which Mrs Gaskell
was always returning, the one thing she valued so dearly in
Molly, and demanded, in greater or lesser degree, from all
her other heroines. This was a restful presence. If Molly
ever had any external stimulus towards this ideal, it was the
example of a family peacemaker like Mrs Hamley; but most
of her tact and sympathy was intuitively developed. Other
people gladly recognised the unconscious power of her
influence. Mr Gibson smiled to himself when he remembered
that she was to accompany Cynthia and Mrs Gibson on their
visit to Hamley Hall, where she was "sure to be a peacemaker,
and a sweetener of intercourse."—When Osborne came to
her with his agitated confession, she knew at once how to
deal with him;—"Rest. No one will interrupt us; I will go on
with my sewing; when you want to say anything more, I shall
be listening."—While Mrs Gibson accused Cynthia of jilting
her lovers, Molly stood by, "very hot," hoping to come in
"as sweetener, or peacemaker, or helper of some kind."—
We have referred already to the "balm" of her presence that
night when she sat at the Squire's feet without uttering a
word of consolation. Later on she weaned him from his
griefs by reading him Aimée's letters to his dead son.—"The
Squire was never weary of hearing them; the very sound of
Molly's voice soothed and comforted him, it was so sweet
and low."—When Aimée and the Squire were living dis-
cordantly under the same roof, Roger saw but one way out of
the difficulty. He went to Molly, and said;

I think you could help us at home. Aimée is shy and awkward
with my father, and he has never taken quite kindly to her—yet
I know they would like and value each other if some one could
but bring them together.

But Molly was scarcely aware of her power. In no sense
did she strive to become a professional consoler. She was

impetuous, and even hot-tempered on occasion; yet, wherever she went, she seemed to put things into harmony. We have referred to the remarkable endurance of the intimacy between her and her father. Few relationships could have survived the strain to which theirs was subjected. Yet it was Molly, far more than Mr Gibson, who kept the friendship alive. If it had been left to her father, the two would have drifted apart, and he would not have known how to help it. It was Molly's steady, unspoken loyalty, her abstinence from criticism or regret, that made estrangement impossible. What she did in her own affair, she repeated without fuss or parade, for other people who came across her path. Mrs Gaskell made no comment; but she leaves us with the impression that if this is a woman's work, it is well worth the doing.

VI

THE SOCIAL PROBLEM

MRS GASKELL produced very little that could be called systematic sociology; yet two of her novels were written with a social and philanthropic purpose. The existence of industrialism could not easily be ignored by a person living in Manchester. That first—and last—of the *Sketches Among the Poor*, written in collaboration with her husband, was Mrs Gaskell's first exercise in slum-studies. That poem reminds us vaguely of Wordsworth; but in many respects he differed from Mrs Gaskell. Mary Lamb laid down his poems—if we are to believe her brother—wondering if a mere dweller in towns had a soul to be saved. Mrs Gaskell had no such misgivings. Very often she defended town life from the charges of external ugliness, not by denying them, but by proving the co-existence of human and spiritual excellences. In *Libbie Marsh's Three Eras* she told how the holiday-makers looked back towards the great town.

And that was Manchester—ugly, smoky Manchester; dear, busy, earnest, noble-working Manchester; where their children had been born, and where perhaps, some lay buried; where their homes were, and where God had cast their lives, and told them to work out their destiny.

Then came *Mary Barton*, with Manchester for its setting. This story is almost entirely a defence of the working man. Mrs Gaskell admitted that there was another side to the question; "but," she added, "what I wish to impress is what the workman feels and thinks." She made a new interpretation of the so-called "faults" of the poor—John Barton's "improvidence," or Mary's reasons for disliking the restrictions of a domestic servant's life. Against these dubious faults are set the positive virtues of the poor.

"The vices of the poor sometimes astound us *here*," she wrote; "but when the secrets of all hearts shall be made known, their virtues will astound us in far greater degree. Of this I am certain."

These working people of hers had a wonderful innate delicacy. Job Legh told how he had seen the childless mother opening a little drawer; but, he added, "I were sorry to be prying." At other times Mrs Gaskell reminds us of the good feeling, or the magnificent endurance of poor people. John Barton as a child had given up his share to the younger children, and told "the noble lie that 'he was not hungry, could not eat a bit more.'" Though Mrs Gaskell was the kind of person to care for the dainty accessories of refined life, there was no disdain in her mind as she noted Alice's homely preparations for receiving company. Probably she meant us to feel that, given the means, Alice would have set as elegant a table as any cultured lady, and in far better taste than a "sham" lady like Mrs Gibson.

We hear also of the rich, but almost invariably in condemnation of their indifference to the trials of the poor. John Barton would hear nothing of the plea that they did not know how poor people lived. "I say, if they don't know, they ought to know." With a touch of revealing insight Mrs Gaskell laid bare the fallacy which embittered his life. He was going to help Davenport—"on an errand of mercy; but the thoughts of his heart were touched by sin, by bitter hatred of the happy, whom he, for the time, confounded with the selfish." Yet, as he himself confessed, there had been a time when he tried to "love" the masters; and towards the close of the book we feel a strong implication that whatever the masters might have done, the men had on the whole tried to be just and charitable. Job Legh told Mr Carson that they were ready to take the will, even if it produced no deed.

If we saw the masters try for our sakes to find a remedy—even if they were long about it—even if they could find no help, and at the end could only say, "Poor fellows, our hearts are sore for ye; we've done all we could, and we can't find a cure"—we'd bear up like men through bad times.

The whole of his speech may affect us as out-of-date—too calm and unembittered to be true; yet, if this be so, the loss is all on our side.

North and South is a much more careful attempt at an impartial and reasoned philosophy. Both masters and men were given credit for that "granite" quality which impressed not only Margaret, but even a casual outsider like Mr Henry Lennox. These impressive people were set in an atmosphere of big things. Captains of industry like John Thornton were stirred by the grandeur of the industrial life—its power and width of horizon; it drew out latent resource and talent, and enabled men of force to play a big game in a big way. Mr Bell accused him of spending his life in gathering together the materials of life.—"I wonder," he said, "when you Milton men intend to live." Mr Thornton retorted that he was living all the time; it was exertion, and not enjoyment, which gave a zest to life.

There was, of course, another side to this almost spectacular conception of commercial progress. Thornton may have defended industrial abuses by pointing out the abnormal rapidity of the Industrial Revolution. "The survival of the fittest" was a test which appealed to his courage, and resource; but he did not like Margaret to attack the romantic core of his theory by accusing him of antagonism to the unsuccessful. He saw the large, impersonal March of Progress; Margaret saw the individual victims. She could not feel the spell of a wide theory when she had brought before her eyes its cruel, personal implications.

They differed likewise on their conceptions of authority. Thornton claimed the right to a benevolent despotism over his men during working hours; at any other time he respected their right to liberty of independent action. Margaret insisted that as masters and men were mutually dependent, they could not cut their days or lives into such arbitrary divisions. They disagreed again on the question of mutual confidence. At first Thornton held strongly to the privilege of keeping his own counsel; yet in the end he came round to Margaret's standpoint, by taking Higgins, and then others, into consultation. In fact he became a complete convert to Margaret's opinions; and Mrs Gaskell seems to imply that she also was on Margaret's side.

Still she did justice to the masters. Thornton, unlike

Mr Carson of the earlier study, was a man of heroic type—generous, open-minded, just. Though Mrs Gaskell's sympathies were with the working men, she did not represent them as impeccable. In *Mary Barton* she portrayed only the best men of their class; here she included a weakling like Boucher, whose hysterical actions overturned the schemes of moderate men like Higgins.—Margaret felt that the men in combination were as tyrannical as the masters. They treated one another as if they were calculable, like machines. She was shocked beyond measure when Higgins told her the methods by which the Union strengthened its claim "to force a man into his own good." For answer she pointed to the example of Boucher—a foolish man, forced into the Union, and driven by frenzy into discrediting its authority. "You have made him what he is," she said—the system of force had made him an obstacle to any rational progress.

All these things are commonplace to us now-a-days. Yet, looking back over the years, it is rather surprising to find how little further we have gone. Either we have travelled very slowly, or Mrs Gaskell was already far ahead of her generation. Other writers of her period wrote on social questions, but hardly from the same standpoint. *Mary Barton* was preceded by Disraeli's *Coningsby*, and followed by his *Sybil*. In the first novel he evinced, like Mrs Gaskell, an interest in the significance of industrial towns.—"Rightly understood, Manchester is as great a human exploit as Athens." Where he felt the romance of machinery, Mrs Gaskell was more deeply moved by the human power which mastered machinery. Particularly in *Sybil*, Disraeli made use of a constant appeal to the spectacular, and turned his story into a series of rather "stagey" pageants. He looked at the same evils as Mrs Gaskell, but was prone to dress them up for public exhibition. Mrs Gaskell cared more for the solution than the display of the problem; she took this solution to be a new spirit of mutual comprehension and respect.

North and South suggests comparison with Dickens' *Hard Times* which preceded it in *Household Words*. He, as much as Mrs Gaskell, recognised the neighbourly kindness of the poor. John Barton was crushed by the hopeless situation of his class, placed in a world where reason seemed of little avail. More whimsically Stephen Blackpool expressed the same conviction to Mr Bounderby;—"Look...how yo are awlus right, and how we are awlus wrong, and never had'n no reason in us sin' ever we were born." Mr Bounderby asked him how he would put this "muddle" to rights; and in reply he set forth from the negative side, what Mrs Gaskell had stated in positive terms, as the social philosophy of *North and South*.

The strong hand will never do't. Vict'ry and triumph will never do't. Agreeing fur to mak one side unnat'rally awlus and for ever right and t'oother side unnat'rally awlus and for ever wrong will never, never do't. Nor yet lettin alone will never do't.

Mrs Gaskell would have agreed with Dickens' satire, not of the "Coketown Hands," but of the mechanical, deadening system which could be satisfied to consider human beings under such terms.—These and other isolated comparisons might be made. The chief matter for emphasis is the fact that Dickens was not ahead of Mrs Gaskell. They travelled, with different gestures and mannerisms, along the same road, but they did not always look at the same objects. They both knew the social evils from which they were trying to escape; sometimes Mrs Gaskell saw if anything more clearly the social ideal to which both were setting their faces.

*   *   *   *   *   *

It is rather amazing to consider the versatility which could produce both *Mary Barton* and *Cranford*. George Eliot might have striven to be scrupulously fair to the "gentility" and the populace; but she was too much given to theories to have been capable of writing two separate studies, each unshadowed by the other. It is true that *Cranford* satirised shabby attempts after aristocracy. Quite as much as Mr Vachell's spinsters in *Blinds Down*, those old maids lived with their eyes closed to reality. But in Mr Vachell's story the maiden ladies were blind to the suffering outside their windows; in *Cranford* they blinded themselves to their own poverty—which was a quaint, but harmless delusion. They had their limitations no doubt, and thought Captain Brown "very eccentric" if not improper, when he carried home an old woman's dinner. Mrs Gaskell laughed at such manifestations of class prejudice, but knew they did not amount to much.—It proves her remarkable breadth of sympathy that she could deal with such contrasted types—the actual poor who struggled for a living, and the comparative poor who tried to keep up appearances.

Margaret Hale was another person with distinct class prejudices. "I am sure," said she, "you don't want me to admire butchers and bakers and candlestick-makers, do you mamma?" But Margaret became a convert to the spell of commerce, for she married John Thornton—a great captain of industry, no doubt; but in her earlier days she would have set him down as a "tradesman."

Mrs Gaskell also drew many pictures of genuine aristocrats such as Lady Cumnor or Lady Ludlow; she seemed to meet them on the same terms of common humanity as Alice Wilson or Bessy Higgins. The fact that they were grand ladies "gave them an air," or added a new opportunity for kind-hearted satire; otherwise it made no difference whatever. —Lady Harriet and Molly had a most edifying discussion of their social relationship; Lady Harriet, however, remained an aristocrat, and Molly persisted in being regarded as a member of the middle class; but this was a trifle of no consequence to the growth of a true and enduring friendship. This was typical of Mrs Gaskell's general attitude to class distinctions. She regarded them as somewhat amusing conventions; but they never worried her excessively. She was often unconventional, not from any sense of pose, but because she could not help it. She was made in that way.

VII

MORAL THEORY OR MORAL EFFECT

MRS GASKELL always disclaimed any attempts after elaborate theories. Like Lamb she was not given to judging "system-wise" of things, but fastened upon particulars. This tendency appeared even in her discussion of character. In writing her *Life of Charlotte Bronte* she made it clear that she had no intention of giving psychological expositions. Quite early in the book she wrote:

I do not pretend to be able to harmonize points of character, and account for them, and bring all into one consistent and intelligible whole. The family with whom I have now to do shot their roots down deeper than I can penetrate. I cannot measure them, much less is it for me to judge them.

She concluded her book in the same strain.—"If my readers find that I have not said enough, I have said too much. I cannot measure or judge of such a character as hers. I cannot map out vices, and virtues, and debateable land."

If this were the case with the psychology of human experience, still more did it apply to its underlying philosophy. Mrs Gaskell ended *Libbie Marsh's Three Eras* with a sly reference to having heard "in the year 1811, I think"— well, she was born in 1810—of a deaf old lady, living by herself, and possessing the "amiable peculiarity" of reading the moral, concluding sentence of a story. From the very beginning Mrs Gaskell had rather a suspicion of avowedly "moral" tales. As she developed further, she seemed to imply that the moral of a story should be something seen and felt, but not expressed or heard in spoken words. At first she used direct religious phraseology entirely free from any trace of cant. Alice Wilson spoke openly of her religion; yet Job Legh expressed almost as much in an occasional phrase. He remembered how he had last seen the childless mother, quietly wiping her eyes, and preparing her husband's breakfast. "But," he added, "I shall know her in heaven."

Passing on in order we notice that Mrs Buxton of *The Moorland Cottage* dealt much in moral observations. Now Mrs Buxton has often been considered as a first sketch for the more finished portrait of Mrs Hamley in *Wives and Daughters*. It is interesting to notice how much more solemnly Mrs Gaskell regarded the earlier heroine. We always feel that she really loved Mrs Hamley more, even though she laughed at her a little. And somehow Mrs Hamley does us more good, possibly because we do not survey her with a preternatural gravity.

Returning to the earlier books, we must pause for a moment at *Ruth*. We need not consider the definite religious background which was often characteristic of Mrs Gaskell's work at this period. Yet, even here, it is well to remember that Sally had a sturdy, practical suspicion of metaphysical discussion.—"Now," said she, "if we've talked doctrine long enough, I'll make th' beds."—It is, however, the treatment of Ruth's own experience and character which gives most call for discussion. Ruth was by no means the only person in the story who did wrong; there were besides Mr Bellingham, Mr Bradshaw and his son, Dick. (For the sake of brevity we must leave out the last figure.) This being so, how was it that Ruth suffered so much more than anybody else? If motives are to be considered—and what else should we consider?—she was by far the least guilty. Yet she was the most heavily punished. If Mrs Gaskell had been telling the story, simply as a record of the world's way in such matters, we might not have been made so uneasy. In actual life it is highly probable that the world would apportion blame in exactly the way she described. Still no person with a spark of justice could be content with such an unequal, external judgment. But Mrs Gaskell scarcely hinted at any dissatisfaction. She implied that Ruth would have been wrong if she had resented what she received. The whole issue is complicated by the fact that she concealed her past; yet for that matter Mr Bellingham concealed his share in that past, and Mr Bradshaw concealed his acquiescence in bribery. If the question of deceit comes in, they were worse, not better, than Ruth; for she sanctioned deception only in

the interests of her child, and not for her own sake. We know
that Mrs Gaskell cherished and respected Ruth; but we
cannot help feeling that she was not sufficiently hard on those
who judged her with discouraging severity.—If we put aside
the question of external punishments and reputations, the
moral issue becomes clearer. We may consider, not what
happened to these people, but what they became; and the
achievement of a moral standard is undoubtedly a high,
internal reward which more than compensates for any unjust,
external penalty. If we look at it in this way, Ruth received
the supreme award. Mr Bellingham received none at all—
only the shame of his own deterioration. By the end of the
story Mr Bradshaw had come to the point of acknowledging
his offence, but unlike Ruth, he had not redeemed his error.
She stood high above him. Evidently this supremacy of
inward justice was the moral effect which Mrs Gaskell meant
to convey.

North and South is more definitely theological in its
implications. Margaret and Bessy were both devout and
orthodox. The remoteness and beauty of the *Revelations*
brought comfort to Bessy. "It's as good as an organ, and
as different from every day, too." But Margaret clung to the
clear, simple sources of inspiration,—passages like the fourteenth chapter of St John's Gospel. Both these women were
brought into close contact with unorthodox parents. Yet
Higgins was not quite so unorthodox as he gave himself out
to be. He was almost infuriated by the very suggestion that
he might not believe in God. That fact was "the one sole
comfort" left to him after Bessy's death.—"There's but one
thing steady and quiet i' all this reeling world, and, reason
or no reason, I'll cling to that." On the other hand Mr Hale
was an avowed "heretic." To Margaret this was a "great
blighting fact," and she could not entirely conceal her disapproval, even though she felt sorry for her father.—"It
is bad to believe you in error," she said. "It would be infinitely worse to have known you a hypocrite." We are never
told the exact nature of Mr Hale's doubts. If George Eliot
had been his creator, she would have spoken more fully out
of her own experience. Possibly also, she would have made

him less timid and hesitating. We should have felt more keenly the courage of his honesty, and less acutely the unfortunate consequences of his resolution. Mr Hale might not have appealed to George Eliot; yet, wistful, unobtrusive and kindly, he was a very true type. Mrs Gaskell seems to have regarded his heretical views as unfortunate, but not fundamentally serious. Though they made things uncomfortable for him and his family, they did not shake the foundations of his faith, or alter the gentleness of his character.

While we are on this subject, we should refer to Mrs Gaskell's religious tolerance. She had nothing, for instance, of Charlotte Bronte's antagonism to Roman Catholics. In *The Poor Clare* she spoke with sympathy of Bridget's religion, and with admiration of Father Bernard's character. In *French Life* also, she praised the practical benevolence of the priests who were responsible for a "ragged church" in Paris. Indeed Charlotte Bronte seems to have thought her friend too broadminded.—"Good people," she wrote to Mrs Gaskell,—"*very*, good people, I doubt not, there are amongst the Romanists, but the system is not one which should have such sympathy as *yours*."

Returning to the course of Mrs Gaskell's stories, we very soon observe a marked tendency to abstain from definitely moral or religious comments. Though the religious impulse is shown in its working, it is not subjected to much discussion. Thus, in *My Lady Ludlow* we are drawn to respect the differing forms of piety manifested by Lady Ludlow and Mr Gray; and Miss Galindo's reference to Martha and Mary would seem to imply that a person's religion is to be judged by its practical results. Sometimes the religious sentiment of a whole family is quietly described and left without elaborate comment. In *The Crooked Branch* we read of simple, family prayers which made the old parents feel "quiet and safe in the presence of God." In *Cousin Phillis* also, we read of household prayers; and Mrs Gaskell evidently liked the minister to pray for the cattle and live creatures —it made his religion so near and real. We have noticed that he could not bear to speak glibly of his griefs or to

receive wordy consolations, when Phillis lay in danger.—
"As for spiritual help at such a time," he said, "it is God only,
God only, who can give it." When it was only a question
of Daisy, the cow, he could pray aloud without difficulty;
when his heart was full of gratitude for his daughter's re-
covery, the words were choked in his throat. At the time
when his religion meant most to him, he could not bring it
into speech.

As the religious impression deepens, the actual phrases
of religion decrease. We get only occasional references such
as this from *French Life*;—"Is not Christianity the very core
of the heart of all gracious courtesy?" In *Wives and Daughters*
there are few, if any, definite allusions to religion. Yet it
would be a strange person who fancied that Mrs Gaskell
had become less "religious" when she wrote this book so
full of that gracious courtesy and tenderness which she had
identified with Christian practice. Molly passed only three
words which could be considered to have a definitely im-
proving tendency. Cynthia had said, "I wish I was good."

"So do I," said Molly simply. She was thinking again of
Mrs Hamley.—

> Only the actions of the just
> Smell sweet and blossom in the dust;

and "goodness" just then seemed to her to be the only enduring
thing in the world.

And Molly *was* good; perhaps all the better because she was
too humble and too reverent to speak to the Squire of his
grief.—On one occasion she refused to argue about Cynthia's
relations with Roger;—"I don't want to discuss it, and paw
it over with talk." This had come to be Mrs Gaskell's feeling
with regard to the deepest experiences of the human soul.
She could not "paw them over" with talk.

The moral effect of *Wives and Daughters* has yet another
aspect. Less obtrusively, but no less firmly than George
Eliot's novels, it preaches a doctrine of consequences.
Mr Gibson paid for his mistaken second marriage. Mrs Gibson did not die conveniently; neither did his influence
improve her beyond all recognition. For that matter, she

was worse after her marriage than before it. There is a quietly implied justice in the fact that Mr Gibson, who alone was responsible for the error, alone paid the unending penalty. Molly must have escaped from it when she married Roger; but the only thing her father could do was to make the best of his encumbrance. This small point convinces us that for all her serenity, Mrs Gaskell was not given to facile sentiment. She was firm in her adherence to truth.

There is little else to be said. "We read as superior beings," said Emerson. Mrs Gaskell's books make us superior beings, not only while they are being read, but whenever they recur to the memory. We feel cleansed and sweetened after living with them. We have not quoted many laudations of Mrs Gaskell. Comparatively few people have taken the trouble to praise her. Yet there are two remarkable eulogies which can hardly be omitted. It satisfies every lover of Mrs Gaskell to know that they were made. The first came from George Sand. "She has written novels which excite the deepest interest in men of the world, and yet which every girl will be the better for reading." The second is taken from the remarks placed by Mr Frederick Greenwood, editor of the *Cornhill*, after her last, unfinished instalment of *Wives and Daughters*.

While you read,...you feel yourself caught out of an abominable, wicked world, crawling with selfishness, and reeking with base passions, into one where there is much weakness, many mistakes, sufferings long and bitter, but where it is possible for people to live calm and wholesome lives; and what is more, you feel that this is, at least, as real a world as the other.

This, after all, is Mrs Gaskell's highest achievement; she convinces us of goodness.

*   *   *   *   *   *

This is in no sense an exhaustive study of Mrs Gaskell. It is more like a series of hints and suggestions. Everybody who cares for her at all will wish to go further in her company, to walk with her by small footpaths, as well as the beaten highways. They could follow her, for instance, as she travelled away from sensation. In *Mary Barton* she often attempted

themes which might have lent themselves to a Dantesque
severity, as where she tells how Mary's dreams were haunted
by the faces of desperate, hopeless men. Sometimes indeed,
Mrs Gaskell trod on the frontiers of melodrama; but she
grew out of that.

Or again, it would be interesting to consider her feeling
for the supernatural. She records how she was once on the
point of telling Charlotte Bronte "a dismal ghost story" just
before bed-time; but her friend shrank from such an agitating
form of entertainment. Mrs Gaskell's best "uncanny" tales
are probably *The Old Nurse's Story*, *The Poor Clare*, and
Charlie Kinraid's story (in *Sylvia's Lovers*) of a voyage to the
mouth of hell. Particularly in the first two examples we feel
the extraordinary delicacy of suggestion which gradually
prepares us for unearthly sensations. In the one it may be
the falling of "white dazzling snow" which seems to build
up an atmosphere of fragile enchantment; in the other we
are vaguely warned by the sound of a jarring laugh; we are
never plunged into a cold shock of terror. When the sense
of awe comes fully upon us, it is always associated with a
few unforgettable details, such as those clinging to Bridget's
recollection of the ghastly Double. "I closed [the window]
up with my shawl, and then *I saw her feet below the door* as
long as it was light."

We have no space to discuss one most important aspect
of Mrs Gaskell's character study. She handled growing
personalities. We observe the whole process by which John
Barton was embittered. We see "Clare" dwindling in
importance from the moment that she became Mrs Gibson;
she lost all wit, for the simple reason that she was no longer
compelled to live by her wits. Best of all, we can watch some
gracious personality growing to full maturity—a temperament such as Molly's, which unfolded like the petals of a
flower. We cannot discuss these things here; but we can
reserve them for our private hours of solace.

We must now turn very briefly to consider Mrs Gaskell's
place among other women of literary type. Doubtless she
owed something to Jane Austen. Both women were alike
in their exquisite transparency of style, their avoidance of

unusual topics, and their general disposition to find life amusing. But Mrs Gaskell had quick-glancing eyes which looked at everything with interest; whereas Jane Austen trained her vision to detect specific details. Mrs Gaskell acquired a beautiful reticent pathos; Jane Austen allowed no implication of strong emotion to break through her deliberate reserve.

George Eliot admired Mrs Gaskell, and wrote to her (in 1859) expressing gratitude.

While the question of my powers was still undecided for me, I was conscious that my feeling towards life and art had some affinity with the feelings which had inspired *Cranford* and the earlier chapters of *Mary Barton*.

There was a similarity between the two women; but the dissimilarity was greater. Mrs Gaskell seemed to be by intuition what George Eliot had become by discipline. They were both sympathetic; but Mrs Gaskell's compassion required less education. They were both women of wide general interests; but Mrs Gaskell was never like George Eliot, vaguely dissatisfied with all that she knew. This may be partly because she was interested in persons rather than theories. She liked people of Minister Holman's type, "with a prodigious big appetite" for learning; but she never became, like George Eliot, morbidly learned. Perhaps she was not so scholarly; certainly she was far less depressed. At bottom this distinction between the two women was very largely a question of temperament and religious conviction; Mrs Gaskell's creed was more human than George Eliot's philosophy. They both worked hard. Mrs Gaskell collected the material for *Sylvia's Lovers*, perhaps not so laboriously as George Eliot would have done, but with a truly careful accuracy. Yet she never seemed to make herself tired. George Eliot built up her plots; Mrs Gaskell's grew like carefully tended flowers. Building is heavier work than gardening; yet—"God Almighty first planted a garden." Building is all very well, and, no doubt, extremely necessary. It may be, notwithstanding, that gardening is the better occupation.

Most significant of all is Mrs Gaskell's relation to Charlotte

Bronte. It is a case of more and less. She was less sensitive
to the spiritual influences of Nature, but more impelled by
many human emotions. She possessed, for example, what
Charlotte Bronte almost completely lacked—the maternal,
protective impulse. She had wider, truer conceptions of
democracy and religion. Mr Thornton, for instance, was
more open-minded and generous than Mr Moore; and on the
religious side we know that Charlotte Bronte was narrow.
She disliked Roman Catholics, and thought Mrs Gaskell was
running great risks in choosing a "heretic" like Mr Hale for
a prominent figure. More than that, every reader feels a
certain check and restriction in Charlotte Bronte's attitude
to "personal" religion; its development in her seemed unnaturally arrested. Mrs Gaskell laid her spirit open to the
influences of religion. It was like the sunshine which lights
up all the colours in a garden. We may not always think
of the sunlight; but without it there would be no flowers.
Again Mrs Gaskell had a wider capacity for friendship. She
was far more contented with ordinary people. Charlotte
Bronte thought almost too much of intelligence—certainly
too much of "bookish" culture. "We keep Latin for the
evenings," said Phillis Holman, "that we may have time to
enjoy it." That was the kind of heroine for Charlotte Bronte!
Yet, Mrs Gaskell, who created Phillis, saw further into the
heart of true culture. Phillis loved Latin, but many other
things besides—Rover, the chickens, the bird-notes which
she copied, the daily round of simple home pleasures. Her
interest in books was only one aspect of a wholesome many-
sided interest in life. Charlotte Bronte could never have
made an intellectual heroine so normal and girlish as Phillis.
She would scarcely have looked at Sylvia—who in truth was
very nearly illiterate. As for Mrs Gaskell, she never worried
about such matters; and who can say that she was any the
worse for it?—"Everybody," said Emerson, "knows as much
as the savant."

Mrs Gaskell was happier by temperament than George
Eliot; she was happier by circumstance than Charlotte Bronte.
She tells us that Charlotte had come to expect little from
life; she believed that some "were appointed to sorrow and

disappointment," and others were destined to "the pleasant places."

I took a different view (wrote Mrs Gaskell); I thought that human lots were more equal than she imagined; that to some happiness and sorrow came in strong patches of light and shadow (so to speak), while in the lives of others they were pretty equally blended throughout. She smiled, and shook her head.

They sincerely agreed in their love of truth. Charlotte, who never shirked tragedy herself, was almost appalled by her friend's rigour. Mrs Gaskell had given her an outline of a story she was writing—it must have been *Ruth*—and Charlotte wrote back in warm approval with only one note of protest.

Why should she die? Why are we to shut up the book weeping? My heart fails me already at the thought of the pang it will have to undergo. And yet you must follow the impulse of your own inspiration. If *that* commands the slaying of the victim, no by-stander has a right to put out his hand to stay the sacrifical knife; but I hold you a stern priestess in these matters.

We have already noted the absence of false sentiment in the working out of *Wives and Daughters*. We have quoted, also, in relation to Charlotte Bronte, the letter where she asked Mrs Gaskell if she was never tempted to make her characters "more amiable than the Life." Indeed, Mrs Gaskell usually displayed a resolution to make people out no better than they really were. Ned Browne of *The Moorland Cottage* never became a model character; his creator firmly resisted any temptation to a Dickensian type of repentance. It has been said that Cranford was an idealised village; but for that matter Charlotte Bronte also was an idealist. She saw things tinged and heightened by romance. No more than Mrs Gaskell did she turn out hard photographic pictures. She was true to things *as she saw them*. This also was Mrs Gaskell's way. Of her first number of *Sketches Among the Poor* she said that it was "rather in the manner of Crabbe, but in a more seeing-beauty spirit." This gives us the clue to what she was seeking. Charlotte Bronte looked for the romance, Mrs Gaskell for the beauty of human actions. They both found and described what they sought.

What, then, is the unique gift which Mrs Gaskell had to bestow? In one sense she suffers in comparison with less normal women. She lacked that concentration of passion or reflection which is so often united with peculiarity of temperament. She had so much of everything, not everything of something. It is not certain, however, that this is a disability. Mrs Gaskell's peculiar achievement was her power of combining the life of genius with a round of common interests. She resembled Lamb very strongly in this utter freedom from the affectations or idiosyncrasies of genius. She did not appear to feel or behave differently from other women. Just because she was so little restricted by self-consciousness, she represented her sex more adequately than any other woman writer of her generation. Herself a perfectly natural woman, she dealt with a woman's natural interests—home and family ties, the tender frailty of childhood and age, the significant details of daily intercourse and friendship. She did all this, hampered by no sense of competition with the masculine point of view. She spoke of the things which interested her most keenly, trusting that others also would find them worthy of attention. Such frankness and simplicity is decidedly engaging. Nevertheless Mrs Gaskell is something more to us than a charming conversationalist. She takes her readers very close to the heart of reality; and she does this without leading them into the wilderness of novel sensation or speculative theory. "The soul," it has been said, "is no traveller; the wise man stays at home with the soul.... He is not gadding abroad from himself." This is the secret of Mrs Gaskell's influence. She speaks to us of the common things which make life dear to the heart. She leaves us at home with our souls.

GEORGE ELIOT
1819-1880

I

INTRODUCTORY

THERE are several ways of approaching the work of
George Eliot. One would be to regard her as "heir of
all the ages," accumulating within her mind the tradition,
wisdom and experience of the race from Aristotle to Jane
Austen; then we would have to consider how far she lay
passive under her wealth, and to what extent she turned it
to active initiative and purpose. The chief objection to this
method is its overpowering vastness. All her life she read
books, and for a part of her life she wrote them; beyond that
she did little else. There is something oppressive in the figure
of this lonely student caught in a dense crowd of the im-
mortals. We watch it, wishing it could beat its way out of
the throng, and escape to some more exhilarating solitude;
or else we lose sight of the single figure, as we surrender
ourselves to the magnetic appeal of greater personalities.

Again, we might adopt the usual method of chronology.
But there is no occasion to repeat what has been done, and
done finely, by Sir Leslie Stephen. Moreover there is
something in the chronological method, which, in this case
certainly, does not yield complete satisfaction. It would be
to put ourselves in the position of a man studying contemporary life from the daily papers. Every day, unless for some
unexampled crisis, there are headlines of the same type; and
the normal reader is, of necessity, unprepared for that crisis.
Possibly, weeks ago, he passed rapidly over some apparent
trifle—the cause of this great effect. How was he to know
that it was going to be a cause? If at the end of a certain
period he wants to know what has been happening, and why
it has happened, he has to go back over the old ground,
adjusting his vision to a truer focus, supplying missing con-

nections, and discovering all the time that he has forgotten
the things he had most need of remembering.—It is true that
every student must follow chronology; but he does not require to articulate his entire process. The chronology is a
means to an end—the apprehension of an author, not as the
originator of a series, but as something living, rounded, and
complete. For anyone who wishes to follow out George
Eliot's achievement from step to step in a sequence, Sir
Leslie Stephen's book is invaluable. It ensures for the
student a personally conducted tour, safeguarded from risks
of missing significant details. But at the end of every journey
there is a retrospect, balancing pleasure and discomfort,
recapturing the mood or tone of swift impressions, reviving
in memory the hours of delight. I shall try to emphasise the
retrospect rather than the sequence. It is the retrospect
which gives meaning and value to the sequence; the passing
emotion finds its fullest justification when it survives to be
"recollected in tranquillity."

The journey, therefore, is to be taken for granted. We
need simply to define the stages, and revive the broad outlines of its course. Marian Evans or "George Eliot" was
born in 1819; by 1842 she had lost belief in Christian doctrine; between 1844 and 1846 she was translating Strauss's
Life of Jesus: in 1851 she became assistant-editor of the
Westminster Review; 1854 is the date of her union with
George Henry Lewes. This stage of her career was the pre-
liminary to achievement. Her work did not rise above the
level of higher journalism, but her experience of life was
laying the bases of all future development.

Between 1857 and 1879, prompted and encouraged by
Mr Lewes, she found her place in literature, though she did
not always keep it with an absolute security. After writing
Adam Bede she felt that she had achieved power, perhaps for
the last time. "I have arrived," she said, "at faith in the past,
but not at faith in the future." Our faith in her is best
assured when we remember the four books written between
1857 and 1861, *Scenes of Clerical Life*, *Adam Bede*, *The Mill
on the Floss*, and *Silas Marner*. We feel that she was treading
safely in this atmosphere of the English country, with its

transforming reminiscences of childhood. In 1863 came *Romola*, that laborious and yet wonderful experiment which "ploughed into her more than any of her other books." From this time onwards her mind moved from one theme to another in a zigzag course, and with an uncertainty which betrayed her latent misgivings. *Felix Holt*, published in 1866, was a return to the English Midlands, stripped this time of zest and glamour. In *The Spanish Gypsy* (1868) she not only handled a remote topic, but abandoned prose for verse. Then she slipped back to the familiar, homely atmosphere of the English provincial town and re-captured in *Middlemarch* (1871) something of her old power. In 1874 she published a collection of poems. Then came *Daniel Deronda* (1876) with its extraordinary blending of melodrama and sincerity. Last of all she wrote *Theophrastus Such*, showing a certain pungency in the first essay, and then sinking into desolate apathy.

Mr Lewes died in 1878; but he had read *Theophrastus* in manuscript. After his death George Eliot wrote no more. "The world's winter is going, I hope," she wrote to Mrs Burne-Jones, in February 1879, "but my everlasting winter has set in." In May 1880 she married Mr John Walter Cross, and died in the following December.

That is the bare record of her life, and even if it were filled out with intimate details drawn from her letters and journals, nobody could call it inspiriting. There is something disheartening in the story of this quest after greatness—the late and laborious start, the straining to reach the summit, the uncertain foothold, and the weary descent to the plain. Yet she did rise above the plain and "the little hills on every side." She reached the mountain level, and saw the great peaks lifting themselves above and below her. She knew what it was to visit the high altitudes. We remember her who toiled so long in the "windless valley" because of her moments on the heights.

Looking back over the difficult struggling course pursued by this persistent woman, we can follow out two lines of thinking which may help to interpret her achievement. Much of her work is personal, reflecting her own experiences and beliefs; yet, judging from her letters, her personality was lacking in magic. There is another side of her work, which is not a reflection of self, but an escape from it. It was in the combination of the personal and the impersonal that she attained distinction. She had to lose her life to find it. We can best understand her work by studying it, first as the expression of an individual temperament; and then as the contribution of an impersonal artist.

THE EXPRESSION OF TEMPERAMENT

IF we wish to understand George Eliot, the woman, we must take into account four things: She was a woman; she was a student; she stood apart from dogmatic Christianity; she formed an "irregular" connection with Mr Lewes.

As a woman of very marked opinions, she could not avoid having theories of womanhood. We know that she approved of the higher education of women, and was one of the first subscribers to Girton College; but she also realised that rapid emancipation might endanger the closeness of family ties. We are told that she was not a "masculine" woman, and certainly her best female characters have the domestic impulse. Whereas Charlotte Bronte had laid stress on the woman as a home-maker, George Eliot felt more keenly a woman's protective and maternal impulse. Charlotte Bronte had an instinctive love of home, with its quietness and shelter. George Eliot lacked this soothing touch. Her mind was too strenuous to appreciate and to feel the serenity of a well-ordered house, where all things go smoothly without bustle or apparent effort. The tranquillity of a woman's duties appealed to Charlotte Bronte; George Eliot felt more strongly the vigorous claims on her service and compassion. (It is worth noting that Mrs Gaskell combined the conceptions of service and domesticity.) After the death of her father George Eliot expressed her desire for this life of service.—"The only ardent hope I have for my future life is to have given to me some woman's duty, some possibility of devoting myself where I may see a daily result of pure calm blessedness in the life of another." To Mrs Beecher Stowe she wrote with a touch of wistfulness: "You have had longer experience than I as a writer, and fuller experience as a woman, since you have borne children, and known a mother's history from the beginning." Writing to Mr Frederic Harrison in late life, she quoted Wordsworth's

Buonaparte Sonnet, in admiration of its "precious" lines;
and she underlined the following words: "Wisdom doth live
with children round her knees." The woman's chief glory lay
for her in the human relationships of the wife and mother.
When Romola's marriage proved a failure, she was said to
have "lost her crown."

Yet she recognised the fact that many women have to
beat out a passage to their true vocation. "A woman must
choose mean things," said Esther Lyon, "because only mean
things are offered to her." Many women, like Maggie
Tulliver, have to wrestle for their souls, in the midst of dingy
sorrows. Other women, like Romola, have "a man's nobility
of soul," yet cannot fill a man's place effectively; they can
exclaim with Brutus's Portia: "I have a man's mind, but
a woman's might." On others is laid, not the burden of a
narrow lot, but the constricting pressure of genius. When
she described Daniel Deronda's mother, George Eliot must
have been feeling the intensity of her own experience: "You
may try—but you can never imagine what it is to have a man's
force of genius, and yet to suffer the slavery of being a girl.
To have a pattern cut out—'this is what you must be; this
is what you are wanted for; a woman's heart must be of such
a size and no larger, else it must be pressed small, like Chinese
feet; her happiness is to be made as cakes are, by a fixed
receipt.'" In *Armgart* she expresses the same difficulty—
the problem of the artistic life. Armgart claims that genius
does not rob a woman of her womanhood:

> Yes, I know
> The oft-taught Gospel: "Woman, thy desire
> Shall be that all superlatives on earth
> Belong to men, save the one highest kind—
> To be a mother. Thou shalt not desire
> To do aught best save pure subservence:
> Nature has willed it so!" O blessed Nature!
> Let her be arbitress; she gave me voice
> Such as she only gives a woman child,
> Best of its kind, gave me ambition too,
> The sense transcendent which can taste the joy
> Of swaying multitudes, of being adored

For such achievement, needed excellence,
As man's best art must wait for, or be dumb,
Men did not say, when I had sung last night,
" 'Twas good, nay, wonderful, considering
She is a woman"—and then turn to add,
"Tenor or baritone had sung her songs
Better, of course; she's but a woman spoiled."

In her own heart George Eliot seems to have regarded genius as yoke rather than diadem. To her it was like the heavy caps pressed on the brows of the hypocrites in Dante's vision, gold without, "but leaden all within" ("*Ma dentro tutte piombo*"). In the case of Charlotte Bronte the metaphor had been reversed. Her genius was lead without and gold within —an obstacle from the standpoint of the world with its round of conventional duties, a glory and solace in the privacy of her own heart.

There still remains the question how far George Eliot's sex reflected itself in her books. We know that Dickens immediately acclaimed the writer of *Adam Bede* as a woman, while Thackeray was equally positive that only a man could have produced such a book. Mrs Carlyle thought the author must be a middle-aged man with a wife, from whom he had obtained his "beautiful feminine touches." Sir Leslie Stephen asserts that George Eliot gives away her sex in her scorn of feminine blandishments: "She is...a little too contemptuous when the Samson yields to the Delilah." He also claims that she fails to portray men successfully unless they are effeminate—"women in disguise"; and he points to some of her most unpleasant men—Tito and Grandcourt, for instance—as evidence of his theory. No woman can be flattered to hear that the most objectionable features of these characters are essentially feminine; yet one must agree with Sir Leslie Stephen that even her "manly" men are described from the woman's point of view.—In addition to this feminine approach to character-study, we should notice her handling of emotional situations. We feel the difference of sex immediately when we put side by side Scott's description in *The Antiquary* of Steenie Mucklebackit's funeral, and George Eliot's account of Lisbeth Bede mourning for her husband.

In Scott's picture there is a massive weather-beaten grandeur;
it is stern, weird, and deeply moving like the scenes painted
by Josef Israels. Yet all the time it is a picture, and we are
the observers. It is different with Lisbeth Bede. We hear
her voice, and the words open out dim vistas of unexpressed
grief.—"But now," says she to Dinah, "do ye make the tay
as ye like it, for I'n got no taste i' my mouth this day—it's all
one what I swaller—it's all got the taste o' sorrow wi' t." In
studying Scott's picture we feel the strange exaltation brought
by death. "A corpse," says Emerson, "is a solemn ornament
in a house." Lisbeth in her narrow way felt the same
exaltation; the importance of the "burial," the special service,
and the funeral psalm acted as "counter-excitement to her
sorrow." The difference is, that in the case of Scott, it is we,
the readers, who feel the exaltation; in George Eliot's account,
the feeling is pitched within the hearts of her characters.
The man stands outside and watches emotion with awe; the
woman passes inwards to live in its fellowship. Shakespeare
made a *woman* say: "Here I and sorrows sit."

George Eliot was not only a woman. She was a student,
and this to such an extent, that she puts us out of tune with
all study. Her learning chills us like a dripping garment.
It is rarely, if ever, a guiding beacon or a comforting fire.
After her father's death she wrote from Geneva, "I...take
a dose of mathematics every day to keep my brain from
becoming quite soft." She hungered for knowledge, as
others hunger for bread.—"There is so much to read, and the
days are so short! I get more hungry for knowledge every
day, and less able to satisfy my hunger." Later she said—
"I could enjoy everything, from arithmetic to antiquarianism,
if I had large spaces of life before me." When she was studying
Spanish grammar in preparation for writing *The Spanish
Gypsy*, she declared, "I find it so much easier to learn anything
than to feel I have anything worth teaching." Her learning
comes upon us with even more sense of chill, in a passage
from one of her letters. She had been describing her household anxieties, and proceeded to set forth her compensations:

But then I have by my side, a dear companion, who is a perpetual fountain of courage and cheerfulness and of considerate tenderness for my lack of these virtues. And beside that I have Roman history! Perhaps that sounds a bitter joke to you, who are looking at sea and sky, and not thinking of Roman history at all. But this too, read aright, has its gospel and revelation. I read it much as I used to read a chapter in the Acts or Epistles.

Perhaps it was meant as "a bitter joke"; there is no doubt, at all events, about the bitterness of placing human love, Roman history, and the glory of the sky, in the same category. Somewhere Lamb has eagerly described the completely satisfactory appearance of a man who has never learnt his multiplication table. We remember also how the schoolmaster left him (Lamb) in "comfortable possession of (his) own ignorance"; and when we read George Eliot we often feel that a so-called ignorance can be more educative than scholarship.—Perhaps this is what she was thinking when she wrote these words in *Middlemarch*:

If we had a keen vision and feeling of all ordinary human life, it would be like hearing the grass grow, and the squirrel's heart beat, and we should die of that roar which lies on the other side of silence. As it is the quickest of us walk about well wadded with stupidity.

At times she seemed to feel that there was something wrong with her. We can hear her own heart crying through her quotation from Margaret Fuller's Journal: "I shall always reign through the intellect, but the life! the life! O my God! shall that ever be sweet?"—We know how she studied for her books. Before writing *Felix Holt* she read through *The Times* for 1832 and 1833. The list of authorities read in preparation for *Romola* is positively astounding. And yet, what came of it all? We feel that the passages in *Romola* which bear most trace of study are the very places where all normally-constructed readers taste the forbidden fruit of "skipping." She wanted to contrast the frivolity of the Florentine citizens with the "high seriousness" of her central figures; and she laboured to demonstrate that frivolity. Shakespeare had the same problem before him in *Julius Caesar*. He had to mark the distinction between the irresponsible rabble, and the deeply conscientious rulers of

Roman society; but he did not do this by taking great stupefying draughts of Roman history. It may be that his crowd was not Roman at all, but frankly Elizabethan. That is not the point. He wanted to mark, not the national character of the crowd, but its levity; and he knew better than to look for that in books of solid learning.

George Eliot had a theory about study, as about most other things. Daniel Deronda's words may have had a personal reference: "Receptiveness is a rare and massive power, like fortitude." She would not exercise her fortitude without a reason; and I think we shall find it in her doctrine of the escape from self. To her mind the highest escape was that of religious feeling; but she recognised other methods of slipping from the restraints of self-love. When Daniel Deronda urged on Gwendolen the shelter of religion, he took music as a "small example" which "answers for all larger things." His words are significant: "The refuge you are needing from personal trouble is the higher, the religious life, which holds an enthusiasm for something more than our appetites and vanities. The few may find themselves in it simply by an elevation of feeling; but for us who have to struggle for our wisdom, the higher life must be a region in which the affections are clad with knowledge." It is, of course, true that the fullest escape is that which leads us to the thought of God; but George Eliot recognised the value, in a lesser degree, of any worthy object—human service, art, knowledge—which distracts us from ourselves. She sought books that she might forget herself. She went there to get rid of her own defects. "I am taking a deep bath," she wrote, "of other people's thoughts."

It must never be forgotten that although she loved learning, she never wished to place her life apart from those who were unlearned. Doubtless, she had scant patience with the stupidity which is so often unconsciously cruel. This is a factor which, to quote Sir Leslie Stephen, diminished "her appreciation of fools." Among her short notes we find a sentence ending with a sudden snap: "Though a certain mixture of silliness may lighten existence, we have at present more than enough." Once, in a moment of depression at

Geneva, she exclaimed that she was with people "so little worth talking to." But the habitual tendency of her mind was all in the opposite direction. Nothing delighted her more than to be trusted with a confidence. In *Theophrastus* she spoke scornfully of the person who yearns for superior society: "I have usually found that it is the rather dull person who appears to be disgusted with his contemporaries because they are not strikingly original, and to satisfy whom the party at a country house should have included the prophet Isaiah, Plato, Francis Bacon, and Voltaire." Comparisons with Charlotte Bronte are usually to the disadvantage of George Eliot; but here it is all the other way. Charlotte Bronte never abandoned, like George Eliot, all traces of "intellectual snobbery."

The most essential thing about George Eliot's bookishness was her feeling for the tragedy of the bookworm. Difficult though it may appear, she wished us to be sympathetic towards Mr Casaubon. His soul, we read, was "sensitive without becoming enthusiastic; it was too languid to thrill out of self-consciousness into passionate delight; it went on fluttering in the swampy ground where it was hatched, thinking of its wings and never flying." As we read, we feel that she was diagnosing her own case. It is, of course, possible, as Milton's example would prove, to combine scholarship and genius; Dr Johnson remarked of him: "His heat sublimates his learning." Without that fervour learning cannot be sublime; and George Eliot was often very cold indeed.—Philip Wakem told Maggie that he yearned for a faculty to raise him above the dead level of provincial life; and then he added: "A passion answers as well as a faculty." The pitiful fact about George Eliot was this: she had the faculty, but she sometimes lost the passion. We remember Stevenson's verdict on her: "A high—but may we not add?— a rather dry lady."

There is a passive suggestion in the phrase "a learned lady." George Eliot was something more—an active rebel. She refused to acquiesce in a creed which she no longer believed. Her rejection of Christianity may have been in the first place a matter of contra-suggestion. She may have revolted, first against a certain crudeness with which great ideas were presented to her. In *Janet's Repentance* she refers to this coarsening of high things:

Religious ideas have the fate of melodies, which, once set afloat in the world, are taken up by all sorts of instruments, some of them woefully coarse, feeble, or out of tune, until people are in danger of crying out that the melody itself is detestable.

She may have felt, not only crudity, but narrowness in the form of Christianity around her. Probably at one time she had been, like Daniel Deronda's mother, confined by tradition:

I knew (said she) what was in the chest—things that had been dinned in my ears since I had any understanding—things that were thrust on my mind that I might feel them like a wall round my life—my life that was growing like a tree.

Nevertheless there was in George Eliot's rejection of Christianity something more than reaction against environment. It seems a startling thing, that, according to her own account, the reading of Scott's novels did more than anything else to unsettle her faith. Yet we must call to mind what Walter Bagehot said of Scott: "He omits the delineation of the soul." In a certain sense Scott's characters are soulless; they are sane, brave, honourable, and often singularly lovable; and they seem to achieve all these qualities without any articulate religion. This strengthened George Eliot's conviction that dogmatic beliefs have no necessary connection with practical actions: in other words, that virtue can be acquired apart from Christianity.—Even this standpoint, though it may weaken faith in a creed, is hardly a justification for its absolute rejection. In the last resort, it was not so much a matter of reason as of emotion; the inspiration faded. She wanted to believe in Christianity, but could not muster up the old fervour; and she was not the kind to go on "pretending that things are better than they really are." When translating Strauss's *Life of Jesus*, she worked under an almost overpowering reluctance. She wrote with Thorwaldsen's figure of the risen Christ before her; and we have an authentic report of her depression.—"She is Strauss-sick—it makes her ill dissecting the beautiful story of the crucifixion, and only the sight of the Christ-image and picture make her endure it." Above all things she was honest. She objected to the facile optimism which displays "pleasing pictures to the exclusion of all disagreeable truths." "I think," she said, "the highest and best thing is rather to suffer with real suffering than to be happy in the imagination of an unreal good." She refused to close her eyes to unpleasant consequences; it will be remembered how she imagined Romola, not "shutting eyes and ears," but watching the removal of her father's library. Perhaps the most characteristic of all her utterances occurred in a letter: "The 'highest calling and election' is *to do without opium*, and live through all our pain with conscious, clear-eyed endurance."

This is not a place for Christian apologetics. George Eliot lost her faith; and she never ceased to regret it. We see this everywhere—most of all in the extraordinary wistfulness with which she handled all cases of deep religious emotion. This affords one of the most surprising contrasts between her and Charlotte Bronte. Charlotte, while possessing a certain measure of religious experience, was curiously dead to the mysterious friction and conflict of the spiritual life. George Eliot, who stood apart from formal creeds, felt to the end of her days the magnetism and dominance of the religious impulse. In later years she came to regard Christianity as the highest of actual religions; but she did not accept it as a final revelation. Hot scorn broke from her when others underrated her lost love: "What pitiable people are those who feel no poetry in Christianity!" When agony enters her stories, the Christian consolation comes unbidden. Maggie found *The Imitation of Christ*; and there is a pregnant comment on Hetty's desolation: "No wonder man's religion has so much sorrow in it; no wonder he needs a suffering God." Passion and poignancy are never lacking when George Eliot writes of spiritual loss or disillusion. Romola felt herself driven to resist Savonarola's standpoint; yet, "in the act of rebelling she was bruising her own reverence." Esther's dread of going to see Felix in prison is described with a significant comparison: "It was what the dread of the pilgrim might be, who has it whispered to him that the holy places are a delusion, or that he will see them with a soul unstirred and unbelieving." There is the same poetry and intensity in her delineation of Rufus Lyon wrestling to regain his old supremacy of faith. He prayed "that some great discipline might come, that the dullest spiritual sense might be roused to full vision and hearing as of old, and the supreme facts again become supreme in his soul."

She never lost this conviction of the soul's infinite hunger. Tito represented the crudest form of pagan selfishness; he had no place in his heart for the servile religion "which lies in the renunciation of all that makes life precious." But it was not only Tito who fell under her condemnation; even Bardo was convicted of inadequacy: "My father," said Fra Luca, "has lived amidst human sin and misery without believing in them; he has been like one busy picking shining stones in a mine, while there was a world dying of plague above him." To George Eliot's mind paganism was ineffective because it lacked spiritual hunger. She laughed kindly at the people who sought moderation in all things—for instance, Mrs Linnet, when she said: "It's right enough to be spiritual —I'm no enemy to that; but I like my potatoes mealy. I don't see as anybody 'ull go to heaven the sooner for not digestin' their dinner—providin' they don't die sooner, as mayhap Mr Tryan will, poor dear man!" She could smile with these apostles of common sense, but her natural bent was towards asceticism. Though she appreciated "the daylight" of Celia Brooke's understanding, she was more at home among "the strange coloured lamps by which Dodo habitually saw." Whether it were the coloured lamps of quixotic impulse or self-denying passion, George Eliot preferred them to the clear, cold searchlight of prudence. She admitted that in the white light one sees more clearly what to avoid.—Tom Tulliver was self-denying; his character was "strong by its very negations." He had a definite goal; and he reached it. Yet we feel all the time that it is better to be like Maggie, struggling along dim paths, and ready—

> To contend for the shade of a word, a thing not seen
> with the eyes.

George Eliot abandoned Christian dogma, but she could not carry on without some theory. As has been suggested, her religion came to be a matter of self-forgettal. It would be possible to multiply instances of this tendency. Self-absorption and irreligion were for her almost synonymous terms. As Adam Bede said, "The best of working is, it gives you a grip hold o' things outside your own lot." Hetty had no curiosity to distract her from self. She took no interest in Adam's conversation unless it were personal; he bored her when he embarked on "the difficulties of ant-life." These things are not trifles; they are meant to carry weight.—The same doctrine burns through Zarca's words to Fedalma:

> 'Tis a vile life that like a garden pool
> Lies stagnant in the round of personal loves;
> That has no ear save for the tickling lute
> Set to small measures,—deaf to all the beats
> Of that large music rolling o'er the world:
> A miserable, petty, low-roofed life,
> That knows the mighty orbits of the skies
> Through nought save light or dark in its own cabin.

At the critical point of Gwendolen Harleth's career we find a note of comment. It is in moments of stress, we are told, that religion is manifested: "Even in the eyes of frivolity life looks out from the scene of human struggle with the awful face of duty, and a religion shows itself which is something else than a private consolation." George Eliot denounced the poet Young's religion because it was nothing better than "egoism turned heavenward." We have already referred to her conception of the intellectual life as a refuge from egoism; but this quotation deserves to be noted: "It is piteous to see the helplessness of some sweet women when their affections are disappointed—because all their teaching has been, that they can only delight in ideas as an experience which they could not confess without being laughed at. Yet surely women need this sort of defence against passionate affliction even more than men." One more tense quotation, and then we are done: "Is it not possible," asked Theophrastus, "for me to enjoy the scenery of the earth without saying to myself, I have a cabbage-garden in it?"—This conception of religion, however arduous, has at least the advantage of being extremely practical. A man may be thinking of anything—his neighbours, a sunset, a symphony, or (presumably) mathematics; so long as he is not thinking of himself at the same time, his mood is religious. Stated baldly like this, the conception seems rather inadequate. It embraces *a* truth, though it does not express *the* Truth, absolute and complete.

In connection with religious outlook we must consider the question of George Eliot's "pessimism."—She herself denied the charge: "I need not tell you," she said, "that my book (*Middlemarch*) will not present my own feeling about human life if it produces on readers whose minds are really receptive the impression of blank melancholy and despair." She called herself a "meliorist"—that is, one believing most firmly that the world could afford to be made better, and cherishing somewhat uncertain hopes of its ultimate improvement. At times she was afflicted with personal depression—"self-distrust and despair of ever being equal to the demands of life."

Everything I do (she wrote) seems poor and trivial in the doing; and when it is quite gone from me, and seems no longer my own, then I rejoice in it, and think it fine. That is the history of my life.

Towards the close of her days she was able to say, "I have entirely lost my *personal* melancholy." Yet, whatever she may have said, we cannot lose the impression that she was a woman unable to cast off sadness. Part of this may have been due to ill-health. We get a sudden glimpse into her daily life in a stray sentence from a letter to Mr John Blackwood: "Having no grand-children to get up a Christmas tree for, we had nothing to divert our attention from our headaches."—She had, moreover, a critical tendency, which does not conduce to gaiety. *A propos* of her garden, she remarked, "Some people are born to make life pretty, and others to grumble that it is not pretty enough." As a matter of fact she could never settle down in the belief that life is pretty.—She quoted with approval the remark of an acquaintance: "'Life is a bad business, but we must make the best of it'; to which philosophy I say, Amen." Adam Bede confessed he was not "the only man that's got to do without much happiness i' this life." Always George Eliot gives the impression of expecting disappointment rather than joy.

It has been much discussed whether such pessimism was the result of temperament or creed. Personally, I think that a gloomy disposition is an evil which causes as much pain and requires as drastic treatment as a violent temper; and George Eliot was far too conscientious a woman to indulge herself in groundless or capricious melancholy. If she was gloomy, she must have had a reason for it; and I think the reason is to be found in her severance from the Christian tradition. To her, above all people, the loss must have been incalculable. At heart she was a Conservative, loving old associations with the utmost force of her nature. It will be remembered how insignificant a trifle brought home to Maggie Tulliver the cleft made in her life. It was after the sale, when she looked in vain for the treasured books of childhood.

"Our dear old *Pilgrim's Progress* that you coloured with your little paints; and that picture of Pilgrim with a mantle on, looking just like a turtle—O dear!" Maggie went on half sobbing as she turned over the few books.—"I thought we should never part with that while we lived—everything is going away from us—the end of our lives will have nothing in it like the beginning!"

In parting with Christianity, George Eliot made the end of her life unlike its beginning. Her action cut her adrift from the old beliefs, the old loyalties, the old affections. She was so made that she could not help looking backward rather than forward; and she looked with the eyes of a stranger.

The only other personal experience which cut deeply into her life was her union with Mr Lewes. Long before she had any personal bias—before she had even met Mr Lewes—she dropped some hot words on the marriage problem as it is set forth in *Jane Eyre*: "All self-sacrifice is good, but one would like it to be in a somewhat nobler cause than that of a diabolical law which chains a man soul and body to a putrifying carcase." This is certainly not the place to defend or criticise the marriage-laws. When her time came, George Eliot decided that the existing marriage-law was wrong;

and so she broke it. She lived with Mr Lewes for nearly twenty-five years, called him her "husband," received his children, and dedicated all her books to him. After his death she said, "I had thought that my life was ended, and that, so to speak, my coffin was ready for me in the next room." The full and private facts are not sufficiently known for any adequate enquiry into the morality of her action; and, in any case, this is not the place for such investigations. The chief point to be noted is this: George Eliot's single defiance of the social tradition set up in her mind a permanent antagonism to conventions. It is true that in her writings she insisted, with an almost unexampled emphasis, on the sanctity of marriage and the binding character of its obligations. While she was in full accord with the wholesome tradition that marriage is a permanent relation, she attacked the prudential tradition which turns matrimony into a bargain. When Catherine Arrowpoint wished to marry Herr Klesmer, a man below her in social station, she exclaimed, "I will not give up the happiness of my life to ideas that I don't believe in, and customs I have no respect for." What an irony gleams sharp-edged through the bland worldly-wisdom of her father!—"'It would never do to argue about marriage, Cath,' said Mr Arrowpoint, 'It's no use getting up the subject like a parliamentary question. We must do as other people do.'" George Eliot refused to do things simply because other people did them. Comparatively early in life she had called England "a land of gloom, of *ennui*, of platitude"; and she could never throw off her aversion to platitudes. She felt that there is nothing so narrow, or so unjust as an unintelligent tradition. Mrs Poyser was "overawed" by her warm-hearted husband's unbending condemnation of Hetty; but the writer supplies an explanation: "We are often startled by the severity of mild people on exceptional occasions; the reason is, that mild people are most liable to be under the yoke of traditional impressions." Tradition may limit the sympathy of a kindly man like Mr Poyser, but it may do worse. It can overlay sympathy with worldly prudence. When Tom rejected Maggie without proof of her guilt, he gave her what he considered a satisfactory reason: "The world shall know that I feel the difference between right and wrong." It came to this—that he sought the praise of man rather than the praise of God.

If we wish to study George Eliot's satire of conventional opinions, we shall find it nowhere more penetrating than in *The Mill on the Floss*. This seems to be the underlying conception of the entire book. St Ogg's was another Vanity Fair where Maggie was an alien, from the bitter griefs of childhood to her final isolation. Tom represented the principalities and powers against which she waged a blind unceasing warfare. He had his moral code, and so far as it went, it was a good one; but it was in a clear-cut pattern which could not admit of variation. When Maggie upset his card-houses, he "turned white with anger, but said nothing; he would have struck her, only he knew it was cowardly to strike a girl, and Tom Tulliver was quite determined he would never do anything cowardly." The external blow could not have hurt Maggie more than his internal feelings towards her; but he was entirely satisfied to have kept his surface smooth and flawless.—His serene common-sense saved him from the lure of romance. Unlike Maggie, he saw nothing entrancing in gypsies—they were "thieves, and hardly got anything to eat, and had nothing to drive but a donkey." The blend of morality and materialism in his verdict was highly significant. He liked things to be normal, and had "a sort of superstitious repugnance to everything exceptional"; thus his radius of sympathy could not extend to Philip Wakem, the hunchback. This affection for the commonplace was shared by every person of any weight in the neighbourhood. Mr Stelling had not wasted his time in acquiring "abnormal" culture, and Stephen was attracted by Lucy just because she was not "a remarkable rarity."— It will be remembered how Dickens' respectable gentleman, Mr Magnus, saw no charm in Sam Weller's originality.— "'Ah,' said the red-haired man, 'that, you see, is a matter of taste. I am not fond of anything original; I don't like it; don't see the necessity for it.'" The society of St Ogg's saw no necessity for unusual people like Maggie Tulliver; and so it cast her out.

Before leaving this study of George Eliot's individual temperament, we must take into account the doctrine which lay at the core of her thinking, till her novels seemed to become an embodiment of her personal outlook. There is nothing in her life to account for her tremendous insistence on the fact of retribution. Why she felt it so mightily we cannot tell. It may have been the outcome of an intensely logical mind. To her, retribution was as certain as the successive stages in a mathematical argument. The cause produces the effect from which it is impossible to escape. This is not the retribution of Greek Drama or *King Lear*; here there is hardly any reference to avenging gods. Rather it is a mechanical, impersonal process which cannot be arrested. It is not malignant or cruel; it is simply inevitable.

In Gwendolen's dread this shadow of fate took upon it a certain semblance of personality: "All the infiltrated influence of disregarded religious teaching, as well as the deeper impressions of something awful and inexorable enveloping her, seemed to concentrate themselves in the vague conception of avenging power."—More often the conception takes the form of a process or growth.—"I'll face the progeny of all my deeds," cried Silva.—In *Romola* we find the same metaphor more fully expounded:

Our deeds are like children that are born to us; they live and act apart from our own will. Nay, children may be strangled, but deeds never; they have an indestructible life both in and out of our consciousness; and that dreadful vitality of deeds was pressing hard on Tito.

The heading of a chapter in the same book expresses this truth by another metaphor: "Fruit is Seed."

Though the retribution may be a process acting like a scientific law, it selects instruments to perform its functions. The penalty is something sharper and more revolutionary than mere pangs of conscience. In the story of Arthur Donnithorne we find this sentence: "Nemesis can seldom forge a sword for herself out of our consciences—out of the suffering we feel in the suffering we have caused; there is rarely metal enough there to make an effective weapon."—

Sometimes the sword moves in the hands of a person like Tom Tulliver, obsessed with zeal for "punishments," till he becomes a representative of vengeance. Sometimes the agent of retribution is as reluctant as the victim; it was Caleb Garth who was compelled to throw the first stone at Bulstrode. At other times the blow falls from the hands of the callous and indifferent, as when Maggie passed, an outcast, through the streets of St Ogg's.—"Retribution," says the writer, "may come from any voice; the hardest, cruellest, most imbruted urchin at the street-corner can inflict it." Looking at the face of life it seems that almost anything can be turned into a channel for punishment.

With the dread of retribution there may arise a struggle to avert it. Mr Bulstrode believed "that if he spontaneously did something right, God would save him from the consequences of wrong-doing." The struggle is never protracted. Most victims submit without question. Some, like Silva, stand erect to meet the blow:

> If I must sink
> At last to hell, I will not take my stand
> Among the coward crew which could not bear
> The harm themselves had done, which others bore.
> My young life still may fill a breach,
> And I will take no pardon, not my own,
> Not God's—no pardon idly on my knees:
> But it shall come to me upon my feet,
> And in the thick of action, and each deed
> That carried shame and wrong shall be the sting
> That drives me higher up the steep of honour.

This redemptive sting is not always a part of the penalty. There was no tonic, no regeneration of deed, for Mr Bulstrode.—"A man may do wrong," said Caleb, "and his will may rise clear out of it, though he can't get his life clear. That's a bad punishment."—Often, as in the case of Godfrey Cass, the doom is beyond all remedy, and subtle in its bitter irony.—"'I wanted to pass for childless once, Nancy,' he said, 'I shall pass for childless now against my wish.'" The punishment is terrible because it is so appropriate. It is like

Dante's conception of the wrathful, tormented by their own permanence of mood:

> *Tristi fummo*
> *Nell' aer dolce che dal soll s' allegra,*
> *Portando dentro accidioso fummo:*
> *Or ci attristiam nella belletta negra.*

> Sad once were we,
> In the sweet air made gladsome by the sun,
> Carrying a foul and lazy mist within:
> Now in these murky settlings are we sad.
>
> (Carey's translation.)

It should be remarked, however, that in her last study of retribution, George Eliot struck a single chord of alleviation. It was a chord with two notes—the pity of one friend, and the possibility of an ultimate goodness. When Gwendolen confessed to Deronda, she told him of her sleepless nights at sea: "It was not my own knowledge, it was God's, that had entered into me, and even the stillness—everything held a punishment for me—everything but you."—Deronda, as he listened, had but one thought in his mind: "If he had opened his lips to speak, he could only have echoed, 'It can never be altered—it remains unaltered—to alter other things.'" Elsewhere George Eliot laid a firm and heavy pressure on the weight of fruitless remorse. Here she leaves us with the hope of a purifying and impassioned repentance.

III

THE IMPERSONAL ARTIST

A SOMEWHAT awkward line from *The Legend of Jubal* might serve as motto for this chapter:

"Hearing myself," he said, "hems in my life."

There is also a passage in *The Spanish Gypsy* where George Eliot drops a suggestion with regard to the impersonal, character of the artist.—Juan, the minstrel, had been singing to Pepita. As he told her, he loved her "in the song," but not "out of it"; then he explained his position:

> Listen, little one.
> Juan is not a living man all by himself;
> His life is breathed in him by other men,
> And they speak out of him. He is their voice.
> Juan's own life he gave once quite away.
> It was Pepita's lover singing then—not Juan.
> We old, old poets, if we kept our hearts,
> Should scarcely know them from another man's,
> They shrink to make room for the many more
> We keep within us.

George Eliot sought the impersonal life of art as a fundamental religion. It was an extra channel of escape from self —a privilege of genius superadded to normal human experience. Genius opens another door through which the few may pass on their voyage out of themselves. Mr Masefield's Dauber thought of his art in relation to other men:

> He was a door to new worlds in the brain,
> A window opening, letting in the Sun.

George Eliot saw the vocation as an illumination of the artist; Armgart partially expressed her own theory:

> My song
> Was consecration, lifted me apart
> From the crowd chiselled like me, sister forms,
> But empty of divineness.

This was only a partial expression of her theory, for she condemned Armgart's sense of aloofness. She condemned the
isolation of art, but accepted its divinity as the burden of
a great responsibility:

> Thy gifts to give was thine of men alone.
> 'Twas but in giving that thou could'st atone
> For too much wealth amid their poverty.
>
> (*The Legend of Jubal.*)

If, then, art were a divine calling, it demanded rigorous
training. "In authorship," she said, "I hold carelessness to
be a mortal sin." In all departments of life she sought
thoroughness as something which brings its own reward.
Many of her characters laboured under that impulse—for
instance, Denner, the lady's maid.—"There's pleasure,"
she said, "in knowing one's not a fool like half the people
one sees about. And managing one's husband is some
pleasure; and doing all one's business well." Stradivarius
could not bear to turn out second-rate violins:

> 'Twere purgatory here to make them ill.

To come back to the professional artist—Armgart swept
from her mind the very suggestion of second-rate achievement:

> I will not feed on doing great tasks ill,
> Dull the world's sense with mediocrity,
> And live by trash that smothers excellence.

Somewhere, speaking of Columbus, George Eliot commented
on "the passionate patience of genius." She meant every
word of Klesmer's advice to Gwendolen—"Genius at first
is little more than a great capacity for receiving discipline."—
Zarca, urging on Fedalma the glories of a high destiny,
told her:

> You must take wingèd pleasures, wingèd pains.

If George Eliot felt the pain of a great labour, she experienced
something of its joy.—"She told me," wrote Mr Cross, "that,
in all that she considered her best writing, there was a 'not
herself' which took possession of her and that she felt her
own personality to be merely the instrument through which
this spirit, as it were, was acting."

So much for the method and spirit of the artist: what is his goal? George Eliot very clearly conceived it as an extension and deepening of human sympathy. After reading *Adam Bede*, Mrs Carlyle felt "in charity with the whole human race"—a result after the writer's own heart. She wished her appeal to the emotions to act with an unconscious moral value.

My function (she said) is that of the *aesthetic*, not the doctrinal teacher—the rousing of the nobler emotions which make mankind desire the social right, not the prescribing of special measures, concerning which the artistic mind, however strongly moved by social sympathy, is not often the best judge.

At another time she wrote: "I think aesthetic teaching is the highest of all teaching, because it deals with life in its highest complexity. But if it ceases to be purely aesthetic—if it lapses anywhere from the picture to the diagram—it becomes the most offensive of all teaching." Matthew Arnold defined religion as "morality touched with emotion"; George Eliot would have accepted the same phrase as definition of the artistic goal. Her writings required the warmth and colour of emotion before they could achieve their purpose. The peril besetting all authors is this—that they should recall faded emotions to do duty for fresh and present opportunities. What she said of Savonarola's preaching had its implication for her own task: "It is the lot of every man who has to speak for the satisfaction of the crowd, that he must often speak in virtue of yesterday's faith, hoping it will come back to-morrow." Notwithstanding, she never lost her faith in the value of artistic achievement. She had nothing but scorn for the shabby, tawdry aims of the author without conscience.—"He really cares," she said, "for nothing but his income. He carries on authorship on the principle of the gin-palace; and bad authorship of the sort called amusing, is spiritual gin."

Possibly it was a part of her altruism that she did not seem to spend much thought on her own reward. She spoke very little of fame or immortality. In 1868 she wrote rather sadly, "I am not yet engaged in any work that makes a higher life for me—a life that is young and grows, though in my other

life I am getting old and decaying." She did not nerve herself with the courageous hopes of a poet like Keats. Her
experience was different, for she had tasted fame, and found
it insipid. Who can say whether she was thinking of herself
at all when she wrote of Jubal's final consolation?

> Thy limbs shall lie dark, tombless, on this sod,
> Because thou shinest in man's soul, a god,
> Who found and gave new passion and new joy
> That nought but Earth's destruction can destroy.

When we come to consider the quality of George Eliot's
art, we are instantly conscious of its ironic flavour. This
command of sharp piercing words came to her early. It
appears in her essay on Young, with its zigzag antithetic
style—the survival of a past literary tradition: "He is equally
impressed with the momentousness of death and of burial
fees. He languished at once for immortal life and for
'livings.'" Later on, this ironic manner developed into a
faculty, inherited from Jane Austen, of giving portraits in
a single sentence. The *Scenes of Clerical Life* are full of
sentences and phrases with a shimmering edge of wit. In
the first chapter of *Amos Barton* we hear of Mrs Hacket:
"In her utmost enjoyment of spoiling a friend's self-satis-
faction, she was never known to spoil a stocking." Or we
see Mrs Patten: "Quiescence in an easy chair, under the
sense of compound interest perpetually accumulating has
long seemed an ample function to her"; we are let into her
motives for respecting Mr Hacket, who was "too well off
to want to borrow money"; and we are told—what Jane
Austen would have omitted—the state of her soul.—"If I'm
not to be saved," she declares, "I know a many as are in
a bad way." A few pages ahead we meet Mr Bridman, with
his science of polite conversation—a subject dear to the
heart of Jane Austen. In *Mr Gilfil's Love Story* we get Jane
Austen's type of irony applied to a subject rather out of her
compass: "Mrs Hacket expressed herself greatly edified by
the sermon on honesty, the allusion to the unjust weight
and deceitful balance having a peculiar lucidity for her,
owing to a recent dispute with her grocer; but I am not aware

that she ever appeared to be much struck with the sermon on anger." To take only one sentence from *Janet's Repentance*, we have Mr Pilgrim, the doctor, who "looked with great tolerance on all shades of religious opinion that did not include a belief in cures by miracle." To my mind the ironic humour of the *Scenes* is infinitely fresher and truer than its pathos; it has the charm of Jane Austen's laughter, with a slight elasticity stretching it out to include themes beyond her range.

This humour, which consists in the portrayal of ordinary figures, tended afterwards to pass into the more dramatic faculty which creates humorous characters, and leaves them to maintain the stock of wit. When we hear Mrs Poyser talking we can do quite well without many humorous by-comments. We want nothing more, so long as we can listen to her. George Eliot never repeated anything so good in its own kind as Mrs Poyser. Mrs Cadwallader, for instance, does not come within miles of her charm; Bob Jakin is of a different sex, and he is not, like Mrs Poyser, more of a humorist than anything else; he is also a disguised knight-errant. The creation of Mrs Poyser was something unique, which calls for an unceasing gratitude; so also was the glorious idea of giving her such an entirely suitable husband.—"'Ay, ay,' said Bartle, 'a terrible woman!—made of needles—made of needles. But I stick to Martin—I shall always stick to Martin. And he likes the needles, God help him! He's a cushion made on purpose for 'em.'"

Mrs Poyser is so irresistible that she has led us away from the question of Jane Austen. There is not much more to be said about it, except that her type of humour appears most completely in *Silas Marner* and *The Mill on the Floss*.—Some phrases from *Persuasion* seem to be re-echoing through the reference to the "timeless origin" of the Osgoods—"the Raveloe imagination having never ventured back to that fearful blank when there were no Osgoods." Or we come across the Dodson family, with its "painful inability to approve the condiments or the conduct of families ungoverned by the Dodson tradition." We have explained to us the use made by Mrs Clegg of her front and back parlours:

"She had two points of view from which she could observe the weakness of her fellow-men, and reinforce her thankfulness for her own exceptional strength of mind." Lastly, we have the two uncles with their remarkable faculty for keeping clear of philanthropic adventures: Mr Clegg, fond of petting animals "which required no appreciable keep"; and Uncle Pullet, who "after silent meditation for a period of several lozenges, came distinctly to the conclusion, that when a young man was likely to do well, it was better not to meddle with him." It is all like Jane Austen—and yet with a difference; for we get the impression of something savage lurking behind the swift darting strokes.

In the later books this lightly-falling satire became less marked though it never passes away completely. We have it, for instance, in *Felix Holt*, when election feeling ran high: "Some regarded it as the most neighbourly thing to hold a little with both sides....It seemed an invidious thing to vote for one gentleman rather than another." But the general tendency is for the irony to acquire a graver tone; either with a suggestion of pathos, as in the description of Mr Casaubon's mind, weighted with unpublished matter; or with a fierce stab of anger as in the rumours about Grandcourt: "It is well known in gambling...a man who has strength of mind to leave off when he has only ruined others, is a reformed character."

All this consideration has been restricted to the ironic phrase. George Eliot never reached Jane Austen's unswerving control of the ironic paragraph. She never did anything so perfect in its kind as the description of Catherine Morland in *Northanger Abbey*. The sight of one of George Eliot's pages with long paragraphs unbroken by conversation gives the reader a premonition of dullness. She was, however, a master of the ironic situation. This power reaches its height in the description of Peter Featherstone's illness, and its effect upon his relations. Dickens treated a similar topic when he pictured Martin Chuzzlewit dying "in a state of siege." But there the whole atmosphere is different.—We seem to see relations heaped upon relations in a grotesque medley; there is a clamour of voices, with the falsetto note rising above them all; it is like some gigantic nightmare; and—if it is not irreverent to quote Keats in such a connection—we feel, after reading the passage, something like the final sentiment of his *Ode to a Nightingale*—

> Fled is that music: do I wake or dream?

No such doubts assail us when we read George Eliot. We are quite sure of being in a world very much awake. We have not the same accumulation of relations, and they make less noise. Unlike the Chuzzlewit family, they do not revel in words, but they have no deficiency in the quality of smiting speech:

"Brother Peter," he (Solomon) said, in a wheedling yet gravely official tone,...."the Almighty knows what I've got on my mind...."

"Then He knows more than I want to know," said Peter.

Dickens regarded the business as an exuberant joke, with a dash of malice in it to give it flavour. The terse realism of George Eliot arouses no laughter, for it reveals the grim fires smouldering in human hearts.

George Eliot's humour is Janus-faced, looking two ways. One is the direction of fierce scorn, and there her humour beats like a scourge. The other is the way of fellow-feeling or compassion. There is very little rancour, for instance, in the description of the music contributed by David, Tim, and Kester at the Poysers' harvest-supper. There is nothing but sweetness in the laughter which touches little children. Shepperton Church, so full of childish memories, is described with touches of winsome grace like those in the first chapter of *David Copperfield*: "(There were) tall dark panels, under whose shadow I sank with a sense of retirement through the Litany, only to feel with more intensity my burst into the conspicuousness of public life when I was made to stand upon the seat during the psalms or the singing." When her humour is tinged with fellow-feeling, its dark strokes lose their harshness of outline. We cast off our severity as we come near to "the God within us holding up the mirror and the scourge for our own pettiness." We are no longer judges, but prisoners at the bar; and we feel the great comradeship of human frailty. "Take a large enough area of human life," says Theophrastus, "and all comedy melts into tragedy, like the Fool's part by the side of Lear."

Although George Eliot sounded rich and deep notes of pathos, this faculty did not come to her quite so naturally as her humour; it took more out of her. She summoned compassion, and yielded herself up to it; but it rarely came unbidden. We have the feeling that the ironic word often slipped out in spite of herself; but she always knew when she was approaching deep emotion.

It will probably be admitted that her command of pathos matured later than her humour. In this she was the direct antithesis of Mrs Gaskell. Pathos found very little place in her early journalism; and the *Scenes of Clerical Life* possess it only in a limited degree. While the emotion there is wistful and delicate, it never becomes heart-searching or impassioned. In writing *Adam Bede*, she first sounded the deep stern waters of pain. Tennyson placed Hetty's fruitless quest beside Thackeray's description of Colonel Newcome's griefs, accounting them "the two most pathetic things in modern fiction." We see Hetty walking heavily towards the pool—black, motionless, and soundless—with the darkening sky above her. As she lies down among the sheep, sobbing for joy, we watch her till we seem to cast ourselves behind, and enter into the "deep heart's core" of her emotion: "The very consciousness of her own limbs was a delight to her; she turned up her sleeves and kissed her arms with the passionate love of life."—Or we hear her confession in prison with its haunting monotony of refrain: "I went back because it cried....Its crying went through me....It was the baby's crying made me go....Dinah, do you think God will take away that crying?"

In *Silas Marner* George Eliot returned to the gentler tones of the earlier *Scenes*—the pity of a barren, purposeless life, the love of gold rooting itself therein, and growing quietly like a weed; the loss of the hard, gold coins, and in its place, the finding of another "gold on the floor in the front of the hearth."..."The heap of gold seemed to glow and get larger beneath his agitated gaze"; Silas leaned forward to handle it, and touched "the soft, warm curls" of a child.

Of Maggie in *The Mill on the Floss* we have already spoken much. The compassion aroused by her story is something unique in literature. Nowhere out of Shakespeare—and perhaps not even there—do we find a character which inspires affection like Maggie. She is as near to her readers as if she had lived and suffered beside them.

Dim pathos, heightened with an element of majesty, surrounds the personality of Bardo. It comes to us through the words of Politian, as Romola reads to her blind father of the blind Tiresias: "He calls Tiresias happy, since, without dying, and with the loss of his eyesight merely, he had beheld Minerva unveiled, and thus, though blind, could for evermore carry her image in his soul."—George Eliot was a voluminous writer, but she could restrain her words under the swift, subduing pressure of death.—"Still Bardo was silent, and his silence was never again broken."—In the same book we meet Baldassarre fiercely hungry for vengeance, and dead to everything else. We feel the spell cast over him by Savonarola's preaching:

In that great sob of the multitude Baldassarre's had mingled. Among all the human beings present, there was perhaps not one whose frame vibrated more strongly than his to the tones and words of the preacher; but it had vibrated like a harp of which all the strings had been wrenched away except one.

Long afterwards his words cut Romola like short, sharp stabs from a dagger: "My mind goes—everything goes sometimes—all but the fire. The fire is of God; it is justice; it will not die."—We thrill to his exaltation as memory and faculty revive, till on the printed page "the black marks become magical"; and then everything fades like mist. He tells Romola of a yearning—"to find all my thoughts again, for I was locked away outside them all." "And," he proceeds, "I am outside now. I feel nothing but a wall and darkness."

Even in *Felix Holt*, so faulty and laboured, we sometimes feel the release of a great compassion, coming through the tragedy of a life apparently faded.—Mrs Transome had "a woman's sensibility and dread which lay screened behind all her petty habits and narrow notions, as some quivering thing with eyes and throbbing heart may lie crouching behind withered rubbish." It will be remembered how Mr Arnold Bennett, in his *Old Wives' Tale*, has pictured Sophia Baines, scanning in old age the degraded features of her dead husband; in that pitiful moment she felt crashing around her the fallacy which tells us that to be old is to have outlived misery. In like manner Mrs Transome turned to Esther, with life shaking under her feet: "I am old, and expect so little now—a very little thing may seem great. Why should I be punished any more?"

There was much sadness in the neighbourhood of Middlemarch. It brooded over the Yew Tree Walk that day when Lydgate placed before Mr Casaubon the possibility of sudden death.—We feel sorrows multiplying through Lydgate's career in the town; even after he leaves it and the story, we are hurt at hearing casual references to his inner dissatisfaction and failure;—he deserved something better.—Possibly George Eliot never wrote anything more poignant or stirring than her study of Mrs Bulstrode's humiliation. This plain, dull woman felt within her the solemn exaltation of a great fidelity:

This imperfectly taught woman, whose phrases and habits were an odd patchwork, had a loyal spirit within her. The man whose prosperity she had shared through nearly half a life, and who had unvaryingly cherished her—now that punishment had befallen him, it was not possible to her in any sense to forsake him. There is a forsaking which still sits at the same board and lies on the same couch with the forsaken soul, withering it the more by unloving proximity. She knew, when she locked her door, that she should unlock it ready to go down to her unhappy husband, and espouse his sorrow, and say of his guilt, I will mourn and not reproach. But she needed time to gather up her strength; she needed to sob out her farewell to all the gladness and pride of her life. When she had resolved to go down, she prepared herself by some little acts which might seem mere folly to a hard onlooker; they were her way of expressing to all spectators, visible or invisible, that she had begun a new life in which she embraced humiliation. She took off all her ornaments, and put on a plain

black gown, and instead of wearing her much-adorned cap and
large bows of hair, she brushed her hair down, and put on a plain
bonnet cap which made her look suddenly like an early
Methodist....

At the sight of her husband

a movement of new compassion and old tenderness went through
her like a great wave....His confession was silent, and her promise
of faithfulness was silent. Open-minded as she was, she nevertheless shrank from the words which would have expressed their
mutual consciousness as she would have shrunk from flakes of
fire. She could not say, "How much is only slander, and false'
suspicion?" and he did not say, "I am innocent."

Still Mrs Bulstrode comes before us with more elaboration
than the earlier women—than Hetty, for instance, or Maggie;
and in *Daniel Deronda* there is a still wider distance from
spontaneous simplicity. The characters and ideas are more
intricate: "The generations," says the dying Mordecai, "are
crowding on my narrow life as a bridge; what has been and
what is to be are meeting there; and the bridge is breaking."
When Deronda's mother speaks to him of her physical
suffering, we cannot help feeling that there is something
pathological in her case:

Sometimes I am in an agony of pain,—I daresay I shall be to-night.
Then it is as if all the life I have chosen to live, all thoughts, all
will, forsook me and left me in spots of memory, and I can't
get away; my pain seems to keep me there.

She feels, not the pain, but its uncanny effect on her mind,
like a presentiment of approaching retribution, making
"ghosts upon the daylight."

Humour and pathos are like threads woven into the texture
of an atmosphere wrapped as a garment round each character.
Sometimes we are conscious of the atmosphere, but can
hardly analyse it.—A few words seem to create it;—for
instance, the picture of Baldassarre "seated on the straw
with something that shone like a white star in his hand"; or
in another sentence a few pages further on: "Baldassarre was
still sitting on the straw when the shadow of Tito passed by."
—At other times we are moved by a sympathetic element in

the setting of the figures.—We see Romola young and dreary in a room full of lifeless objects—" the parchment backs, the unchanging mutilated marble, the bits of obsolete bronze and clay"; when she goes to see her brother for the last time, she looks on "a pale crucified form rising high and pale on the frescoed wall, and pale faces of sorrow looking out from it below." Or we have the wonderful passages where her very surroundings become symbolic of her lot.—The white and gold wedding robes lay in the same chest with a dark coarse bundle—the habit of a nun; the garments represented to her mind the joyous life which was over, and the new hard life which was beginning; the taper died out, like her early hopes, and she sat in total darkness. When she passed out into the bare wintry dawn, its austerity refreshed the sternness of her resolution; but with sunrise came the awakening of shadows, bringing their subtle reminders that however much she might try to escape from her past, she could never escape from herself: "For the last few moments she had been looking at nothing but the brightness on the path and at her own shadow, tall and shrouded like a dread spectre."

George Eliot sometimes placed Nature in the background of her human stories, but hardly ever in the manner of Wordsworth. She denied most positively the claims made for the beneficent influences of Nature: "The selfish instincts are not subdued by the sight of buttercups, nor is integrity in the least established by that classic rural occupation, sheep-washing. To make men moral something more is requisite than to turn them out to grass."—Yet she felt very strongly the fascination of water, and even more deeply the power, appeal, and mystery of the sky. Janet was ashamed to look up through the rent clouds to the "dim light of stars"; it seemed to her "like a cruel finger pointing her out in her wretchedness and humiliation." Hetty shuddered when the moon looked out on her guilt—"It never looked so before."— When Romola drifted out in the boat, "the gold was shrinking and getting duskier in sea and sky"; she rowed out till the stars disclosed themselves "like a palpitating life over the wide heavens"; as the boat glided over the water, she lay and "watched the deepening quiet of the sky." But—and here lies the point—the tranquillity of Nature held no message for her:

Romola felt orphaned in those wide spaces of sea and sky. She read no message of love for her in that far-off symbolic writing of the heavens....She...covered her face, choosing darkness rather than the light of the stars, which seemed to her like the hard light of eyes that looked at her without seeing her.

This brings to mind a cross-comparison with Charlotte Bronte. It will be remembered how Lucy Snowe felt her solitude intensified by the harsh glare of lights flashing across the bay of a continental harbour; but these lights were man-made. Nowhere in Charlotte Bronte do we find any suggestion of harshness in the light of God's stars. She would have contrasted the lamps of earth and the stars of heaven in the same manner as Lear contrasted the glances of his daughters' eyes:

> Her eyes are fierce; but thine
> Do comfort and not burn.

Charlotte Bronte found in the lights of man, fierceness; in the lights of God, comfort. We should remember, however, that George Eliot did not always fail to find sympathy in the heavens. Maggie Tulliver read in the skies judgment and resolve.—She went to sleep on deck, with Stephen, when the sun was flushing the west, but awakened to behold an "awful, starlit sky." Dawn came, and "the reddening eastern light," with its summons to decision; as she looked at "the slowly-rounding sun," she made her resolution; she strengthened herself for the opening day of resistance.—In the later books the backgrounds become less vital, as the emphasis presses more firmly on the inner life. Yet in the latest novel of all, Mordecai went out to watch the lights on sky and river—a life "that can shiver and mourn, be comforted and rejoice."

We have said that the tendency in the later novels is to pass from externals of setting into the inner life. It is in an early book that we see Hetty with her black lace scarf and coloured glass earrings, gazing into the dim mirror till the shadowy room seems alive and throbbing with her joy. But

in *Middlemarch* we have those strange night conversations
between Dorothea and Mr Casaubon; we see nothing to
arrest us—the light of a candle, the dull glow of a dying fire,
and two faint, unexcited figures. The power of such an
atmosphere lies in its negative quality; Dorothea felt her
words to be all the more forcible, "falling clear on the dark
silence."—As George Eliot became older, her art passed into
psychology apart from picture. She approached the standpoint of Fra Lippo Lippi's advisers:

> Paint the soul;
> Never mind the legs and arms!

George Eliot did not always "paint the soul." She was
sometimes content to paint a portrait suggesting more or
less of the soul. In the case of children she often attempted
nothing more than some quaintness or delicacy of manner.
For instance we have Totty,—as Arthur called her, "a funny
little fatty." She appears only in pen pictures, but who wants
anything more? It gives the reader a thrill of expectant
delight to look down the pages and find Totty's name appearing. Or we see Eppie, happily settled on the muddy
margin of a pool:

Here, however, sat Eppie, discoursing cheerfully to her own small
boot, which she was using as a bucket to convey the water into
a deep hoof-mark, while her little naked foot was planted com-
fortably on a cushion of olive-green mud. A red-headed calf was
observing her with alarmed doubt through the opposite hedge.

The mere fact that she painted the external "legs and arms"
of children is no argument for believing that George Eliot
found no soul in childhood. She told us all about Maggie
Tulliver; and after that, there is nothing more to be said.
    The minor characters are sometimes sketched, like her
children, from the outside. We are spared an intimate
acquaintance with such people as Mr Brooke. George Eliot
invites us to look at him like a delightful curiosity; but we
have no desire to understand him. Yet he is not a caricature.
Dickens would have painted him wrapped about with ridicule.
To write on the theme of the election speech would have

filled him with ecstasy. But his Mr Brooke would have borne to George Eliot's personage the relationship of a forty-second cousin. To the reader Mr Brooke cannot be like Mr Micawber—purely a source of recreation. We have to take him more seriously; he is linked on to responsible people—to their decided inconvenience. In a museum of humanity he would do well to be placed in the same corner as Mr Woodhouse from *Emma*.

Nevertheless, such characters, glanced at in passing, do not express George Eliot's deepest convictions about human nature. Whenever she pierces below the surface, she reveals a conflict. She seems to have known many people like Gwendolen, with natures "liable to difficulty and struggle." Sometimes as in the case of Mr Tulliver, the obstruction takes the form of a "puzzling" world; but more often the contest is a matter of spirit rather than intellect. It may be waged between spirit and spirit—Romola and Tito, Rosamond and Lydgate. There is something wonderful in the psychology of these battles—the deftness of assault, the pressure of soul upon soul. Perhaps the most subtle contest of all takes place during the interview where Gwendolen accepts Grandcourt. Here we are put into the position of intelligent spectators. After each cut delivered by Grandcourt the writer delivers a comment like a physician's statement of injuries received by his patient; and yet, with all our alertness we can hardly foretell the result. The interview has the unforeseen quality of all George Eliot's writing. It appears constantly in her plots; we cannot guess the last page from the opening chapters. In this at least she possessed what is assumed to be a masculine characteristic—she knew how to keep a secret.

Very often the battle takes place in the privacies of the individual soul. The ultimate issue then becomes the degradation or elevation of the soul. The result is a survival of its fittest—or in other words, of its strongest—elements. The evil in Tito's nature was stronger than the good. At one time he may have appeared more good than bad; but any deficiency in the quantity of his evil was made up by his quality. His few really bad actions had far deeper conse-

quences than his every-day good-nature. It was all an
instance of cause and effect. Each lapse from integrity
cleared a path to the next dishonour; and each lapse became
steadily worse than the one before. In Tito's story it was
scarcely a matter of conflict between good and evil. His
goodness found itself so inconvenient that it gradually
disappeared in favour of his evil. With other characters the
degradation is not always so steady or so final. Some men
start life as egoists, and then repent, but not in dust and
ashes; and they remain modified egoists to the end. Though
Arthur Donnithorne was genuinely sorry for the misery he
had caused, he never lost sight of himself as a penitent figure.
—"You can't think what an old fellow I feel," he wrote to
Mr Irvine; "I make no schemes now. I am the best when
I've a good day's march or fighting before me."—Possibly
it was all quite true; but it would have been better if he had
never mentioned himself.—Again, Rosamond's better nature
asserted itself for a few hours of her life. She cleared Will
Ladislaw of blame, and she would never say a word against
Dorothea. But her goodness could not extend to more protracted struggling; the evil came back into power, and killed
her husband's career: "He once called her his basil plant;
and when she asked for an explanation, said that basil was
a plant which had flowered wonderfully on a murdered man's
brains."

It is good to remember that the conflict does not always
end in the defeat of goodness. Mean men like Harold Transome sometimes show themselves capable—it may be only
once—of behaving honourably, and without certainty of
reward.—Esther's flippant charm was superseded by the rare
courage of her avowal at Felix's trial: "Half a year before
Esther's dread of the ridiculous spread over the surface of
her life; but the depth below was sleeping."—The same
process of "conversion" worked through Gwendolen. It
may be that neither Esther nor Gwendolen is particularly vivid
to us; still they have the value of representing George Eliot's
philosophy. We know that for Gwendolen's redemption,
some external influence was needed; and it came to her in
the personality of Deronda. She had a "capability of recti-

tude," and acknowledged her error. She was not so "narrow-brained" as to be without a sense of justice—"She had a root of conscience in her." It must be confessed, however, that it is impossible to muster up an excessive love for any of the people in *Daniel Deronda*; they are often the vehicles of a philosophy, and nothing else.—Before leaving this subject we should go back to one of the earlier books to find somebody a little more human. Well, there is Mrs Tulliver. Her small, drab mind was enlightened by no philosophies. She seemed incapable of understanding anything apart from her china. She preserved the inanimate furniture of her house, but the family who lived there had no home—no shelter, unless for their bodies. Nevertheless, when all had turned against Maggie, Mrs Tulliver stood by her, risking even the displeasure of her idol Tom: "But the poor frightened mother's love leaped out now, stronger than all dread. 'My child! I'll go with you. You've got a mother.'" Not only did she do this; she did something far more difficult than the sudden impulse of courage. In the old days, when both her children were independent, Mrs Tulliver had burdened them with incessant, querulous complaints; but now that Maggie was broken, she learnt to repress the grumbling habits of a life-time. Only once did she let slip a lamentation in Maggie's presence; and for this lapse she had the abundant excuse that she had just come from visiting Mrs Glegg.

It is customary to dismiss George Eliot's poetry with the scantiest respect. It does not seem reasonable to expect anything noteworthy in this line from a woman who started writing it as an experiment after she was forty. A learned lady attempting such a feat is sure to startle the world and his wife; and, as often happens, their opinion is not altogether wrong. Neither is it altogether right. George Eliot plodded too much to be a great poet. Still it is hardly just to call her a minor poet.

One thing that "marks down" her poetry is its want of continuous excellence. She gets a spark; and then it is smothered with grey ashes. The Prior warns Silva that he will carry about with him a double self—

A self that will be hungry while you feast,
Will blush with shame when you are glorified;
Will feel the ache and chill of desolation
Even in the very bosom of your love.

It is a *facilis descensus*, hastened possibly by the awkward
redundance in the third line, but toppling in any case before
it received this impetus. There is very often some technical
error to account for the flagging lines; for instance, in the
appeal for friends to support Fedalma—

Hearts such as wait on beggared royalty,
Or silent watch by sinners who despair.

The flaw in the second line is its ugly and excessive alliteration. Sometimes the flash comes abruptly, and dies away
from pure exhaustion.—Silva cries:

O God, we know not yet
If bliss itself is not young misery
With fangs swift growing.

For this reason George Eliot's poetry does not stand continuous quotation. Very often the fault lies in arrangement
of the pauses, giving the rhythm not a rest, but a gasp. We
frequently feel that she was glad to reach the haven of a full-
stop.

Yet, if we choose, we can find jewels, placed in a shabby
setting. George Eliot claimed kinship of spirit with the
Elizabethan poets, and sometimes a phrase sparkles as if it
had come from an old play-book. We would not be surprised
to find in *The Duchess of Malfi* the line where Fedalma compares herself to a caged bird:

Like me, who have no wings, but only wishes.

At least one of the following lines bears the same distinction:

Oh, I have fire within;
But on my soul there falls the chilling snow
Of thoughts that come as subtly as soft flakes
Yet press at last with hard and icy weight.

It is not like Webster at his highest. The alliteration is over-
done; and there is a want of suppleness in the rhythm,
especially in the last line. Still, the resemblance is there.

Again we catch the Elizabethan echo in Fedalma's words to
Juan:

> Oh, you will never hide your soul from me;
> I've seen the jewels flash, and know 'tis there,
> Muffle it as you will.

Or we hear Juan speaking:

> No matter whether I am here or there,
> I still catch sunbeams.

When Zarca felt impulses of pity he said—

> I needs must bear this womanhood in my heart,
> Bearing my daughter there.

If any of these quotations were slipped among the lines of
an Elizabethan dramatist, they would seem at home in their
surroundings.

There was another side of George Eliot's poetry in which
she seemed to catch a reflection from Browning. She tried
to reason and "psychologise" in metre, but lacked the verve
which transforms metre into poetry. For instance she said:

> Earth and heaven seem one,
> Life a glad trembling on the outer edge
> Of unknown rapture;—

but put beside it the well-known lines from *Abt Vogler*:

> And the emulous heaven yearned down, made effort to reach the
>   earth;
> As the earth had done her best, in my passion to scale the sky;
> Novel splendours burst forth, grew familiar and dwelt with mine,
> Not a point nor peak but found and fixed its wandering star,
> Meteor-moons, balls of blaze; and they did not pale nor pine,
> For earth had attained to heaven, there was no more near nor far.

The one poet spoke smoothly of an untasted rapture; the
other struggled to find words for an experience that "broke
through language and escaped."—Again we hear Browning
speaking through Fedalma's fragment of conjecture:

> If the earth
> Broke off with flower-fringed edge, visibly sheer,
> Leaving no footing for my forward step
> But empty blackness....

Browning sometimes assumed a casual pose to cloak dramatic

emotions; for instance, in the concluding words of *Count Gismond*, or the last line of *Porphyria's Lover*:

And yet God has not said a word!

George Eliot tried to capture the same manner in *Armgart*, where the singer speaks of her dead joy in song, and the rival taking her place:

O, it is hard
To take the little corpse and lay it low,
And say, "None misses it but me!"
She sings,——
I mean, Paulina sings Fidelio,
And they will welcome her to-night.

She tried to assume the indifference which beats down and conceals a turbulent passion; but the turbulence was lacking.

There is also a reminiscence of Tennyson's *Morte D'Arthur* in the last paragraph of *The Spanish Gypsy*, where Silva watches Fedalma's vanishing ship and sees

The waters widen slowly.

It is true that one could find a few beautiful lines which call up no reminiscences; for example, the description of Silva entering the rich chamber, and finding it poor without Fedalma:

It was the lute, the gems, the pictured heads
He longed to crush, because they made no sign
But of insistence that she was not there,
She, who had filled his sight, and hidden them.

Nevertheless it is the general rule that when we find anything of value, it invariably reminds us of some other poet's treasures—a sure evidence that George Eliot cannot claim the rank of an original poet.

Most of these illustrations have been drawn from *The Spanish Gypsy*, but the same conclusions apply to *The Legend of Jubal*.—This, which was to have been a defence of George Eliot's poetry, seems to have reversed the policy of Balaam. It was intended to bless, but the blessing has turned to a curse. It looked as if it would be easy to praise; in reality, it is difficult not to blame. However, it sounds ungracious to close on a note of blame. When all is said, George Eliot's poetry was mainly tentative; and one does not judge experiments with rigour.

This is probably the best place to draw a few conclusions and set up a few contrasts between George Eliot and practically the only other Victorian woman-novelist who competed with her in fame or in influence. As technical artists the distinction between them is so marked as to render comment almost superfluous. George Eliot began writing novels when Charlotte Bronte had left off; and looking at the matter superficially, it would appear that she had the benefit of the late start. The ground had been broken before her, the pioneering experiments had been tested. As a matter of fact she had to set to work as if no one had been there before her. Technique has its devices which are commonly transmitted from one artist to another; but Charlotte's technique—such as it was—could hardly be transmitted; it was fragile, and without a trace of self-consciousness. Moreover, the spirit can be communicated from author to author; but in spirit Charlotte Bronte and George Eliot were almost anti-pathetic. Their achievements were distinct and independent. Each writer approached life from different aspects, and left records which stir different tones of appreciation. Only a few of these contrasts can be noted.

In the first place, Charlotte Bronte sought concrete stories, definite adventures, and of these she made a record; George Eliot considered a story with the additional weight of its after-impressions. She studied, not so much the story, as its psychological implications; she endeavoured to give both record and interpretation. Each method fostered a distinctive treatment of character. Charlotte Bronte took men and women simply. She quickly made up her mind as to their leading characteristics. For instance, she had an instinctive contempt for the frivolous type of woman—Miss Rosamond Oliver, or Miss Ginevra Fanshawe; and having once decided that these women were trivial. she felt there was nothing more to be done—unless to tolerate them. When George Eliot had to deal with a shallow girl like Hetty Sorrel, she laboured to do her justice. Instead of putting her aside as a trifle, she made her very smallness the occasion of overwhelming tragedy.—The same tendency is apparent in the handling of certain masculine types. If Charlotte Bronte wished to depict the flaws in a man's character, she made him hard to the verge of brutality; George Eliot made him an egoist. The brutal type is simple; he figures constantly in any child's romantic tale, with a character fixed from the very beginning. But there is nothing childlike in the egotistic type. His character evolves—like Tito's—from charm to repulsion. It requires a certain intricacy of temperament to comprehend such natures.

Secondly, where Charlotte Bronte was apt to confide, George Eliot was prone to question. Jane Eyre trusted her traditions, recognising them in a moment of crisis as her only defence; but, as we have seen, George Eliot disapproved of her attitude. It was her way to scrutinise authority before yielding respect; she was staunch, however, to any principle which satisfied her reason. Charlotte Bronte put aside the rational aspects of a matter, and trusted to the health of her own impulses. She never felt, like George Eliot, the clogging harshness of conventions. Maggie Tulliver's life was broken because it was out of tune with a stupid and worldly convention; Jane Eyre also was "a discord" at Gateshead, but her unconventionality had nothing to do with the matter. It was her diffidence and reserve, that—to the ears of Mrs Reed —jangled out of tune the sweet bells of her nature.—In the same way Charlotte Bronte trusted Nature, while George Eliot stopped short with an awed admiration. We have seen Romola drifting seawards under "the hard light" of callous stars; when Jane Eyre lay friendless on the moor, she looked up to "a kindly star" twinkling in the "pure" sky. Romola hid her face, because she could not bear to look at that cold beauty; as Jane watched the soft glory of the Milky Way, she felt the "might and strength of God."—"Night was come, and her planets were risen; a safe, still night, too serene for the companionship of fear."

In one sense George Eliot was more trustful than Charlotte Bronte; her temperament was more religious. If George Eliot had believed what Charlotte Bronte believed, it would have filled her life, as it never filled Charlotte's. It is not that Charlotte was irreligious; she was genuinely devout. But her natural intensity never carried her into the glowing heart of religious experience; she halted on the outer surface. If she, with her swift instincts, had let herself go, she would have travelled much further than George Eliot, with her patient, laborious gait, and scanty, impoverished creed. Charlotte would not, or could not, realise the tremendous sweep of spiritual forces; she would not have comprehended subtle cases of conscience. George Eliot would have recognised a deep spiritual emergency; she might not have been adequate to the occasion, but she would have tried her best. It is likely that Charlotte would have passed by on the other side. She was not altogether fair to St John; George Eliot would at least have tried to do him justice.

It all comes back to the single conclusion—these women were of entirely different types. On the one side we have George Eliot, with poor vitality and varied experience, seeking escape from self by the pathway of knowledge, and attaining to a remarkable efficiency without the magical touch. On the other side we have Charlotte Bronte, with rich vitality and poor experience, seeking self-realisation through knowledge, and attaining to a faltering beauty flushed with glamour. It is like placing an eager little girl beside a sad and experienced woman. Both writers were poor—one in finish, the other in charm; both were rich—one in instinct, the other in instruction.

* * * * * *

George Eliot held that no author had a claim to be heard unless he had something unique to give.

I will never write anything (she said) to which my whole heart, mind and conscience don't consent, so that I may feel it was something—however small—which wanted to be done in this world, and that I am just the organ for that small bit of work.

By her novels she justified her calling; they expressed something which she alone could offer;—this was her attitude of mind. Scott and Charlotte Bronte had felt the romance and poetry of the human story; Dickens its fresh and irrepressible oddity; Jane Austen its piquancy; and Thackeray its piquancy with something of its sadness. George Eliot felt its complexity. Modern life has become an enigma, but she did not write much of contemporary problems. Rather, she felt that uneasy current which flows beneath articulate questions. It was Dickens who dealt with specific problems—in *Oliver Twist*, for instance, or *Nicholas Nickleby*. The modern problem-novel has inherited something from both writers. To take an illustration, *Joan and Peter* is descended from *Nicholas Nickleby* and *The Mill on the Floss*.—Dickens told an educational story, but drew no obvious conclusions: George Eliot studied Tom Tulliver's education, and hinted plainly at her own conclusions; Mr Wells has told an educational story, and expounded his conclusions.—It must be remembered that George Eliot did not hint at her conclusions when the problem was one of permanent human interest. She suggested her views on the current education of her time; but she openly expressed her opinions on human life and destiny. The modern problem-novel is a dovetailing of parable and comment; from George Eliot it has acquired the interpreting habit.

As we have seen, George Eliot did not openly express her opinions except on questions of perennial human value; these questions are usually matters of psychology. Before her time there had been many great delineators of human characters; and in a certain sense they were all psychologists. But their method was spontaneous rather than scientific. Prof. Elton has accounted it an honour to Shakespeare that he was not "an amiable psychologist." The scientist must be dispassionate; he must examine, classify, and judge, without emotion—and, even as Prof. Elton suggests, without morality. He adopts not an immoral, but a non-moral standpoint. Though he sees the "soul of goodness in things evil," goodness and evil, as such, are irrelevant to his purpose. His sense of justice is restricted by the want of emotional insight; he tabulates deeds and motives. A certain type of modern realist handles unpleasant facts without any moral repugnance, simply because they are facts. He represents one of the tendencies of scientific psychology applied to literature. The scientific bias was only a part of George Eliot's outlook.

She walked by faith as well as by sight; sometimes she trusted her instincts. In her judgments of character we often feel a conscientious straining after accuracy. She is very particular to exhibit "the bad in the best of us, and the good in the worst of us." Undoubtedly this is a scientific tendency. There was no such effort in Shakespeare. When he made his dying villain say, "Yet Edmund was beloved," it seems to have come from his heart with a flash of sympathy; he sprang naturally to the highest, truest justice. In a lesser degree George Eliot had those gleams of intuition. In a passage already quoted from *Daniel Deronda*, she spoke of the affections being clad with knowledge. Though her knowledge may hang like a heavy garment, her affections carry the burden with a vivid, stately presence.

MRS BROWNING[1]
1806–1861

I

THE NEGATIVE APPROACH

IT is difficult to write of Mrs Browning with justice or temperance. She has been so foolishly and so extravagantly praised that it is easy from sheer contra-suggestion to descend to folly and extravagance of blame. At the very outset it must be confessed that Mrs Browning's poetry was feeble. This was inevitable in the case of a woman feeble in spirit as well as body. It is a paltry thing to stand staring at weakness; and there is no justification for writing at length of faults now generally recognised, unless it be with the sincere intention to discover in the process some elements of worth. In spite of her defects Elizabeth Browning enjoyed an extraordinary popularity. All the world knows now what Robert Browning thought of her—and all the world acknowledges that he was "no fool." Although to us her failures are obtrusive, somewhere in this woman there must have been something which commanded respect; and it is our task to look for it. Whether we shall find it is another matter; but at least we can try; and we shall search honestly without any pretence at finding anything, good or bad, which is actually non-existent.

The only possible method is to proceed "from the known to the unknown"—from the recognised weakness to the undiscovered power. It may be that Mrs Browning was not one of those who "out of weakness are made strong"; still she was at times made convalescent, and even for this we should be thankful.

We can take the facts of her life for granted—the years of study, retirement, and bodily weakness, broken on the one

[1] The study of Mrs Browning is placed here, as she is nearest in subject-matter, though not in chronology, to Christina Rossetti.

hand by the death of her favourite brother, and on the other by the entrance of Robert Browning; then the secret marriage and flight, followed by fifteen years of almost perfect happiness. All these matters have become hackneyed. What will never become hackneyed is any trace of artistic vitality.

We begin then, in somewhat ungracious fashion, with Mrs Browning's faults; of which almost the most striking is her acute self-consciousness. If this feeling is analysed, it will be found to contain three distinct elements. She was conscious of her sufferings, of her sex, and of her vocation as artist.

"I am morbid, I know," she wrote. "Like the lady who lay in the grave, and was ever after of the colour of a shroud, so I am white-souled, and the past has left its mark with me for ever." References of the same nature are to be found everywhere in her poetry, and leave on it the desolating taint of all self-depreciation, so closely related to self-pity. Even the *Sonnets from the Portuguese* have this flaw, this limpness of introspection:

> For frequent tears have run
> The colours from my life, and left so dead
> And pale a stuff, it were not fitly done
> To give the same as pillow to thy head.
> Go further! Let it serve to trample on.

In the second place she could not forget her sex—and for the simple reason that she was, or tried to be, an artist. Occasionally she may speak in general terms of the negative position of women, who are only praised—

> As long as they keep quiet by the fire,
> And never say "no" when the world says "ay."

Nevertheless when she speaks of "the woman's movement," it is nearly always the literary woman of whom she is thinking. The high-spirited Brontes sprang to the adventure of literature. Whereas they felt the zest of pioneering, Mrs Browning was cast down by its loneliness and difficulty. Not born to lead, she searched in vain for predecessors.—"I look everywhere," she wrote, "for grandmothers, and see none. It is not in the filial spirit I am deficient, I do assure you—witness

my reverent love of the grandfathers!" At all points she
seemed baffled by ignorance of the way. On the one side
we hear her speaking through Aurora—

> No perfect artist is developed here
> From any imperfect woman.

On the other side, we find her constantly struggling against
the current opinion that the artistic vocation robs a woman
of her completeness, till she becomes

> A printing woman who has lost her place
> (The sweet safe corner of the household fire
> Behind the heads of children).

Whereas a woman more sure of her own position would have
been content to live down popular prejudices, Mrs Browning
weakened her energy by voluble protests. We feel this in
Aurora's retort to Romney:

> I perceive!
> The headache is too noble for my sex.
> You think the heartache would sound decenter,
> Since that's the woman's special, proper ache,
> And altogether tolerable, except
> To a woman.

She could not admire even Florence Nightingale without an
aftertaste of personal bitterness. The noble work done by
women in the Crimea she declared to be no solution of the
woman's question—in other words, of the literary woman's
question.—"Every man," she cried, "is on his knees before
ladies carrying lint, calling them 'angelic she's,' whereas,
if they stir an inch as thinkers or artists from the beaten line
(involving more good to general humanity than is involved
in lint), the very same men would curse the impudence of
the very same women, and stop there."—The singularity
and detachment of the woman artist seemed to lie upon her
spirit even when she herself had escaped from solitude into
a perfect fellowship. In the comfort of her own home, kindled
by the praise of her own husband, she could yet exclaim:

> How dreary 'tis for women to sit still
> On winter nights by solitary fires,
> And hear the nations praising them far off,
> Too far!

In spite of all her protests Mrs Browning listened too attentively for the world's estimates—and particularly for its estimates of censure. She seemed unable to clear her mind of misgivings as to the possibility of artistic supremacy for women. She was deeply hurt by the popular conception, so bitterly voiced by Aurora, that women are

> Poor to think,
> Yet rich enough to sympathise with thought.

In Romney Leigh's criticism of Aurora she seems to be declaring her own experience of the world's depreciation. Women, says Romney, are too personal to become great artists :

> All's yours and you,—
> All, coloured with your blood, or otherwise
> Just nothing to you......
> ....This same world,
> Uncomprehended by you, must remain
> Uninfluenced by you.—Women as you are,
> Mere women, personal and passionate,
> You give us doating mothers, and chaste wives,
> Sublime Madonnas, and enduring saints!
> We get no Christ from you,—and verily
> We shall not get a poet in my mind.

This alternative—the choice between apprehension of the multitude and love of the individual—seems to have been definitely placed before both Charlotte Bronte and George Eliot. St John, for instance, with his devotion to a great cause, is in some ways a parallel to Romney Leigh. But Jane Eyre, battling for the privacies and liberties of the individual soul, finds no fitting counterpart in Aurora, whose many words carry less conviction than Jane's decisive actions. The whole distinction is this :—while Charlotte Bronte—and George Eliot also—made up their minds about their attitude to large impersonal matters, Mrs Browning hesitated and faltered.

Some years before the creation of Aurora she had written to Robert Browning in words of great significance.—" I am, in a manner, as a *blind poet*. Certainly there is compensation to a degree. I have had much of the inner life, and from the habit of self-consciousness and self-analysis, I make great guesses at Human nature in the main." Herein lies the clue to much of her weakness. If she had been as sincere as Christina Rossetti, she would not have made guesses; she would have accepted her narrow restricted life as the one reality of which she could speak with conviction. By an unswerving fidelity to the truths which she knew and experienced, she would have extracted from meagre resources some treasure of beauty. But this is precisely what she did not do. It is not at all astonishing that she became tired of her uninspiring self. There are not many people, who, when forced upon themselves, can, like Christina Rossetti, probe bravely to the very core of their unrest,—to find in the intense reality of the inner life both solace and revival. Many people, afraid to face their own inadequacy, run away from themselves, and seek shelter in impersonal things. This is a form of self-forgettal based, not on denial and sacrifice, but on timidity.—It is impossible to close one's eyes to the working of this tendency in Mrs Browning. "My only idea of happiness," she wrote, "...lies deep in poetry and its associations. ...You throw off *yourself*." Instead of developing the poetry latent in her own soul, she often contented herself with a species of metrical journalism. Like Tennyson, she allowed herself to be caught in the web of current events. She declaimed and argued about Italian freedom, the slave-trade, or social abuses; but nearly always there is something lacking. Too often disregarding what Matthew Arnold called "the buried river" of the inner life, she spoke on the surface of experience; and her words failed of power—

'Tis eloquent, 'tis just, but 'tis not true.

While reading *Casa Guidi Windows* or the *Poems of Progress*, we constantly hear ringing in our ears Hamlet's outcry against the Player's simulated emotions—

What's Hecuba to him, or he to Hecuba?

What, we exclaim, was Italy to Mrs Browning?—Is there not something artificial, something almost of pose, in this wordy devotion to what was, after all, a foreign cause?—It was good that she should be interested in Italy; but had she no other interest, more vital and intimate?—She very rarely attains to the

> Words that breathe, and words that burn.

Indeed the prevailing characteristic of her utterance is that it pants and flickers. As we read, we fall back upon King Lear's wistful appeal to Cordelia—

> But goes thy heart with this?

Unlike Lear, we cannot obtain an affirmative answer. Mrs Browning often seems to have written with only part of her heart; and we cannot be expected to make a whole-hearted response.

So far we have been dealing with her artistic consciousness in its relation to sex. But Mrs Browning had other theories of art which, though personal, were not necessarily feminine. In common with her husband, she felt keenly the detachment of the literary creator, and expressed this sentiment most strongly in Aurora's bitter outcry to Lord Howe:

> Love, you say?
> My lord, I cannot love. I only find
> The rhymes for love,—and that's not love, my lord.

In another place she hints at the possibilities of inarticulate art—the tragedy of the "mute, inglorious Milton";

> I called the artist but a greatened man,
> He may be childless also, like a man.

Notwithstanding, it is her general custom, when writing of the personal life of the artist, to deal with its compensations—its privacies and high communions.—"Most of my events," she wrote, "and nearly all of my intense pleasures, have passed in my *thoughts*....The Greeks were my demi-gods, and haunted me out of Pope's Homer, until I dreamt more of Agammemnon than of Moses the black pony."—A few years later we find her writing—"Men and women of letters are the first in the whole world to me, and I would rather be the least among them than dwell in the courts of princes."—It is not always easy or desirable to feel sympathy for this attitude

of detachment.—"I am one," she said, "who could have
forgotten the plague, listening to Boccaccio's stories."—It is
doubtful whether any genuine artist could have found power
in neglecting the dreadful reality for the pleasing fiction;
it is certain that Robert Browning would have looked the
plague, as all other evils, full in the face. His wife failed to
recognise that it is the great courage which produces the
great art.—Some of her other declarations as to the absorption of the artist do not tally with her own practice. Writing
to the *Athenaeum*, she remarked:

When Milton said that a poet's life should be a poem, he spoke
a high moral truth; if he had added a reversion of the saying, that
a poet's poetry should be his life,—he would have spoken a critical
truth, not low...."Art," it was said long ago, "requires the
whole man," and "Nobody," it was said later, "can be a poet who
is anything else"; but the present idea of Art requires the segment
of a man, and everybody who is anything at all is a poet in a
parenthesis.

She did not apply her theories or carry them to their logical
conclusions. She had before her the chance of being like
Christina Rossetti, a poet and nothing else—living and writing
out of her inner resources; but she tried to be something else
as well—a political and social theorist. The real difficulty was
that she could not make up her mind between two ideals—
poetry of the inner life, and poetry, like her husband's, of a
penetrating and general humanity. She could not decide
which ideal was best in accord with her own temperament,
and reaped the inevitable harvest of halting between two
opinions. She did not devote herself wholly to either ideal,
and quite against her own intentions, only the "segment"
of herself made itself felt in her writings.

These are theories of the artistic life. Mrs Browning also
had her opinions on the artistic function. She most indig-
nantly cast back the challenge made by such "practical" men
as Romney, that Art is not of much use in a workaday world:

> When Egypt's slain, I say, let Miriam sing!
> Before..............Where's Moses?

In the teeth of such taunts Mrs Browning maintained that

Art could be of the highest efficiency, and this by virtue of
its spiritual testimony. It affords an explanation of material
symbols—

> Earth's crammed with heaven,
> And every common bush afire with God;
> But only he who sees, takes off his shoes;
> The rest sit round it, and pluck blackberries.

The artist teaches men to see the mystic fires of God—

> Art's the witness of what Is
Behind this show.

This witness must be most thorough and painstaking. It must
describe the show as well as interpret its meaning.—It
appeared to Mrs Browning that the "show" must be a matter
of common experience; and for this reason she usually chose
themes of current, modern life. For these themes she claimed
an utter freedom of speech.—

If a woman ignores these wrongs, then may women as a sex continue to suffer them; there is no help for any of us—let us be
decent and die. I have spoken therefore, and in speaking have
used plain words—words which look like blots—...words which,
if blurred or softened, would imperil perhaps the force and
righteousness of the moral influence.

Thackeray, as is well known, reluctantly refused one of her
poems for the *Cornhill*, on the grounds that it was too outspoken.—"There are things," he wrote, "which *my* squeamish
public will not bear on Mondays, though on Sundays they
will listen to them without scruple."—From Mrs Browning's
answer we quote one significant line: "I am deeply convinced that the corruption of our society requires, not shut
doors and windows, but light and air." The modern reader
objects to Mrs Browning's frankness, but not from the
Victorian standpoint. He objects, not to the attack, but to
the method of attack. It may be a writer's duty to deal with
unpleasant subjects; but it is also his duty to curb and select
his phrases. He should aim, not at "words which look like
blots," but at speech which burns like flames. No doubt
he should be merciless; but the fiercest utterance has an
element of terseness; and Mrs Browning never learnt that
secret.

This brings us to the second of Mrs Browning's radical faults—her lack of self-control, so clearly evidenced by the disorderly behaviour of her words. It is difficult not to believe that she had a furtive affection for excitement, mistaking it for a sign of vitality.—

Headlong I was at first (she wrote to Robert Browning) and headlong I continue—precipitously rushing forward through all manner of nettles and briars instead of keeping the path; guessing at the meaning of unknown words instead of looking into the dictionary—tearing open letters, and never untying string—and expecting everything to be done in a minute, and the thunder to be as quick as the lightning....I do not say *everything I think* (as has been said of me by master-critics), but *I take every means to say what I think*, which is different!—or I fancy so!

About a month later we find her referring to people who "have to write a poem twelve times over, as Mr Kenyon says I should do, if I were virtuous." "I consider myself," she adds, "a very patient, laborious writer, though dear Mr Kenyon laughs me to scorn when I say so."—The consciousness of slipshod work left her without any sense of mortification. Speaking of the defective rhythms in *The Cry of the Children*, she wrote—"the first stanza came into my head in a hurricane, and I was obliged to make the others look like it—*that* is the whole mystery of the iniquity." Later we find her writing to Ruskin with the same complacency: "I do think, if I may say it of myself, that the desire of speaking or *spluttering* the real truth out broadly, may be a cause of a good deal of what is called in me careless and awkward expression." She apologised as if she had been guilty of paying herself a compliment; she was content to "splutter." After that nothing can be said in way of extenuation.

This lack of control left its mark upon every page of her writings, so faint in outline, and weak in emphasis. She wrote a "vision" of *forty-two* poets; and a strange medley they are, heaped together with hardly any distinctions of precedence. It is as if she had mapped out a country of mountains and "little hills"; and running short of the strong darker browns to differentiate her contours, had washed it all in with an indeterminate drab.—There were times like these when she said too much; there were other times when she would have been wiser to say nothing at all. With an almost incredible deficiency of tact she made her Seraphim talk through the agony and mystery of Christ's Passion. She did not seem to realise that there are times when it is impossible to speak, and things which it is not lawful to utter. Those inarticulate impulses of ours—how sacred they are while we leave them alone in the darkness of our hearts! How cheap and tawdry do they appear, when we drag them out into the public glare, decked with ill-fitting words!—Yet, with a rather naïve inconsistency, she frequently referred to the appeal of silence. Lucifer fell from heaven "trampled down" by the stillness of the watching archangels. Adam and Eve fled—

> Wordless all day along the wilderness.

She herself seemed incapable of silence, or the smiting words which cleave their way out of reticence. In fifty-one lines she declaimed against the material aims of the Crystal Palace Exhibition (*Casa Guidi Windows*, No. 20); yet Kipling was able to point a similar moral in a single line—

> All valiant dust that builds on dust.

This lack of restraint could not fail to slacken her fibre. Her anger was turned to rant, and her pathos to feeble sentiment. Of *Lady Geraldine's Courtship* she wrote—"In that poem I had endeavoured to throw conventionalities (turned asbestos for the nonce) into the fire of poetry, to make them glow and glitter as if they were not dull things." She failed, because the fires of poetry are best kindled within strong souls. In the same way her pathos often came short, simply because she had not the heart to discard unworthy ideas. The conception of motherhood in *Isobel's Child* is most forced and unnatural. Possibly it appealed to the writer as touching; but nothing is permanently touching unless it is true; and the sincere reader has scant patience with Isobel and her emotions.—On the first reading, similarly, *A Child's Thought of God* seems quaint and pretty. But when we proceed to ask whether a healthy child thinks in this way, the appeal is instantly weakened. Not many people would be fond of a precocious child like this. They would be much happier with

the daring child of Francis Thompson's *Little Jesus*—more
daring because more intimate, and more lovable because
more lifelike.—In fact Mrs Browning was too easily pleased
with her ideas. She accepted pretty things until they left
no room for what was really beautiful. Her poetry is so
full of references to angels, that familiarity breeds contempt;
and we begin to understand the wisdom of the privilege
which allows men to entertain angels *un*awares. It comes to
this—that Mrs Browning's seraphs make no more appeal to
us than the pretty angels on a Christmas card. This is not
the case with Christina Rossetti. And why?—If Christina
mentioned angels, she spoke out of a full heart, because they
were an essential part of her dreams; they did not serve for
embroidery, but were woven into the texture of her visions.
It is this firm hold of truth which makes Christina the higher
poet; it gave to her what Mrs Meynell finds lacking in
Mrs Browning—" the *impassioned peace* of the greatest poetry."

It is this want of discrimination—or perhaps a deliberate
refusal to exercise discrimination—that runs like a flaw
through Mrs Browning's poetry. She did not choose between
the texture and the embroidery of her imagination. She
wished to keep both, and usually achieved the result of
covering her texture with disfiguring embroideries. Occasionally we get glimpses of the real stuff—the true material
of poetry. Throughout *Casa Guidi Windows* we see flashes
of quickly fading beauty. Or we light on a phrase worthy of
Christina Rossetti—and this in *Isobel's Child*, where the
mother looks down at her sleeping infant:

> O warm quick body, must thou lie,
> When the time comes round to die,
> *Still from all the whirl of years,*
> *Bare of all the joy and pain?*

In the poem to the memory of Mrs Hemans there is a single
line which seems to anticipate the richer music of Swinburne:

> Lay only dust's stern verity upon her dust undreaming.

In *Confessions* we catch a few phrases glimmering through
the mists:

> Thou couldst carry thy light like a jewel, not giving it like a star.

Often we find expressions arresting or original, but without the full cry or throb of the highest poetry:

> 'Twas hard to sing by Babel's stream,
> More hard in Babel's street!

Such phrases are interesting or clever, but they do not lay a spell upon us; they have no magic. And how could they? It is very wonderful that Mrs Browning, cumbered with many words, ever touched the fringe of the eluding Enchanter's garment.

II

THE POSITIVE APPROACH

So far we have been dealing chiefly with negatives. It should be possible to find something more positive and satisfying before we leave this study. There are at least two lines of investigation open to us. One is *The Drama of Exile*, with its specifically feminine contribution to a great theme; the other is the artistic significance of the fact that Miss Elizabeth Barrett became the wife of Robert Browning.

In *The Drama of Exile*, as everywhere else in her poetry, we have abundance of external, superadded matter. Sometimes, in fact, these additions are remarkably effective—as where the lion feels

> The new reality of death.

Superadded also is the atmosphere of "pathetic fallacy," all nature being subtly moved by the human catastrophe. There is a broken yet strangely appealing music about many of the Spirit choruses:

> We shall triumph—triumph greatly,
> When ye lie beneath the sward!
> There, our lily shall grow stately,
> Though ye answer not a word—
> And her fragrance shall be scornful of your silence.

However, Mrs Browning's essential contribution to the theme does not lie in such matters, but in her peculiarly feminine attitude to some figures of the drama. This appears very strongly in her conception of Lucifer. He has entirely lost the magnificence of Milton's Satan. He is obstinate rather than defiant. There is a real distinction here; for defiance is sometimes reasonable, but obstinacy never. Whereas Milton's Satan had some grounds for rebellion, Lucifer has no grievance, and in his heart he knows it. This weakens both his self-respect, and the impression he makes. From the very beginning we feel that he is not invulnerable.

—Unlike Satan he has not entirely subdued the old loyalties; he seems to be trampling them down when he cries,

> *I* too have strength—
> Strength to behold Him, and not worship Him.

He is sadder than Milton's Satan or Marlowe's Mephistopheles—sadder because less single-minded. He prophesies that in future ages, men regarding human life with its strange minglings of hope and fear, of evil and goodness, will feel his touch upon the world; they will discern

> The heart of a lost angel in the earth.

Wistful and lonely, he cannot, like Satan, find solace in his own personality:

> None saith, Stay with me, for thy face is fair!
> None saith, Stay with me, for thy voice is sweet!
> And yet I was not fashioned out of clay.

He is driven to seek satisfaction in his superior intensity of feeling:

> Go—I curse you all—
> Hate one another—feebly—as you can.

Satan neither made nor implied such comparisons, for he was above them. He found his satisfaction in the power of his determination, which is in itself a more exhilarating and abiding solace than any reliance upon evanescent emotions. —Finally, Lucifer is overcome, not by violence, but by the very subtlety of the destiny which brings him on common ground with Christ. For Christ, in choosing like Lucifer the path of exile from Heaven, claims the same crown of sorrow. The distinction lies solely in the redemptive motive of Christ. No longer unique, Lucifer utters his last word—

> All things grow sadder to me, one by one.

Possibly this is a somewhat effeminate portrait; but it is undeniably original. It is natural also that Mrs Browning, as a woman, should have something new in her conception of the first woman. Her Eve is less submissive than Milton's, but a more genuine helpmeet. She is prepared to renounce the companionship of Adam—to see him forgiven, and go

out from Paradise alone; and Adam responds to her loyalty
with prayers of thanksgiving:

> Thanking Thee,
> That rather Thou hast me out with her,
> Than left me lorn of her in Paradise;—......
> ....Because with *her*, I stand,
> Upright, as far as can be, in this fall,
> And look away from Heaven, which doth accuse me,
> And look away from Earth, which doth convict me,
> Into her face; and crown my discrowned brow
> Out of her love; and put the thought of her
> Around me, for an Eden full of birds.

It would be vain to seek in Milton for such equality or perfection of fellowship.—Moreover Eve, with her maternal
impulses, thrills to the "voices of foreshown Humanity."

> I hear a sound of life—of life like ours—
> Of laughter and of wailing,—of grave speech,
> Of little plaintive voices innocent,—
> Of life in separate courses flowing out
> Like our four rivers to some outward main.
> I hear life—life!

In *Paradise Lost* the interest of the future centres round
Adam. Here it centres round the woman, as mother of the
race, and as the agent of compassionate service. It is thus
that Adam comforts Eve:

> A child's kiss
> Set on thy sighing lips, shall make thee glad;
> A poor man served by thee, shall make thee rich;
> A sick man helped by thee, shall make thee strong;
> Thou shalt be served thyself by every sense
> Of service which thou renderest. Such a crown
> I set upon thy head.

Other points of comparison with Milton suggest themselves
—such as the extraordinary difference of outlook and result
between *The Dead Pan* and the description in Milton's
Nativity Ode of the silenced oracles. But here the comparison
lies principally between artist and artist, and not, as in the
portrayal of Adam and Eve, between man and woman. It is
hardly fair to consider Mrs Browning's art, even at its finest,

side by side with the noble and perfect achievements of a
higher artist.

From Mrs Browning's study of Milton we may take a
few words capable of a more personal and intimate applica-
tion. In one of her essays she wrote: "Yet the poet Milton
was not made by what he received; not even by what he
loved." Immediately the question arises—How far was
Elizabeth Barrett made by what she loved? Side by side
with it rises a parallel query—How far was Robert Browning
made by what *he* loved?

We shall take the second question first. It may be that
Elizabeth Barrett will be permanently remembered, not for
her own writings, but for the new vistas which she opened
in the mind of a superior poet. Robert Browning did not
reach his heights before he met Miss Barrett, and made her
his wife; nearly all his great poetry was written during her
lifetime, or shortly after her death. These things are universally admitted, and can hardly be explained as a mere
coincidence. It is true, of course, that most poets write at
their best during youth and early middle age; but this is not
sufficient to account for the intellectuality, the dryness, which
seemed to harden over Robert Browning's later poems. He
was a man in whom buoyancy died hard, and not by the
mere accumulation of years.

Miss Barrett, it will be remembered, was attracted to the
author of *Paracelsus* as "king of the mystics"—a phrase
capable of a two-edged interpretation. She was drawn to
him, either by the kindred frailty of obscure speech, or by
the kindred excellence of spiritual insight. It is probably
more just as well as more charitable to take the second alternative. To her Robert Browning always remained a king;
but to him she became an ideal. "She has genius," he said,
"I am only a painstaking fellow. Can't you imagine a clever
sort of angel who plots and plans and tries to build up something; he wants to make you see it as he sees it, shows you
one point of view, carries you off to another, hammering
into your head the things he wants you to understand; and
while all this bother is going on, God Almighty turns you

off a little star. That's the difference between us. The true creative power is hers, not mine." There are few things more warming to the heart than Robert Browning's generosities, his free frank affections. He had a "big" way of looking at things—himself included. It is good to feel how blind he was to his own superiority; and it is greatly to his wife's credit that she never took herself at his estimate. She wished to serve rather than to be served.—

> How, Dearest, wilt thou have me for most use?
> A hope, to sing by gladly?...or a fine
> Sad memory, with thy songs to interfuse?...
> A shade, in which to sing...of palm or pine?
> A grave, on which to rest from singing?...Choose.

It would be possible to go through Robert Browning's poetry, and find something to tally with each of these different aspects. Hope lies at the heart of all his great utterances. He also recognised the dominance of memories:

> How sad and bad and mad it was—
> But then it was how sweet!

In spite of all his sturdiness, he had his music for soothing in quiet shadowy places—the folk-tunes which David sang to Saul, or occasional descriptions, cool, peaceful, and with an implied fragrance:

> And all day long a bird sings there,
>   And a stray sheep drinks at the pond at times;
> The place is silent and aware;
>   It has had its scenes, its joys and crimes,
> But that is its own affair.

Mrs Browning would have had him to "rest from singing" on her grave, but rest was not natural to Robert Browning. We owe to his wife's grave the glorious wrestling of *Prospice*.

It would also be possible to go through his poetry, and find there certain themes parallel to those chosen by his wife. As has often been noticed, *Prince Hohenstiel-Schwangau* is a sort of counterpart to her political poems. What is much more noteworthy is a correspondence of mood, or of opinions coloured by emotions.—The conviction of immortality was one of their common joys.

What would this life be, dear Mr Ruskin (wrote Mrs Browning), if it had not eternal relations? For my part, if I did not believe so, I should lay my head down and die. Nothing would be worth doing, certainly. But I am what many people call a "mystic," and what I myself call a "realist"; because I consider that every step of the foot or stroke of the pen has some real connection with and result in the life hereafter.

In *Casa Guidi Windows* she wrote:

> For if I write, paint, carve a word, indeed,
> On book or board or dust, on floor or wall,
>   The same is kept of God who taketh heed
> That not one letter of the meaning fall
>   Or ere it touch and teach His world's great heart.

Immortality, it is true, is not definitely mentioned in these lines; but in the thinking of both poets it was very strongly implied that no good thing is permanently lost, for if it fails of use here, it will find its function hereafter. This lies at the core of Robert Browning's exhilaration; he believed what Abt Vogler believed:

> Eternity confirms the conception of an hour.

He and his wife thought alike; the distinction is that he felt his thoughts and expressed them with a grander passion.

There is one mood so frequent in Mrs Browning that it could not fail to impress her husband. This is the wife's apprehension lest death should snap the loyalties of life. It makes itself felt in the midst of the false, weak sentiment running through *The Lay of the Brown Rosary*:

> How could I bear to lie content and still beneath a stone,
> And feel mine own Betrothed go by—alas! no more mine own?

In *Catarina to Camoens*, which, be it observed, was Browning's favourite among her poems, the same idea found a slightly worthier expression:

> You may cast away, Beloved,
> In your future, all my past;
>   Such old phrases
>   May be praises
> For some fairer bosom-queen—
> "Sweetest eyes were ever seen!"

She rose to her utmost height in *The Sonnets from the Portu-*

guese, where she spoke with the added stimulus of an avowed personal feeling:

> But I look on thee...on thee...
> Beholding, besides love, the end of love,
> Hearing oblivion beyond memory,...
> As one who sits and gazes, from above,
> Over the rivers, to the bitter sea.

We have quoted at length, and of set purpose. This idea, expressed so frequently and so gently by Mrs Browning, found more impassioned utterance in Robert Browning's *Any Wife to Any Husband*. We need quote only one of the great stanzas to feel the difference:

> But now, because the hour through years was fixed,
> Because our inmost beings met and mixed,
> Because thou once hast loved me—wilt thou dare
> Say to thy soul and Who may list beside,
> "Therefore she is immortally my bride,
> Chance cannot change that love, nor time impair."

Fragments cut from the poem are pitifully inadequate to testify to its wonderful beauty; but let us be allowed to quote the last three lines, realising that in this abrupt accent of sorrow there is something quite beyond the range of Elizabeth Barrett Browning:

> What do I fear? Thy love shall hold me fast
> Until the little minute's sleep is past,
>   And I wake saved.—And yet, it will not be!

The only satisfactory thing is to read and read again the whole poem from beginning to end; and then we shall feel nothing but gratitude to the woman, who, though often failing herself, made possible the triumph of another. This is probably her greatest gift to Robert Browning—that she gave him certain common things to be intensified, heightened, transfigured. He was probably not thinking of himself when he wrote *James Lee's Wife*; but the transforming power which he found so wonderful in the lives of other people worked also within his own heart.—

> For all, love greatens and glorifies,
> Till God's a-glow, to the loving eyes,
> In what was mere earth before.

There is still the other side of the picture—the influence of Robert Browning upon Elizabeth Barrett. Sometimes she copied him to her own undoing, as when, in *Aurora Leigh*, she attempted conversational, argumentative writing. But the primary effect of her marriage was an emotional experience. This, as the only thing of any magnitude which entered her life, was the one matter of which she was competent to speak. It was the one experience which really counted to her. To say this is to lay myself open to protests. "What!" some will exclaim, "have you forgotten Mrs Browning's religion?" I have not forgotten it but—it is a matter of opinion only—I do not think it was so deep or so real as her love for Robert Browning. Put her religion beside Christina Rossetti's, and the difference is apparent. It is not so much a difference of aspect, as of intensity and pitch. The ultimate evidence for such matters lies within. As Carlyle so often declared, anything spoken from the heart moves other hearts. Whereas Christina Rossetti's religious language stirs us deeply, Mrs Browning's leaves us pretty much where we were; but this is not the case with her language of earthly affection. *The Sonnets from the Portuguese* do not move us so profoundly as Christina Rossetti's poetry—and simply because Mrs Browning was incapable of Christina's intensities; but they move us more deeply than anything else in Mrs Browning. They have the *communicable* effect of all sincerity. It is very remarkable that the prose of the love-letters should so often be of greater value than the poetry of her impersonal art.—"So my rock," she wrote, "...may the birds drop into your crevices the seeds of all the flowers of the world—only it is not for *those* that I cling to you as the single rock in the salt sea."—However, she was capable of a higher music:

> Men could not part us, with their worldly jars,
> Nor the seas change us, nor the tempests bend;
> Our hands would touch, for all the mountain-bars.

It might be casually noted, that here, as in other places where Mrs Browning speaks home, not only her diction, but the structure of her clauses, is extremely simple.

In these sonnets we see Mrs Browning at her best, and never at her worst. Usually, it must be admitted, there is some alloy—and this chiefly in the nature of an over-sensibility. She appears to have reversed the Tennysonian line—

A sorrow's crown of sorrow is remembering happier things.

She seems to have felt that a joy's crown of joy is remembering sadder things. One doubts if the uttermost gladness is ever like that. The great joy, intensely received, blots out all evil memories; or it recalls them voluntarily for the sake of tasting the swift sensation of contrast. Mrs Browning leaves us with the impression that the evil memories came to her unbidden; she could not forget—nor did she try to do so. Undoubtedly her joys were real; her whole heart went out into speech when she described her soul overcome with gratitude—

Because God's gifts put man's best dreams to shame.

Perhaps she was too conscious of her joys, analysed them too keenly, and did not take them sufficiently for granted. We feel sometimes that she interfered too much with her emotions. She could not leave them alone. Whatever may be the reason, the fact remains that *The Sonnets from the Portuguese* do not give the impression of firm and abiding joy. We hesitate to pass harsh judgments, but to the modern reader there is always a suggestion of hypochondria in Mrs Browning's outlook.—What, after all, were her sorrows, if we weigh them in comparison with those suffered by many other women of her own generation?—Put her beside the Brontes, put her beside Christina Rossetti—and hers will appear the lighter burden. All these women endured physical weakness; Mrs Browning was the only one who showed evidences of a broken spirit. In the perfection of her married life she had more cause for happiness than any of these women; but they —even Emily Bronte and Christina Rossetti—had a greater capacity for happiness; and this, possibly, because they had the greater capacity for courage. Mrs Browning thought she behaved bravely in the circumstances of her secret marriage and flight.—"I begin to think," she wrote, "that none are so bold as the timid when they are fairly roused." Certainly there was an element of daring in the proceedings. But think again of the Brontes. It is utterly impossible to imagine Charlotte or Emily doing anything in the dark. No matter how afraid they might have been, they could not have brought themselves to the point of "giving in" to fear; and Christina Rossetti was made of the same invincible stuff. This is not a judgment from the point of view of the twentieth century woman, sturdier in body, but (as we are told) coarser in spiritual texture. Mrs Browning is here rated in comparison with women of her own age, and her own general atmosphere; with women, who, like her, were delicate in body, but, unlike her, were strong in spirit. It will be remembered that, writing to Ruskin, she excused her "sickly" poems on the plea of sickly health. It is kind and charitable to make full allowance for such pleas; but it is only just to consider that we do not come across anything of the kind in the records of the Brontes, George Eliot, or Christina Rossetti.

*   *   *   *   *   *

In one sense Mrs Browning is representative of her age. She exhibits much of the tendency known as "Victorian"—a word used in a definite sense, and with a definite stigma attached. She is not so far away from the heroines of Victorian fiction—its Amelia Sedleys and Agnes Wickfields. It may be that these "heroines" were typical of the age—that they represented the current, average conception of womanhood. On the other hand we remember that Charlotte Bronte and Mrs Gaskell were Victorians; and with that in mind, we begin to think more kindly of their generation. We begin to think kindly; but it is not so certain that we continue. We come back to Mrs Browning and feel the same distaste as before. It is probable that the characteristics which we find so distasteful in her were the very things by which she endeared herself to her public—her "sensibility," docility, and attitude of wifely subjection. It is to be supposed that the Victorians as a whole were quite satisfied with Coleridge's admiration of Shakespeare's women on the score that they were so characterless; they were, he said, the kind of women that a man would like to marry. The novels and even some essays of the day seem to imply the conviction that it was rather a fine thing for a woman to have a personality sufficiently

faint to be absorbed into that of her husband. We do not
take Coleridge quite so seriously now-a-days—and least of
all his conceptions of womanhood. Why, even the Shakespearean heroines whom he praised—tender, sensitive women
like Desdemona or Imogen—were not quite so negative as
his words might lead us to believe. Put aside the women of
positive temperament—Rosalind, Portia, Juliet; he was not
thinking of them. Consider the women of negative type, and
we discover that even Desdemona was something more than
a minus quantity. And Imogen!—So delicate she was, so
fragile, and so winning! But she was a braver woman than
Mrs Browning—braver also than the general run of heroines
in Victorian fiction. She shrank, as Elizabeth Barrett would
have done, from "the hourly shot of angry eyes"; but she
had a stronger nerve, which could face opposition from
Cymbeline with an uplifted serenity:

> I beseech you, sir,
> Harm not yourself with your vexation;
> I am senseless of your wrath; a touch more rare
> Subdues all pangs, all fears.

Not once only, but at all times, Mrs Browning seems to have
missed the rare touch of exaltation. She never stood

> Within this life,
> Though lifted o'er its strife.

There is some justification for her weakness; and we can
give it freely. The Victorian public was quite satisfied with
her as she was. The chief blame lies, not on her shoulders,
but on those of her admirers. She was lacking; so also was
the current ideal of what a woman should be. She attained
the average standard.

One thing remains to be said. It is always not only merciful,
but just, to give credit for motive as well as achievement.
Mrs Browning possessed the poetic motive; that in itself is
a distinction. It implies a reverence for things lovely and of
good report. And Robert Browning's wife has a special
claim for charitable judgment. Using her husband's words,
she can voice her plea against the verdict of apparent failure:

Not on the vulgar mass
Called "work," must sentence pass,
Things done, that took the eye and had the price;
O'er which, from level stand,
The low world laid its hand,
Found straightway to its mind, could value in a trice:

But all, the world's coarse thumb
And finger failed to plumb,
So passed in making up the main account;
All instincts immature,
All purposes unsure,
That weighed not as his work, yet swelled the man's
    amount:

Thoughts hardly to be packed
Into a narrow act,
Fancies that broke through language and escaped;
All I could never be,
All, men ignored in me,
This, I was worth to God, whose wheel the pitcher
    shaped.

CHRISTINA ROSSETTI
1830–1894

I

PERSONAL EXPERIENCE REFLECTED ON
HER POETRY

CHRISTINA ROSSETTI was born in 1830, and died in 1894. Between these dates there lies a very slight quantity of biographical episode; yet the quality of these episodes is deeply significant. A few facts of her own experience provide an explanation of all the colour, poignancy, and intensity of her art.

One is the fact of Death, casting its shadow upon her from her fifteenth year to her sixty-fourth. From the year 1845 Christina never walked in the clear sunlight of perfect health. For many years of her life the prospect of death was a daily and hourly consolation. Like milestones upon her road she marked the coming of death to members of her immediate circle—in 1854 her father, in 1876 her sister Maria, in 1882 her brother Dante, in 1886 her mother. Every funeral must have sounded a summons to her own soul. Unlike most of us, it might be said of her that in the midst of death she was in life. Death startles us as an interruption, an intrusion; to her the mere fact of living was a surprise. Apparently predestined for early death, she kept alive for sixty-four years. She must have felt something magnetic in the dark Shadow which moves through the world of men. She had touched the Shadow, which had taken shape before her gaze; sometimes in hours of pain she had looked into the eyes of Déath. Then the figure had passed away, but rarely out of her sight. She witnessed its dealings with others close by her, and awaited her hour. Yet she showed no signs of fear.—

> Fear death? To feel the fog in my throat,
> The mist in my face—

she never mentioned such things. She never girded herself up to meet

> The Arch-Fear in a visible form.

Her visualisation of Death must have resembled the tall, dim figure of Watts' painting *Love and Death*—a form powerful and yet tender; shrouded, but not in hues of darkness; standing with a gesture steadfast, brooding, and protective. Nevertheless the idea of Death as personality finds little definite expression in her writings; hers is rather the conception of Death as a region—"the shadowy land" to be crossed, while—

> Dim beyond it looms the land of day.

Whether it were conceived as personality or region, her attitude remained unchanging. She always seemed absorbed in her long vigil, and more conscious of death than of life.

The second great fact is renunciation. The long years of waiting might have been filled with the joy of human love; but Christina most deliberately chose the empty life of abnegation. There were, as we know, two love episodes in her life-story. One came when she was a young girl in her teens. The years 1848 and 1849 stand out as the period of intimacy with James Collinson, the artist. In its broad outlines the story is well known.—Collinson had been converted to Roman Catholicism before meeting Christina. On her raising this as an insuperable barrier, he reverted to his original fold —the Church of England. Then came his repentance and return to the Church of Rome—with inevitable results, so far as Christina was concerned. This brought her the first sting of disillusion, and turned her fresh dreams to bitterness:

> I must pull down my palace that I built,
>   Dig up the pleasure-gardens of my soul;
> Must change my laughter to sad tears for guilt,
>   My freedom to control.
>
> Now all the cherished secrets of my heart,
>   Now all my hidden hopes are turned to sin.
> Part of my life is dead, part sick, and part
>   Is all on fire within.

The fruitless thought of what I might have been,
Haunting me ever, will not let me rest.
A cold North wind has withered all my green,
My sun is in the West.

(Three Stages.)

The second love episode, which came in later life, left deeper wounds. Charles Bagot Cayley, a scholar and man of letters, met Christina constantly after the year 1860. Mr William Rossetti has noted the years 1862 to 1867 as the period of their closest intercourse. After that date there was neither question nor hope of marriage, for Christina had made the central and most inflexible resolution of her life. The rest of the story is most fittingly told in the words of her brother William: "Years passed; she became an elderly, and an old woman, and she loved the scholarly recluse to the last day of his life, and to the last day of her own, his memory." That, and not mere physical suffering, strikes the single pervading note of tragedy in Christina Rossetti's life-story. The tragedy was self-calculated and self-inflicted; its roots settled deep within her own nature. Mr Cayley was reverent and unworldly, but to Christina he lacked the one thing needful. Even Mr William Rossetti cannot tell us the precise grounds of disagreement between his sister and her lover. He leads us to suppose that, whereas Mr Cayley's form of Christianity was partial, Christina's was absolute. He did not regard it as the single and ultimate creed, while for Christina it was everything or nothing. These facts presented themselves to her in the form of a sharp and definite choice; she made her resolution, and kept it. The world knows her secret to-day, but it is not for the world to discuss it, with either condemnation or approval.

It is remarkable that Christina did not "unpack her heart with words" about this matter. She did write about renunciation after the year 1867, but rarely in words of throbbing pain. The great poems of renunciation were written *before* her own testing. *Introspective*, perhaps the greatest of all, was written in 1857, three years before the commencement of her intimacy with Mr Cayley. She seems to have written, not from actual experience, but under a premonition

of the impending ordeal. This adds to her intensest poetry
an unique and almost prophetic poignancy. She felt herself
rejecting happiness before it had been offered to her. She
tasted in advance the pangs of martyrdom. This is hardly
too strong a word for one who wrote with such an instinctive
passion on the theme of self-renunciation. Her heart burned
within her whenever she touched the subject. Even when
she approached it impersonally, as in *The Convent Threshold*,
the hidden fires stirred. An inexplicable presentiment seems
to have burned its warning across her heart; and she foretold
—using the *past* tense, like an Old Testament prophet—the
silence which would fall on her after the future evil had come
to pass:

> Dumb I was when the ruin fell,
> Dumb I remain, and will never tell;
> O my soul, I talk with thee,
> But not another the sight must see.

> *(Introspective.)*

This dumbness of spirit did fall upon her. She spoke after
1867, in the sense that she produced many poems; but her
voice lacked the old vital, singing quality. It approached her
own description of the many "subtle stings" which prick
our daily walk—

> A voice which sang, but never sings.

This blankness and dullness of heart is best measured by the
quality of her poetry after 1867. For a time it fell off, even
in quantity; then her voice came back with a halting and
uncertain music. It almost seemed as if in renouncing earthly
love, she had sacrificed her art. Like Rupert Brooke going out
to wage an earthly warfare, she in her spiritual contest
risked poetic vision:

> Our sons we gave,
> Our immortality.

Mr A. C. Benson has declared the *Descent into Hell* a requisite
for the highest artistic development. But, as we have seen,
most of Christina's supreme poetry was written as if in
anticipation of that ordeal. There must have been a new
quality in the music of Orpheus after he returned from Hades

to the upper world. Though he had lost Eurydice, he carried with him his instrument unscathed. Christina made the descent into Hell, but her lyre suffered in the fierce flames of testing.

Indeed, if Christina Rossetti's immortality depended solely on work done after 1867, it would still be impossible absolutely to forget the author of *Monna Innominata*, *Marvel of Marvels*, and *Heaven Overarches Earth and Sea*; but we could have no conception of the rich, rare, and unerring beauty of the earlier day. We should have to search for gold among silver and meaner metals. The gold would be there for the finding, but rarely, if ever, would we light upon the warm colour and radiance of jewels. Christina had to pay the price of her sacrifice, and add it to the sum of increasing physical weakness. This uncertainty of her art testifies to the weariness which fell upon her spirit. It is certain, however, that she never regretted the cost, never wished to go back over the past, taking the other alternative. Possibly we never hear her absolute verdict on her decision—never in words that ring clear from the heart—till we get a poem roughly dated, "Before 1886," and most probably written a good time after the death of Mr Cayley in 1883. It is well known, but surely it can never be quoted too often:

> My love, whose heart is tender, said to me,
>   "A moon lacks light, except her sun befriend her,
> Let us keep tryst in heaven, dear Friend," said she,
>   My love, whose heart was tender.
>   From such a loftiness no words could bend her,
> Yet still she spoke of "us," and spoke as "we,"
>   Her hope substantial, while my hope grew slender.
> Now keeps she tryst beyond earth's utmost sea,
>   Wholly at rest, though storms should toss and rend her.
> And still she keeps my heart, and keeps its key,
>   My love, whose heart is tender.

Literally this is not the story of her life; for in her case, it was the man who died first. In every other respect it fits closely to her experience; and in one line her own conclusion is unmistakably implied—

> *Her hope substantial*, while my hope grew slender.

That substantial hope atoned to Christina for any measure of earthly sorrow. The nun whom she described when a girl of nineteen, used words which she could have applied to herself at the age of sixty:

> I whom prayers and fasts turn pale
> Await the flush of Paradise.

It reminds us of Browning's statement of the consolation fitted for a poet who falls short of attainment. God, he says,

> Just saves your gold to spend.

Christina Rossetti believed in the same truth. Her gold was being saved for her. Though some of it was spent in the world of human turmoil, the great treasure was laid up in heaven. In an early poem she had referred to the fruition which follows pain:

> To-morrow I shall put forth buds again,
> And clothe myself with fruit.
> *(From House to Home.)*

"To-morrow" came to stand before her as a symbol of Eternity, dawning after the night of earthly ruin. It was on this chord that she closed one of the last poems she ever wrote:

> Heaven overarches earth and sea,
> Earth-sadness and sea-bitterness.
> Heaven overarches you and me;
> A little while and we shall be—
> Please God—where there is no more sea
> Nor barren wilderness.
>
> Heaven overarches you and me,
> And all earth's gardens and her graves.
> Look up with me, until we see
> The day break and the shadows flee.
> What though to-night wrecks you and me,
> If so to-morrow saves?

II

SOURCES

THE chief source of all poems is the poet's life. This is the firmest basis for the study of literary biography—not as an end in itself, but as the means which produced an end. The cause is the poet's experience; the effect is his art. The experience is a transitory thing, for the poet dies like all other men; but the art remains as survival of his fittest achievement. Literary biography should always be regarded in this light—as the record of passing hours and months which brought forth an imperishable beauty.

This is particularly true of Christina Rossetti. She was one of the most secluded and detached of English writers. It is almost impossible to take up any of her poems, and say—"Because such-and-such an English poet lived before her, she wrote in this style." Echoes we may catch, lines and phrases from other writers; but they are so faint and rare as to be lost in her own music. In the same way historical movements and great intellectual impulses swept by without ruffling the waters of her pool. Perhaps the Oxford Movement, with its bearing upon Anglicanism, should have come nearer to her than any other influence of her age; yet, all she had to say about it in definite language was contained in one grave, calm sonnet to the memory of Cardinal Newman. Christina Rossetti was not a product of her age. We can imagine her living through successive periods of the Christian era, and achieving the same result in each case. She could project her mind back through the ages and feel quite at ease—more at home with Augustine, Dante, or Thomas à Kempis than with Tennyson, Browning or Carlyle. Mediaevalism was for her the atmosphere of least resistance. Still, it is impossible to determine whether she would have been different if born into the middle ages, and not in the nineteenth century. A sympathetic environment could not have developed more intensity than that which she acquired in solitude. The most essential fact of her nature was her singular independence of environment. It is hardly too much to say that the essentials of her art would not have been materially altered if she had lived in the England of either Elizabeth or Charles II. This can be said of hardly any other English poet—not even of Milton. It may be true of him that his

> Soul was like a star, and dwelt apart.

But it is also undeniable that he represented Puritanism. Christina Rossetti represented nothing apart from her own personality. Hers was the solitude, not of the mountain-summit, but of the locked and darkened room. "In thy chamber," said a writer much loved by her—"In thy chamber thou shalt find what abroad thou shalt too often lose." In Christina's chamber we find something which eludes us elsewhere. This shy, unobtrusive woman, passing self-contained through the midst of intellectual zests and turmoils, in the world and yet not of it, was more unusual, more truly unique than any of the great figures overshadowing her. In the course of English literature she stood unparented—like Melchizedek set apart, "without father, without mother" (and possibly) "without descent."

The literary influence which stirred her most profoundly was that of Dante. Yet here, as always, she transformed what she received. She had something of the Dantesque temperament—its vehemence, flame, delicacy, and ecstasy. But there were in Dante whole worlds which escaped her. His outlook, embracing sun, moon, and stars, and piercing through the "veins o' the earth" to the fierce dark underworld, was concentrated by her into the processes of her own soul. He looked upward and outward; she looked inward. The stars entered his stretching vision as constant symbols of inspiration. It was characteristic of Christina that she sought escape even from starlight, in the close, secret grave, where she might forget all things—

> Forget my body, and forget my soul.
>
> *(There Remaineth Therefore a Rest.)*

Dante walked, a living spirit, through the worlds of the dead, his path haunted with echoing voices. Christina's dreams were full of dim voices, questioning and replying. The spirits who thronged round Dante yearned after knowledge of the world they had quitted, and wistfully sought to be remembered; they asked the poet to speak of them when he returned to the dwellings of men, and the radiant light of the stars:

> Fa che di noi alla gente favelle.
> (*See that of us thou speak among mankind.*)
> (Carey's translation.)

The same thought pervaded much of Christina's writing, and found place in one of her most perfect poems, *When I am Dead, My Dearest*, with its recurring refrain—

> And if thou wilt, remember,
> And if thou wilt, forget.

It found more impassioned and consummate expression in the poem, *At Home*, so highly praised by her brother, Dante Gabriel. There the spirit returns to the earth, seeking recognition, and finding instead the blankness of oblivion:

> "To-morrow and to-day," they cried;
> I was of yesterday.

Another point in which Christina resembled Dante was the beautiful grave tenderness which sweetened the gloom of torment. With what an instinctive sympathy must she have turned to the famous passage where Paolo and Francesca are ashamed to read of Lancelot's guilty passion! In Christina's mind there would have been something akin to Dante's wonderful reticence:

> Quel giorno più non vi legemmo avanti.
> (*In its leaves that day we read no more.*)

In the same way she could have appreciated Dante's courtesy to his old master, Brunetto Latini; for even in the place of torment the pupil greets his master and passes on with him—

> Com' uom che riverente vada.
> (*As one who walks in reverent guise.*)

Still, it was not in the *Inferno*, but in the *Paradiso* that she entered most fully into his spirit. In one of her poems she speaks of the Christian life as a race run—

> In darkness for the city luminous.
> (*Shadows To-day.*)

It was the luminous quality of Dante's imagination which left the deepest impression upon her temperament. His splendour of colour and light, flower and music, reappeared in her brief flashing visions. Like his own, her dreams of Paradise were ethereal, radiant, translucent. It is easy to understand how Christina could not enter into the substantial, massive imagination of Milton; in Dante she could find the kindred touch of fragility. His visions melted and wavered, vibrated with elusive harmonies, flushed and glimmered with changing lights. There was nothing opaque in his structures, but instead an almost transparent clearness of colour, set in the dimmest of outlines. The spirits were amazed to see Dante's shadow cast upon the flames (*Purg*. Canto 26). It is remarkable also that the angels in flight cast no shadows upon the petals of the mystic rose (*Par*. Canto 31). Christina once wrote of the "shadowless hair" of a ghost, but this in itself is a trifling resemblance. The absence of shadow is simply a token of the peculiar, almost immaterial quality of colour in both poets. Sir Sidney Colvin has selected from Keats' description of Madeline praying the one word which suggests the coming and going of colour:

A shielded scutcheon *blush'd* with blood of queens and kings.

There is the same vitality in the colours of Dante Alighieri and Christina Rossetti. They are not permanently painted on a canvas; they flush and fade as if they were alive. It is impossible to enumerate detailed places of contact, such as "the kindling stair" of *The Convent Threshold*, so like the glowing ladder set up in Dante's seventh heaven, and fading high up beyond sight.

Only one more point of resemblance can be noted. This is suggested by the crowning symbol of Dante's vision—the clustered petals of the snow-white rose. Christina never attained to any conception so magical, so overwhelming as this; but to her, as to Dante, the rose was an emblem of Ultimate Beauty. Possibly no literature can have so lifted the wings of her spirit as that passage where Beatrice leads Dante into the yellow heart of the living flower. Christina's soul would follow his into the fragrance and dazzling purity of unutterable visions.

From *The Imitation of Christ*, Christina Rossetti acquired much of her outlook upon Christianity. We have already noticed that her grasp of Christianity was absolute. That is so in the sense that it completely absorbed her life. In another sense she possessed only a partial creed—not the Christianity of the Gospels, not the complete Christianity of Christ, but one intense and intimate aspect of the Christian life. This aspect was most fully expressed by the author of *The Imitation*. It is hardly the creed which uplifts and regenerates civilisations; it is a faith which warms and illumines the inner life of the individual spirit. Its basis is submission—"O dust, learn to be obedient." It insists upon self-renunciation, and for reward it offers communion with Christ. In Christina's poems we find a ringing echo to the dialogues of *The Imitation*—speech between Christ and the Disciple, intimate, searching, urgent. Such disciplined serenity of mood was something into which Christina could enter heart and soul:

Thou oughtest not to be dejected nor to despair; but at God's will to stand steadily, and whatever comes upon thee to endure it for the glory of Jesus Christ; for after winter followeth summer, after night the day returneth, and after tempest a great calm.

In this book she found testimony to her own sources of consolation: "Thou art the true peace of the heart, Thou its only rest; out of Thee all things are hard and restless." She never rose to its abandon of joy, to the swift, radiant delight of the chapter "On the Wonderful Effect of Divine Love":

He that loveth, flyeth, runneth, and rejoiceth; he is free, and cannot be held in. He giveth all for all, and hath all in all....Love ...is able to undertake all things, and it completes many things, and warrants them to take effect, where he who does not love, would faint and lie down.

She could not reach this elasticity and buoyancy of faith; but she held very firmly to the secret which lies at the core of all religious vitality—the fact of close and personal relations with unseen forces:

For who is there, that approaching humbly unto the fountain of sweetness, doth not carry away from thence at least some little sweetness? Or who standing near a large fire, receiveth not some small heat therefrom? And Thou art a fountain always full and overflowing, a fire ever burning and never giving out.

This fire lighted the embers in Christina's own heart; and we, standing without, can feel the warmth of the flame. A fire indeed is not always comfortable; it warms, but it can burn. At times there may be something in the intense isolated flame which makes us shrink back from it. We say that this fire of religion is dangerous—a good servant, but a bad master. Those who wish to master their religion are repelled by Christina Rossetti, who was mastered by her religion; but whatever we may feel, there is one positive fact —her religion never leaves us cold.

Mr William Rossetti has told us that his sister delighted in *The Pilgrim's Progress*; this is in some ways astonishing. The homeliness of Bunyan seems far apart from her ordered reverence; his freshness of speech very different from the concentrated passion of her published writings. Still he is not so far away from the unstudied piquancy sometimes appearing in her letters; and beyond the superficial manner, she would apprehend a meaning where she and Bunyan could meet on common ground. In both Dante and Bunyan she must have noted the comparison which so often took form in her own writing—the likening of earthly life to a pilgrimage, a sojourn, a "progress." It is true that Dante did not use the same definite metaphor of the journey as applied to man's life on earth; but the foundation of his poem and the basis of Bunyan's allegory were alike. Both writers were recorders of a pilgrimage.

Christina has often been compared to the English mystics of the seventeenth century—Herbert, Crashaw, and Vaughan. There again the distinction is more prominent than the resemblance—the distinction between familiarity and intimacy. These men approached God in the spirit of little children, and played with their fancies at His feet. Even in their moments of sincerest devotion they took pleasure in their phrases; and with this clearness of the childlike heart they learned secrets hidden from the wise and prudent.

Christina lacked this youthful innocence. When she was nineteen she described herself as one—

> Grown old before my time.
> (*O Roses for the Flush of Youth.*)

We can imagine that the fantastic exuberance of these poets would have oppressed her with her own sobriety. She might have gone a certain distance with them, and then been pulled up by the sudden sense of an alien atmosphere. For instance she might have started on a passage like this:

> All thy old woes shall now smile on thee;
> And thy pains sit bright upon thee;
> All thy sorrows here shall shine,
> And thy sufferings be divine.
> Tears shall take comfort, and turn gems,
> And wrongs repent to diadems.

She would have halted at the last two lines—not because of their defects in style, but because they are fantastic. She took her religion too seriously to indulge in fancies about it.

Again we are told that she admired Coleridge and Shelley; but she took very little from them. She would find in them the same absence of outline, the shifting evanescent colour which characterises the visions of Dante's *Paradiso*. The "sunless rivers" of her *Dreamland* are reminiscent of a phrase from *Kubla Khan*. There was in these poets something ethereal and unearthly to which she could respond. But apart from the fact that they were dreamers, caught up into worlds beyond the tangible actualities of earth, she had little kinship with them. In Coleridge's personality there was a slackness of fibre which found its way into his writings, thus setting them apart from hers. The direct antithesis of Shelley, "tameless, and swift, and proud," she never seemed to experience his hunger and thirst after freedom, his hot, hopeless struggles against the bars of necessity or convention. Mr Edmund Gosse has found in both Christina Rossetti and Shelley "that *desiderium*, that obstinate longing for something lost out of life"—

> Out of the day and night
> A joy has taken flight.

Perhaps it would be truer to say that Christina's habitual temper was that of one who has lost a sense of delight, whereas Shelley went in constant pursuit of an unknown joy subtly eluding his grasp.

Keats stands out next as a member of the great procession of poetic colourists; and the question arises—Did he transmit anything to Christina Rossetti? To me it appears that Christina felt colour as she did, chiefly because this was an inborn faculty, and also because she lived in the society of artists. I think her colour-sense would have been as perfect if she had never read a line of Keats. Similarly she resembled Keats in her sensitive handling of growing things —grass, and plants, and flowers. She does not show us landscapes. She takes us into a place full of movement and change —a world which seems to lay a physical touch upon our senses. But this again is an attitude, a mood, which cannot be learned from books. It is impossible to believe that she was like this, just because Keats, who lived before her, had felt Nature, while others took observations. This, even more than the sense of colour, is an instinct, not an acquired habit. —One phrase, however, which fell from Keats' dying lips constantly takes shape anew in her poetry—"I feel," he said, "the flowers growing over me." In *Looking Forward* this idea pulses through the dying farewell of a girl to her friends:

> Have patience, with me, friends, a little while;
> For soon, where you shall dance and sing and smile,
> My quickened dust may blossom at your feet.

Yet the idea in itself is not at all singular. What was original in Keats' use of it was his personal and intimate relation to the idea. Christina, also, was capable of feeling in the same way without any external suggestion.

She was always conscious, however, of living in the same world as Mrs Browning. Sometimes she caught a faint reflection from her;—*An After-Thought* displays a slight debt to a few phrases from *The Drama of Exile.*—Christina humbly believed that but for one thing lacking, Mrs Browning could have written a sonnet-sequence better than her own

Monna Innominata. That lack was an impassioned sorrow.—
"Had the Great Poetess of our own day and nation only been
unhappy instead of happy"—she would have given the world
something finer than *The Sonnets from the Portuguese*; and
in that case, it is implied, Christina would not have competed
against it with her *Monna Innominata.* For once we can be
thankful to have missed the might-have-been.

As Christina felt this respect for Mrs Browning, we, even
at the risk of some repetition, must examine her position
more closely. Although she was conscious of Mrs Browning,
it is not so certain that she was influenced by her. We would
think less of Christina if she had allowed her firmness to be
shaken by the weight of Mrs Browning's words. It would
have lowered her to become the disciple of such a teacher.
For Mrs Browning was not like Christina, a supreme poet.
Her genius was weak and intermittent, pushed out of her
in short spasms, and stifled with words.—"The lady protests
too much."—Nothing was kept back. Christina Rossetti was
never garrulous like Mrs Browning's Seraphim. She could
hold her lips firmly closed. Mrs Browning's was not the
case of an empty sounding vessel, for she was not empty.
She had many things to say, and some of them were worth
saying; but by her own action she depreciated their value.
She poured the liquid out of her vessel so that it drenched
the recipient; yet all the time she was trying to satisfy
his thirst. Still there was nourishment in that fluid so care-
lessly wasted; and Christina seems to have recognised the
fact. For our part we should try to find out how much she
tasted of this offered nourishment, and how much she laid
aside.

In the first place she passed over anything which approached
character-study. She had no counterpart to Mrs Browning's
Lucifer; she never scrutinised types like Romney Leigh or
Lord Howe. She had nothing of Mrs Browning's interest
in man's apparent inconsistencies:

> What creature else
> Conceives the circle, and then walks the square?

She could not see life through another's eyes. In this respect

Mrs Browning had an undeveloped germ of insight. There were many grave defects in her rendering of Marian Erle's story. Marian herself is so swathed about with words and sentiment and theories, that we can hardly find the woman underneath all the layers. But Christina could not have felt, like Mrs Browning, the blended "anguish" and "ecstasy" of her mother-love. To do that she would have required to look out from herself; and this she could not do.—She was not a proud woman. She flinched from the revelation of her own spiritual weakness; but she could not stoop to pity degradations deeper than her own. She could not have voiced the cry of Mrs Browning's runaway slave:

> But *we* who are dark, we are dark!
> Ah God, we have no stars!

Christina could not have imagined what it was to exist without the starlight of faith. Neither could she have realised the utter misery of the slave's hopeless cry:

> I look on the sky and the sea—
> We were two to love, and two to pray,—
> Yes, two, O God, who cried to Thee,
> Though nothing didst Thou say.
> *Coldly Thou sat'st behind the sun!*

Christina had known the misery of forsaking God, but never the agony of feeling God-forsaken. It is doubtful whether, for all her intense religious experience, she could have given spiritual consolation to that slave—or to anybody else who differed from herself.

In her world there was not much of physical humanity with its caprice and outward gesture. Her figures were too much like disembodied spirits to have been fitted into a drawing-room or a slum. Mrs Browning believed that poetry must be modern in tone; she distrusted the poet who—

> Trundles back his soul five hundred years;

and that is pretty much what Christina did. To her time and space were mere wrappings on the surface of reality. She allowed her soul to wander wherever it could find a home. She had nothing to say about the spirit of modern London, political upheavals in Florence, the slave-trade, or factory

acts. She hardly knew that these things existed. The solitary
exception is her reference to the Franco-Prussian War.
While Mrs Browning went to one extreme, she went to the
other. She would have been richer, however, if she had
seen more. Having no compassion for the multitudes, she
could not have detected, like Mrs Browning, the emotion of
a crowd:

> A holiday of miserable men
> Is sadder than a burial-day of kings.

We have said that Mrs Browning dissipated her emotions
on the crowd, and that Christina was wiser in describing the
one thing she knew—the working of her own spirit. But
sometimes we cannot help feeling that it was a pity she knew
nothing else. She never felt what was a constant problem to
Mrs Browning—the uplifting and temptation of a great
cause. The ideal which exalts us with its spacious vistas may
deaden us to individual compassions. Mrs Browning knew
that; so did Charlotte Bronte; so did George Eliot; but as
for Christina Rossetti—it is doubtful whether the mere idea
ever entered her head.

For this reason she took no interest in certain topics
discussed by every other woman writer of her time. She
had nothing to say on the woman's question. Mrs Browning
was constantly fretting against the world's estimate of literary
women. Perhaps Christina did not know that it was considered unusual—even unseemly—for a woman to be a
writer. Even if she had known, it would not have given her
a moment's misgiving. Other women tried to make believe
that they did not care for the world's opinion; Christina
simply ignored it.

In the same way she had no conscious theories of art.
Mrs Browning felt the responsibility of her vocation. Art,
as witness to the invisible, demands conscientious discipline:

> Better far
> Pursue a frivolous trade by serious means
> Than a sublime art frivolously.

If Christina hated frivolity, it was not for her art's sake; she
was afraid of cheapening her soul. Mrs Browning felt the

solitude of the artistic life; the vine stoops with its fruit, but—

> The palm stands upright in a realm of sand.

Christina never blamed her art for her loneliness; she had voluntarily renounced a deep and intimate fellowship. Even if she had attained, like Mrs Browning, to "hear the nations praising (her) far off," she would not have felt the poignancy of her aloofness. Neither did she feel a contrast between her life and her writing. "Books succeed," said Mrs Browning, "and lives fail." Christina was not considering the success of her books; she had to make of her life a spiritual triumph. Beside that, nothing else mattered. "He who would write a heroic poem," said Milton, "must first live a heroic life." Christina tried to live a heroic life, and "without taking thought" she produced heroic poems. She seemed as careless of her art, and as faultless as the lilies.

There were certain places where the two women could stand in sympathy. For all her sociology, Mrs Browning was a dreamer. She closed her eyes more firmly than Christina, and less colour crept in among her fancies. She was more sound asleep, but the dream stillness came to her.—

> And between each word you might have heard
> The silent forests grow.

These lines from *The Romaunt of Margret* have the dim haunting quality which lies at the background of Christina's glowing pictures.

Both women had taken up their lives, and felt them meagre.

There is nothing to see in me (wrote Miss Barrett to Robert Browning). If my poetry is worth anything to any eye, it is the flower of me. I have lived most, and been most happy in it, so it has all my colours; the rest of me is nothing but a root, fit for the ground, and dark.

The difference with Christina was that religion, and not poetry, gave the colouring to her life. Her religion grew within her till it sprang and blossomed into poetry. Both women were sufficiently religious to feel the sharp edges of

their souls. Mrs Browning was more afraid of the soul's
contact with the external world; Aurora Leigh carried hers—

> Through all the spilt salt-petre of the world.

Christina, on the contrary, felt her soul grating against her
own flesh. She had to make a different choice from Aurora's,
but in

> Preferring dreary hearths to desert souls,

their motives were the same.

For sheer intensity there is, of course, no comparison
between the two women. Christina's soul was like a radiant
texture, its colours flashing and quivering as if some hidden
life were rippling through its folds. Mrs Browning's soul
was of the same colour, but in a paler shade, and woven of
plainer threads. Her wedding garment was so much clumsier
that she sat ill at ease in the midst of the festival:

> With God so near me, could I sing of God?

Christina never felt that embarrassment. When she felt God
near her, she sang like a child, for sheer gladness of heart;
and even when God seemed more distant, she still sang, like
the same child, holding on to his courage as he passes through
dark places.

Mrs Browning excepted, Tennyson was the only other
writer of her generation who could have left any trace upon
her art. Robert Browning would hardly enter her realm of
thought; Ruskin she regarded chiefly in the light of an art-
critic; but for any Victorian poet there was no possible
evasion of Tennyson. Here and there he cast his shadow on
her; yet in almost every case she escaped out of the shade into
the light of her own individuality. For example, she started
Repining—a very unequal poem—after the style of *Mariana
in the Moated Grange*; but before she had written many lines,
she let fall a touch of that almost uncanny simplicity which
belonged peculiarly to herself:

> She bound her hair up from the floor,
> And passed in silence from the door.

Again, the tone of *The Royal Princess* has been found to
resemble that of Tennyson's narratives; but it rises at the

close to a compression and directness which she never learnt from the Poet Laureate:

I, if I perish, perish; in the name of God I go.

The most striking comparison is to be found in *The Prince's Progress*, which undoubtedly fills in an allegoric framework of the kind handled by Tennyson. The lighter touches, the satire of the "social Prince" are almost identical in spirit with much of *The Princess*. Nevertheless the ultimate and essential beauties of the poem are entirely original. The allegory, so like many things in Tennyson, was an after-thought; it was written, as it were, to herald and introduce the lovely song placed at its close. It may be true that Tennyson apprehended more things in heaven and earth than those which entered Christina's dreams; yet it must also be admitted that she trod certain paths where he could not have followed her. He could not have achieved this poignancy:

Then you had known her living face
Which now you cannot know.

Neither could he have attained to the terseness of compassion which describes the bride's face with "the want graven there." Certainly he could not have written these lines:

Her heart sat silent through the noise
And concourse of the street.
There was no hurry in her hands,
No hurry in her feet.
There was no bliss drew nigh to her
That she might run to greet.

Christina wrote that out of her own heart; and Tennyson could not have done likewise, because his heart was different.

There is also the question of the Pre-Raphaelite Brotherhood. It is beyond all doubt that of all contemporary influences, this stirred her most effectively. She was the sister of a dominating artist, who studied her face, sketched it, and painted it; she sat to him for the figure of the Virgin in two of his pictures. Her other brother was an art-critic; her first lover was an artist; she drew designs and illustrations for some of her own poems. It came naturally to her to regard everything as the possible foundation of a picture. Still the

pictures suggested by her words are not precisely of the type
which her brother Dante Gabriel painted on his canvases.
They are less vivid, less virile, less near at hand. They stand
aloof, glow, and fade, and vanish, like forms seen in a dream.
There was in her outlook some affinity to the paintings of
G. F. Watts. Like him, she set out on a quest for symbols.
As we have seen, his figure of Death was of the kind to satisfy
her imagination. At the foot of his *Sic Transit Gloria Mundi*
he placed words which could have summarised her philosophy: "What I spent, I had; What I saved, I lost; What
I gave, I have."—We see her also in his conception of
Hope patiently fingering her broken lute, and drawing from
its single string fragments of melody. It may be urged that
he did not think of her while he was painting his picture;
he was visualising the spirit of his age, and Christina stood
apart from that age. Still she was like his symbolic figure;
not in its position on the topmost curve of the earth, for she
was one of those who ever seek "The Lowest Room"; not in
the self-bandaged eyes of one who, doubting the heavens,
misses the light of a solitary star; but in the steadfast purpose
which clings to the fragile survivals of ruin, and keeps alive
a song.

III

SYMBOL, ALLEGORY, AND DREAM

FROM Mr William Rossetti we learn that Christina read the *Dialogues* of Plato with the same eager zest as Dante's *Divina Commedia*. Undoubtedly this exercised a formative influence upon her personality and art; it intensified and established her habitual cast of thought. For this reason we have not placed Plato among the "sources" of her work—as a source is a starting-point which may be left behind; whereas Plato's philosophy of beauty formed the basis of her structures. Her love of Plato helps to explain the fact that she did not become a meagre ascetic, purging her soul of beauty. The antagonist of materialism, she had to make a clear decision as to the claims of earthly beauty—whether to reject it as snare and delusion, or accept it as symbol. If it had not been for Plato she might have rejected things seen and temporal for the things that are eternal. She came instead to love them as steps towards an everlasting beauty, "not growing and decaying, or waxing and waning;—pure and clear and un-alloyed, not clogged with the pollutions of mortality, and all the colours and vanities of human life." Through this majestic symbolism the waters of common experience were transformed into wine. She re-captured the "visionary gleam," the glory which tends to pass away from the earth; for she beheld all things as manifestations of God. (In passing it may be noted that her love of elaborate church-ritual was the natural outcome of such an inherent symbolism.)

Sometimes the feeling for what is emblematic found expression in brief snatches of lyric, such as *A Rose Plant in Jericho*, or *Consider the Lilies of the Field*, with its concluding touch—

Thou who gatherest lilies, gather us and wear.

Every metaphor is a symbol, and metaphors came swiftly to her summons. This figurative style, which represents the undeveloped symbolism of her mind, is to be found on every page of her writings. What is more significant is the rich full-grown symbolism that took shape in her allegories. These fall into a few clear groups: allegories of journeying and destination; allegories of ships at sea—another form of the journey; allegories in which personal figures are the central core of attraction. It will be observed that the allegory of the journey often merges into the quest for a personality.

The allegories of journeying are perhaps the most habitual and constant. They were among the first which she wrote. *The Dead City*, which came early, was remarkable chiefly for its flashes of translucent colour; for instance, the birds "with bodies like a flame," or—

> Pure and colourless as dew.

It was remarkable also for the sudden mood which falls upon the reader—its silences, strangely reminiscent of phrases from Keats' *Ode on a Grecian Urn*:

> There were none to buy or sell,
> None to listen or to tell,
> In this silent emptiness.

Then came *Repining*, with its subtle, delicate rhythms, and atmosphere of windless, wordless tension. As a whole it was a defective poem, but it had its promise. Later she wrote that strange sonnet *Cobwebs*—dealing with the destination this time, and not the journey; a land of utter negations, with—

> No beat of wings to stir the stagnant space.

The allegories where the journey merges into a quest for an actual figure are most perfectly represented by *Fata Morgana* and *The Prince's Progress*. The latter, as has been said, is not entirely original in its allegoric portions; its glory is its song. Yet there is something peculiar to Christina Rossetti in the "white room" where the bride waited; or in the delicate pendulum of rhythm:

> The long hours go and come and go;
> The bride she sleepeth, waketh, sleepeth.

But what words can be found to express the loveliness of *Fata Morgana*; its single touch of colour in the "blue-eyed phantom"; its rhythms, stirring, leaping, and sinking in pulses of movement; its sense of something wild, shy, and elusive? There is only one thing to be done with such poems; simply to say they are beautiful, and then re-open the book to enjoy them once again.

There are two important allegories of ships at sea—*Sleep at Sea* and *The Ballad of Boding*. Of these the latter is far more elaborate and, I think, less perfect. It is rich in music and suggestion, but it lacks the terse magic of the earlier poem, its arresting throbbing rhythm, and its wonderful austerity of contrast:

> So dream the sleepers,
>   Each man in his place;
> The lightning shows the smile
>   Upon each face....
> The lightning glares and reddens
>   Across the skies;
> It seems but sunset
>   To those sleeping eyes.

There is something overpowering in the discussion of such beauty. How shall we be equal to these things?—We must pass rapidly over the allegories of personality: *The Triad*, with its contrasted singers of love; the figure of the steadfast woman in *From House to Home*; the dream from *The Convent Threshold* of a spirit "with transfigured face." Interesting, beautiful though they may be, they are eclipsed by *Goblin Market*. This seems *the* poem of poems which Christina was predestined to write; for here she did something which nobody else could do. In the English language there are a few solitary poems, placed apart by their amazing singularity. *Tam o' Shanter* is one; *Goblin Market* is another. It is an allegory, of course, but this soon becomes "an unconsidered trifle." It is more like an adventure across the foam of perilous seas into "faery lands forlorn." There we find movement, flurry, precise grotesque detail, a clashing of incident and dream, stir and silence, sudden vivid anger and laughter. There seems to be no end to our discoveries as we keep turning the pages; it is like Browning's description of a mountain-journey—

> Ledge by ledge outbroke new marvels.

When we reach the last line we do not feel that the story has come to an end; it still seems "young in deed." Here Christina gives us no impression of resources completely used; we can picture her going on—

> For ever singing songs for ever new.

She did this only once; but we need not be like Oliver, crying out for more. We can pass out rejoicing from the festival of beauty.

All this seems a far cry from Plato. We have been revelling in allegories, and deliberately neglecting their meaning. It does not accord with "the philosophic mind." Still, the matter is not so incongruous as it appears. We have seen that Christina loved symbols for their significance. She never intended to exalt the story above its purpose, and most certainly she would have been displeased with us for so doing. We linger over her colour, music, and phantasy, till we forget there is a moral; but she never forgot it. She would have discarded all this rich beauty if it had not led to a moral. It was the moral that saved it for the world.

Christina's symbolism was a means of approach to invisible realities. Her dreams were an escape from the bitterness of actuality. All her poetry is suffused with this dream-quality. She said of the quiet sleeper in *Dreamland*—

> Through sleep as through a veil
> She sees the sky look pale.

Very often Christina dropped a veil between her and the harshness of external things. In poems like *Death's Chill Between* and *A Chilly Night*, she dreamed of haunting spirits —the low voice, the footfall, the "dim hand" feeling at the door, the tossing of "shadowless hair." In *Echo* she appealed for dreams of lost delight—the shadowy presence and touch of vanished memories. This is, indeed, a very beautiful poem; but as a general rule, poems of the type where she sees or feels ghosts of the past are usually surpassed by the more poignant conception (expressed in *At Home*) of her own spirit's return to earth. Here, instead of the dream picture, there is a tense emotion, which blurs the illusion of dream, and gives us the sting of reality.

Dream-Love stands in uncompanioned beauty. This, again, is one of the achievements so wonderful that it can hardly bear words of admiration. It brings us to the standpoint of Browning's lover—

> (I) cannot praise because I love so much!

It is impossible adequately to praise such frail and exquisite beauty; the magical suggestion of white lambs, white doves, and white may-bushes; the sunlight on "rustling forest-tips"; the moonlit waters; the weaving of silent dances; or the blending of light and shade:

> Cool shadows deepen
> Across the sleeping face.

The fittest tribute to such loveliness is—

> Silence more musical than any song.

Like her own dreamer, we halt between the pauses of her melody, while—

> The perfect silence calms.

Her thoughts often tended towards the still dream-world of death, or leapt beyond "the shadowy land" to the rapture of Paradise. The conception of death as a dream, a retreat, an oblivion, found consummate expression in such poems as *When I am Dead, My Dearest*, *Rest*, or *Dreamland*. Here she sought release from the burden of identity; the rest of an absolute negation—with eyes closed to the grey of twilight skies, ears deaf to the nightingale's song, and limbs no longer sensitive to the touch of the silent rain. Her storm-wearied spirit strained forward to the refuge of an absolute oblivion—a passionless state of nonentity:

> Not so much as a grain of dust
> Or drop of water from pole to pole.
>> (*From the Antique.*)

Yet her dreams did not always tarry in this land of dim negations. They sped forward to the ecstasies of spiritual transport. Sometimes, as in *Advent*, she heard echoing the voices of expectation, the speech of the virgins trimming their lamps, and the cry of the watchman as he searched the skies for "speaking signs." At other times, as in *Birds of Paradise*, the flash and rustle of wings came to her as symbol and promise of bliss. Once she rose to the topmost peaks of vision, and bore witness to a glory beyond human utterance. It was with an almost breathless tension that she hastened to set down the evanescent splendour of her imagining:

> Marvel of marvels, if I myself shall behold
> With mine own eyes my King in His city of gold.

The vision burns and flashes across our eyes; the rhymes and vowel-tones accumulate and roll back on one note like the tolling of a bell; then the glory passes—

> Cold it is, my beloved, since your funeral bell was tolled;
> Cold it is, O my King, how cold alone on the wold.

This, the most radiant and noble of her dreams, was recorded towards the close of life, shortly before she passed on to the fulfilment of her visions.

IV

EMOTIONAL QUALITY

MR EDMUND GOSSE has singled out for notice the "penetrating accent" of Christina Rossetti's poetry. As the quintessence of her art, it demands attention; yet there is nothing so elusive and evasive as the breath of emotion, slipping away from any scheme of classification. Nevertheless we cannot talk vaguely of emotions without some attempt after a definite direction. Otherwise the sole result of our reflections will be an "insubstantial pageant faded." The classification which I shall attempt is based on degree of intensity—the pitch or tone of emotion. In the first place, there is in Christina's poetry a constantly recurring strain of wistfulness or patient serenity. There is also a less frequent escape into passion, tension, ecstasy, or the agony of a great weariness. In addition there is a single group of poems, written in an intermediate state between yearning and intensity; this is the great series of sonnets, *Monna Innominata*.

It is not satisfactory to take all these groups in a strictly chronological sequence. For, as is the case with people who live a restricted life, Christina's moods repeated themselves. They did not evolve, or work up to a climax, but recurred like phrases in a piece of music. She struck her note of quiet pathos very early, in a few lines from *The Dying Man to His Betrothed*. The rejected dying lover gives a word of counsel with regard to his fortunate rival:

> And, if he chide thee wrongfully,
> One little moment think of me,
> And thou wilt bear it patiently.

This tone, like that of a muted violin, echoes through the whole course of her poems. It occurs in connection with a Pre-Raphaelite tendency to concentrate on solitary details:

> Led by *a single star*,
> She came from very far,
> To seek where shadows are
> Her pleasant lot.

The note of selfless tenderness rings quietly through the
concluding lines of *After Death*:

> Very sweet it is
> To know he still is warm, though I am cold;

or through the resignation in *Remember* of all claim to remembrance:

> Better by far you should forget and smile,
> Than that you should remember and be sad.

A subdued yearning finds utterance in the wonderful repeated
simplicity of *A Pause*:

> Only my soul kept watch from day to day,
> My thirsty soul kept watch for one away.

In *Three Seasons* and *Mirage*, separated by seven years of
experience, she tells the same story of regret, even as in
The First Spring Day and *Home by Different Ways*, she
catches, in different keys, a melody of hope. *The Last Look*
strikes an impersonal note of the *lacrimae rerum*—the infinitely pitiful sense of waste:

> Heaven lit with stars is more like her
> Than is this empty crust;
> Deaf, dumb, and blind, it cannot stir,
> But crumbles back to dust.

In *Twice* she surveys a human tragedy with a singular and
almost astounding pose of detachment—

> I took my heart in my hand.

There is a wonderful poignancy in the repeated exhibition
of that heart—to self, man and to God. Everywhere the
poetic result is beautiful, but it is in the second part—where
the heart is exposed to man—that she sounds an unusual
note of short but bitter irony:

> You took my heart in your hand
> With a friendly smile,
> With a critical eye you scanned,
> Then set it down,
> And said: It is still unripe,
> Better wait awhile;
> Wait till the skylarks pipe,
> Till the corn grows brown.

As you set it down it broke—
     Broke, but I did not wince;
I smiled at the speech you spoke,
     At your judgment that I heard;
But I have not often smiled
     Since then, nor questioned since,
Nor cared for corn-flowers wild,
     Nor sung with the singing bird.

There are many poems where she painted in dim colours her own quiet story. It appears with an exquisite simplicity in *May* or the later *Love Said 'Nay.'* *Autumn* is a longer and richer reproduction of the same theme. She displays the intangible temper of her mind in *A Wish*, with its expressed desires to be an invisible bird, the "song once heard," the wind-stirred shadow of a lily, the echo of a loving word, or memory of the deferred hope. There is a more deliberate restraint, a smouldering passion, in poems like *Memory*. In *Somewhere or Other* she sings softly what she cried sharply in *The Heart Knoweth its Own Bitterness*—the isolation of the human spirit, and its yearning for kindred sympathies.

In *Uphill* she escapes from a purely private outlook into the articulation of a more universal weariness and aspiration. There is the same kinship with common humanity in the powerful serenity of a later poem—

Lord grant us calm, if calm can set forth Thee;
     Or tempest, if a tempest set Thee forth.

This characteristic firmness can never be forgotten. However low her music may be, it is never feeble.—"Out of the strong came forth sweetness."

Detailed examination of *Monna Innominata* is impossible in this place. It is, I think, the only instance of her yielding to imagination of the might-have-been—love rendered without any pang of renunciation. She achieves here not the affectation of simplicity, but simplicity itself—a frankness, an intimacy, a closeness of touch which seems to bridge the chasms isolating spirit from spirit. In the structure of the sonnet there appears to be some element which retains echoes of former harmonies, and vibrates with the promise of music still unborn. As we read, our minds are sometimes lifted

back to the world of Shakespeare's sonnets; at another moment
they slip forward to the newer music of Mrs Alice Meynell;
everywhere we are reminded of Mrs Browning. Still, while
we hear these voices blending with Christina's it is only as
accompaniment or chorus; hers is the solo part. For a few
lines in the centre of the seventh sonnet Christina's music is
silent, and we seem to hear Shakespeare's voice re-telling
his great theme:

> Let me not to the marriage of true minds
> Admit impediments;

but it is Christina's voice which begins and ends the poem—
all else is a digression. The second sonnet is very like
Mrs Meynell's *Unmarked Festival*, but in lower, richer
chords. The third sonnet again is like her *Renouncement*,
though hardly so beautiful; but there is a note of self-
revelation in Christina's poem, and this gives it a distinctive
touch:

> I blush again, who waking look so wan.

Indeed the most perfect of her sonnets are those where she
speaks alone, and the other voices are still; sonnets like the
eleventh, where she appeals to the final verdict of Eternity;
or the peerless twelfth—so reticent that it hushes excited
words of admiration. It is a rich and consummate version
of the earlier *Remember*. Possibly she never wrote anything
more gracious and penetrating than its concluding lines:

> Your honourable freedom makes me free,
> And you companioned, I am not alone.

Christina's stifled intensity pressed forward at odd
moments in single lines and phrases. It broke out, for instance, in the sudden cry of her nun—

> My life is breaking like a cloud.

Nevertheless it is remarkable that at certain periods of her
life she seemed to write more sternly, more solemnly than
others. It may be that there was some external crisis, unknown to us, which accounted for these moods. With the
biographical materials at our disposal it is hard to assign an
exact psychological reason for the fact that between the

ages of twenty and thirty the passionate quality—and quantity—of her work exceeds that of any other period. There is a certain interest in tracing the line of her life with special reference to a few high, sharp summits of emotion.

In 1849 we see, I think for the first time, the prospect of strong passion. *One Certainty* struck deeper tones of her music, a solemn crescendo that rose, then faded away into stillness. As yet the music was neither loud nor vigorous; but it came like the opening chords of an overture, with the suggestion of something greater to follow.

In 1851 *The Three Enemies* gave a token of religious duty intensely conceived and accepted. There is something which rankles in the simple, searching words of temptation— "Sweet, thou art pale....Thou drinkest deep." A latent power works beneath the outward calm of the answers repelling the Flesh, the World, and the Devil.

In 1854 came the firm portraiture of *A Soul*—

Indomitable in her feebleness.

Here again we approach still closer to the shores of deep, passionate waters.

In 1856 the utterance became more definite. She sang of one "*Shut Out*" from joy. Behind the curbed words we can feel the throbbing of fierce pain.

In the following year she wrote on the same day—the thirtieth of June—two poems of scorching intensity. One was *Introspective*, with its short stabbing sentences, its imagery of desolation; the other was *A Better Resurrection*, written with the same curtness of style, while the soul, stung with its own emptiness, pleads with an ever-increasing fervour, each petition rising higher in spiritual compass: "O Jesus, quicken me....O Jesus, rise in me....O Jesus, drink of me." In August of the same year she wrote *A Birthday*—the single instance in her work of a great poem completely happy. Yet with a fine insight Mr Edmund Gosse has described the reader's reaction from such an overpowering joy: "The impression which its cumulative ecstasy leaves on the nerves is almost pathetic."

The Convent Threshold, certainly the most highly-strung

of all her long poems, was written in July 1858. In October came the most appealing and potent version of an often repeated conception—Christ pleading with the human soul. *The Love of Christ which Passeth Knowledge*—so impassioned, so terse, and so tender—seems too sacred for discussion. It may be observed that six years later she returned in *Despised and Rejected* to the same appeal, made more poignant by rejection. But in the later poem, great though it may be, there is not the same smiting intensity.

In 1860, on the last day of the year, Christina wrote what her brother William considered her supreme poem—*Passing Away, Saith the World*. The sonorous and majestic sweep of her music rises slowly to the culminating speech of God. Most impressive of all is the almost inarticulate awe, the dumbness of response, which falls like a hush on the concluding line of each stanza—

Then I answered: Yea.

About twenty-two years later Christina returned in *An Old-World Thicket* to the fierce probing of her own grief. Nowhere else has she—or perhaps any other writer—expressed more poignantly the ultimate bitterness of defeat, devitalising the soul:

Each sore defeat of my defeated life
Faced and outfaced me in that bitter hour;
And turned to yearning palsy all my power,
And all my peace to strife,
Self stabbing self with keen lack-pity knife.

The indifference of external nature—its "jubilee" and "mere content"—stings the soul to hot and barren anger. After that comes a pause in the intensity, a stage of helpless questioning. To this succeeds a passion for extinction, an overwhelming desire to be done with things for ever—

That which ends not who shall brave or mend?

This burden of Eternity presses on the soul. How shall it "face the perpetual Now"? It was characteristic of Christina that she did not try to argue herself out of misery. She believed in something which transcends argument. The dark mood passed, and she attempted no explanation. A dim music stirred within her, till, like Saul, she was "refreshed," and the evil spirit departed. The warm beauty of sunset stilled the tempest of her spirit, filled and soothed her heart. Sometimes it appears as if the concluding peace of the poem does not ring with the same earnestness and truth as the expression of her despair. If we wish to understand Christina's utmost capacity for suffering, we must go to *An Old-World Thicket*; we do not find in it the sources of her strength. To the sympathetic reader they are an open secret.

V

GENERAL CONSIDERATIONS

WE have spoken of the sympathetic reader; but to many readers Christina Rossetti is uncongenial. She is not now, and probably never will be, widely popular. She has been accused, and truly, of limitation. From her, far more than from Wordsworth, who received the same criticism, "one half the world escapes." Readers complain because it is their half of the world which is neglected. Most people who go to Christina Rossetti, hoping to find a reflection of their own attitude, will meet with swift disappointment. If we are at all like the common run of people, we cannot expect her to represent us. But surely poetry is something more than a reader's looking-glass. It is a poor sort of occupation to sit studying ourselves in the mirror of a poet's mind, when we might be watching, not our own, but another "human face divine." We go to Christina seeking an escape from ourselves. We cross our limiting frontiers, and pass into her province. But, if we travel sympathetically, we are amazed at the familiarity of a common humanity. We do not lose ourselves in following her; we come back to ourselves, enriched by absence. In our own minds we repeat the experience of the discoverers on the high seas:

> Leaving their home behind them,
> By a road of splendour and thunder,
> They came to their home in amazement,
> Simply by sailing on.

It may be objected that it is not a long journey, and that much gathered on the way is of the same type. This must be admitted. Still, if the type is excellent, it seems rather querulous to demand more variety; and it is beyond all controversy that Christina's treasure is unsurpassed in its own kind. If we do not like the type, the charge of limitation can be levelled against ourselves.

"Still," exclaim some, "it is not the limitation that we criticise. We are prepared to admit that—

> In short measures life may perfect be.

What we condemn is the isolation of outlook in these poems. The supreme poets are closest to common things; they praise the daisy as well as the rose." There is only one answer to this censure: Christina was not isolated from all common things—from love, or death, or the "undying fire" of religion. It is true that she seemed to stand far away. For instance she wrote of Nature, in London, looking out from a back bedroom to "the tall dingy walls of adjacent houses"; yet she described the distant country vividly and freshly, and apparently without consciousness of the streets beneath her window. To Christina Rossetti distance implied no inevitable estrangement. She was sometimes most near when she seemed most remote. She may have been far from the restless surface of life, so—

> Dull with din of what and where and why;
> (*For One Sake*.)

but she reached below storm to the calm, untroubled depths—

> Depths no storm can pierce, pierced with a shaft of the sun.

The claim made by Christina Rossetti is something which cannot be demonstrated. Argument never evokes sympathy. Still it is possible to render absolute proof that her craftsmanship was worthy of all honour; and respect is sometimes an approach towards love. No competent critic has failed to recognise the formal excellence of Christina Rossetti's poetry. The general characteristics of her technique were an extreme daring united to a surprising freedom from accidents. Though daring she was not rash. She leaped across barriers, but never without looking. In our study, which is necessarily limited, we shall have to content ourselves with pointing out a few noteworthy features.

Her single lines are remarkably varied in form. Professor Saintsbury has declared the *Sleep at Sea* stanza to be example of alternating rhythms—a dactylic-trochaic passing like a pendulum towards the succeeding

line, and then swinging back to itself. This contrasting
rhythm harmonises effectively with the sharply contrasted
conceptions of the poem.—This concerns the character of
the line as a whole. But Christina makes full use of the
capacity for music latent in single words. Sometimes she
draws out and combines the tones of rich, deep vowels—

> Cool shadows deepen
> Across the sleeping face.
>
> *(Dream Love.)*

At other times she shifts her emphasis from consonants to
vowels, with a set purpose in view:

> It *breaks the* sun*light bound* on *bound*;
> Goes *singing as* it *leaps* along
> To sheep-bells with a dreamy sound
> A dreamy song.
>
> *(Fata Morgana.)*

In the first two lines the quick leaping effect is largely due to
the hard consonants—*b, k, t, d, g*; the *l*'s give a curving grace
to the movement. In the last two lines the full vowels slow
down the time from *andante* to *adagio*. Of course there are
hard consonants in the second half, and full vowels in the
first; but they have less effect on the character of the rhythm.
—Some of Christina's lines seem moulded into curves; and
this is often due to her use of pauses to mark the completion
of each stage in her design. We have already noticed the
swaying, pendulum effect of the lines from *The Prince's
Progress*:

> The long hours go || and come || and go; ||
> The bride || she sleepeth, || waketh, || sleepeth. ||

In *Birds of Paradise*, by this device alone, she imparts to a
series of three identical words the effect of soaring movement:

> Mounting, || mounting, || mounting still, ||
> In haste to scale the skies.

It may be noticed in passing that ease in upward motion,
suggested by the first line, is assisted by vowel effects. In
the second line, difficulty is emphasised by means of guttural
consonants.

Passing on from consideration of the single line, we

come to the grouping of lines into stanzas. This we can regard from two points of view: varying lengths of lines; varying ends of lines—or rhymes.

The most noteworthy feature of Christina Rossetti's line-lengths is her use of the shortened final line. Sometimes, as in *Dreamland*, the shortened lines appear throughout the course of the stanza, giving to it an elasticity of movement— a series of expansions and contractions. But the shortened line at the end of the stanza is—if not a more frequent— a more significant, device. It marks a culmination—and not one of loud, strong chords. Most of Christina's melodies fade away. They are like Tennyson's echoing bugle notes which "*faint* on hill and river." This was characteristic of Christina. She wanted to finish quietly. These dying rhythms of hers are in a way symbolic of her whole attitude towards death as the final silence. She would have wished, like Keats, to pass quietly:

> Now more than ever seems it rich to die,
> To cease upon the midnight with no pain.

In the ceasing of her stanzas there is the suggestion of rich and painless death. They move quietly to their end. The stanza already quoted from *Fata Morgana* would serve as illustration.—Sometimes the shortened line carries with it another implication. In *Passing Away* the great music of God's message swells and fades to its close. The human voice can only respond in the faintest of echoes:

> Then I answered: Yea.

Finally we come to the question of rhyme; but this is too complicated a matter to be discussed at length. We could investigate Christina's effective use of passionate driving couplets in such poems as *Introspective*, or we could study the pulsing quintets of *An Old-World Thicket*. We could lose ourselves trying to follow out the rhyme-patterns of *The Convent Threshold* or *Goblin Market*. But to these things there is no end. We must concentrate on one point alone—Christina's fondness for repeated sounds. She loved to swing back on to previous notes. We find this tendency in the poem already quoted—*My Love, Whose Heart is*

Tender. Here there are only two rhymes in a poem of twelve lines; and of these six are double rhymes. Indeed there is a seventh, if we count a word in the first line, rhyming internally to the end of the second:

My love, whose heart is *tender*, said to me,
"A moon lacks light, except her sun be*friend her.*"

These mathematical computations, so perilous to the soul of poetry, are made to demonstrate Christina's extraordinary command over words. We shall take only one more instance of repeated rhymes, and this from a supreme poem. There is a single rhyme, twelve times repeated, in the wonderful *Marvel of Marvels*; and even that note re-echoes through separate lines:

O saints, my beloved, now *mould*ering to *mould* in the *mould.*

But there is no monotony in this magnificent tolling music. The rich bell-tones are deeply satisfying to the spirit. Here the music does not die away; it rings out to the last vibrating peal:

Cold it is, O my King, how *cold* alone on the *wold.*

The concluding line throbs as if possessed with the glory of a single beautiful tone.

Technique like this stands high above the stigma of "mechanism." It is sometimes urged that the poet's technique is his instrument; and the instrument is subsidiary to the performer. Yet the poet is singular, because he usually makes his own instrument. Like Abt Vogler, he is "extemporising on an organ of his own invention." Christina Rossetti had sufficient respect for her art to fashion in its honour a very perfect instrument.

* * * * *

Sometimes the instrument survives the performer. It may be refashioned by another performer for his own use; its mechanism may provide hints for some future "maker." Christina's metrical devices will probably be perpetuated; or—what is more vital—her fondness for metrical experiment will be passed on to poets of the future. As for her spirit: will it also live again? This is a difficult question. We are too near her in time to estimate the extent of her influence.

It is unlikely that anybody with such an exceptional life and outlook as Christina's should exercise a dominating influence over any other poet of normal experience. Still it may be urged that no poet receives experience in the normal fashion of meaner men. The exceptional thing about Christina Rossetti was not her experience; it was herself. We cannot yet discern the scope of her influence upon more recent poets of the inner life—Francis Thompson or Mrs Meynell. It is certain that the former did not learn her simplicity. If she passed anything on to Francis Thompson it was the almost tropical heat of emotion which over-ran his art; he lacked the severity with which she restrained her fires. Superficial resemblances to Mrs Meynell may be misleading. We have her own testimony that *An Unmarked Festival* was written absolutely without knowledge of Christina's poem almost identical in conception—the second sonnet of *Monna Innominata*. Mrs Meynell has a certain affinity with Christina's quiet precision and delicate simplicity; yet we do not feel with her, as with Christina, that something tumultuous is being held back. For her this stillness of mood seems a natural self-expression; with Christina it was an achievement of discipline. The resemblances of both these writers to Christina Rossetti are confined to inborn qualities of mind and soul—things which cannot be transmitted. What they might have learned from one another was a mode of handling or developing their points of resemblance; but this they did not do. In original temperament or choice of subject they are sometimes alike; but not in manner of self-expression.

Yet we return to Mrs Meynell as the kind of person best fitted to apprehend Christina's ultimate secrets. Her essay, "The Rhythm of Life," contains a sentence which, applied to mystics in general, deepens our understanding of the individual mystic.—"The souls of certain of the saints, being singularly simple and single, have been in the most complete subjection to the law of periodicity."—It is that word "periodicity" which interprets Christina to us. It saves us from any shallow condemnation of her "inequality." We do not call the sea unequal because it ebbs and flows. This coming and going, rising and falling, is a feature of "living" water; if we want regularity and equality, we must go to the stagnant pool. A slurred note follows the accented beat, a rest the phrase of melody. Some modern musicians lay great stress on the beauty of flowing, continuous rhythms; in Christina Rossetti's poetic output there is something which curves and flows. It would be quite possible to draw the graph of her inner life, taking as our basis of measurement the relative intensity of her poems. Or we might draw our line on the basis of subject-matter; it would be constantly curving back to the same topics—renunciation or death; and it would always wind within the strongly defined circle of religion. Christina Rossetti may have written a few poems very close to the circumference of that circle; but none of them crossed it into the "secular" territory beyond.

Yet no matter on what basis we drew our curves, we should soon discover that they were not absolutely symmetrical. There was a pulse in Christina's poetry; and that was a token of its vitality. But the pulse was intermittent. It beat rapidly between the years 1850 and 1860; after 1867 it became slower and fainter. "The law of periodicity" cannot explain everything in Christina Rossetti. These variations in her intensity cannot be estimated solely in terms of the mystical temperament. And of this we are glad. It is good to feel that Christina, so self-contained and lonely, was capable of receiving an external impression; still more, that her whole life could be changed by an external influence. Her poems are full of introspective emotion; but they also prove to us that she could love with all her strength something outside herself. She loved Mr Cayley; and that is why 1867, the year which ended their closest intimacy, marks the zenith of her course; all after that slopes down towards the sunset. From that time onwards, no human influences appear to have shaken her to the core of her being; but she looked out from herself to the visions of the spirit.

Any apparent contradictions and inconsistencies are a moving testimony to her genuine humanity. Though she was an ascetic, her poems are rich in colour and picture. Though she seemed indifferent to the external world, she took its objects as symbols of spiritual truth. Though she became independent of man, she clung to the feet of God. So we leave her—as a human figure, not a mere piece on the chessboard of literary progress. It is for her own sake that we prize her. She may or may not possess a historical significance. In our day we cannot make absolute judgments. It seems probable that the future verdict on Christina Rossetti will assert her extraordinary aloofness from currents of literary progress; she will be remembered as a solitary, exquisite flower, blooming for a season, fading, and casting no seed.

CONCLUSION

The Attitude to Tradition. "Don't let us shut our minds to the infinite possibilities of existence." These words, taken from a recent scientific lecture, would have suited the temper of the Romantic Movement in English Literature. Where the modern scientist considers the latent possibilities of man in his relation to the physical world, the Romantic writers of the late eighteenth and early nineteenth centuries were awakening to the resources within itself of the human mind—its powers of introspection, imagination, and reflection. Men then felt themselves on the edge of new discoveries—on the frontiers of new worlds. These worlds possessed for them an additional allurement and magic; they were radiant in all the glory of their spring season—

The dauntless youth of the year.

While Jane Austen wrote, their trees were budding; but she rarely looked through her windows to the open blossoming spaces; she did not walk out of doors to hear "spring singing in the woods." Nevertheless some scents and echoes of this awakening beauty must have penetrated the walls of her quiet chambers; she could not escape from the quickening influences of the pure strong sunlight.

Spring passed into summer. The Romantic Movement grew up from adolescence into maturity; and with that came a significant change of name. We speak of the writers of the Romantic *Movement*—thereby suggesting that they were passing onwards to some goal; when we mention the writers of the Victorian *Period*, we imply that they had come to a halt, they had reached a destination. Victorianism cannot be regarded as the final goal of Romanticism; for the essential quality of all Romantic art or thought is its love of the never-ending quest. Victorianism marked a stage in the journey. From it we can look back over the road and the country behind us; and as we step out from the Victorian tradition, we can look forward to new highways and footpaths awaiting the adventurers of Romance.

We can never be sure that anything is impossible. This is the keynote of many Romantic melodies. By the end of the Victorian period the world had to acknowledge the disappearance of many traditions of apparent impossibility. One of them—not the greatest perhaps, but still not the least—was the tradition that a woman-writer is by the very nature of things something abnormal and altogether unnecessary. The woman-writer had made herself indispensable.

This tradition, however, did not die of old age; it had to be fought. Every woman-writer except Mrs Gaskell and Christina Rossetti had to deal with it; and, as we have seen, they escaped from convention by the simple expedient of paying no attention to it. Mrs Gaskell had a husband who lectured on English literature, and took a deep interest in her writings. In this way she heard less of the tradition than other women who received no daily encouragement. Even Christina might not have escaped, if she had not happened to be born late in time, and into the midst of a literary circle. It is rather instructive to observe how different women dealt with this problem of opposition. Jane Austen made fun of it; we have quoted already (p. 24) her remarks on the necessity for feminine ignorance. Nevertheless she took precautions. She often assumed an air of simplicity to beguile the ranks of the stupid; and she never interfered with "masculine" topics. This was partly a matter of free choice; but it was also quite possibly a case of discretion. Jane Austen must have revelled in breaking the established conventions with such an air of innocent decorum.

With the Brontes, it was entirely different. Emily probably felt that as she was already singular in so many points she could quite well afford to be singular in this also. But in a most intimate, personal way, Charlotte was brought up against the tradition. In early life she was discouraged by Southey's letter; and in later days she discovered that her husband did not consider novel-writing a wifely attribute. Charlotte had a particularly difficult problem before her. It is comparatively easy to ignore a convention if one is sure that it is nothing else; but Charlotte had to be certain whether in opposing this tradition, she was not fighting against nature. With great conflict of spirit she proved to herself and to the world that she stood on the side of nature. She was not un-sexed by her vocation. It was all the other way; for her art enriched her womanly charm. From the very beginning she knew things would be difficult. She prepared for obstacles, but did not compromise with them. Though she and her sisters disguised their names, they adopted no specifically masculine title: Currer, Ellis, and Acton are not "boys'" names. In their methods of writing they made no attempt to disguise their sex.

With Mary Ann Evans, strange to say, there was a distinct note of compromise. She called herself "*George* Eliot"; and she wrote like a man. Consciously or not, she adopted a great deal of the masculine point of view. In many ways she was a formidable character. Her personality, just because it was not quite natural, carried with it a certain suggestion of awe. It was in her nature to be conscientious. Even if she had been under no sex handicap, she would have worked with an excessive strain. But as it was, the fact of her sex put upon her the necessity for additional effort. She had to prove herself equal to men; thus she could afford to neglect no opportunities for self-culture. She attempted to live down the tradition; Mrs Browning argued about it. Whereas men have been content with an easy disregard of conventions, women, in the past anyhow, seem to have defied them. A woman usually appears conscious of doing anything at all "Bohemian." She may enjoy the sensation, or she may fear it; but she cannot take it for granted. This feminine tendency deepened the self-conscious note in the writings of Victorian women.

The Fact of Limitation. A tradition may be attacked and confounded; but there is no escape from facts. Women could not write long without realising that in certain things they could not be the same as men. They lacked for one thing the inherited tradition of adventure. More than this, they lacked, and always will lack, the faculty for particular types of adventure. There are certain zests—chiefly in the direction of powerful physical energy—from which women are debarred. They cannot fight in battle—which is no great deprivation. They cannot go on exploring parties to the South Pole, or to the top of Mount Everest. At least no woman has yet been discovered with sufficient physical qualifications for such feats. Some enthusiasts, no doubt, will have it that the woman's story is only beginning, and no limits can be assigned to the scope of her future possibilities. That may or may not be true. Looking on the plain facts of the past and present, it does not seem likely that women of the future will ever be absolutely free from certain disabilities and limitations. In any case these conjectures have no connection with Victorian women. Whatever future women may be like, the Victorians had to accept the facts of limitation; and nearly all of them spoke directly on the subject.

As we have seen, all these women fell back upon personal experience. Even George Eliot with all her desire for the impersonal escape, had some pages steeped in reminiscence; and it was through them that she spoke home to the hearts of her readers. These women usually handled common experience in an uplifted fashion. Mrs Gaskell alone touched it with familiar, loving fingers. Jane Austen looked down on it with amusement; Charlotte Bronte—and Emily also— looked beyond it to wide high spaces of the imagination; and George Eliot drew it up towards the altars of artistic consecration. Charlotte Bronte also took her sex as a position of detached observation. We have already noted (p. 53) how she betrayed femininity by the "intensity" with which she described men's faces. The women-writers succeeded only when they submitted to the facts of restriction. George Eliot failed when she struggled to experience all things known to all men. Christina Rossetti and Mrs Gaskell succeeded because they, more than any others, bowed to their destiny.

Women, because of their limitations, are prone to detail. But detail is not always insignificant. Intellectually Portia was no match for Shylock; she could not argue against him. But sheer weight, even of intellect, does not always win the day. How poor a thing was a drop of blood in comparison

with Shylock's overwhelming passion for revenge! Still, like a
woman, she gained her purpose by means of a small weapon.—

> Shed thou no blood; nor cut thou less nor more,
> But just a pound of flesh; if thou tak'st more
> Or less than a just pound,—be it but so much
> As makes it light or heavy, in the substance
> Or the division of the twentieth part
> Of one poor scruple, nay, if the scale do turn
> But in the estimation of a hair,
> Thou diest, and all thy goods are confiscate.

"The twentieth part of one poor scruple"—"the estimation
of a hair"—these are trifles indeed. But think of the consequence which they can bring to pass: "*Thou diest.*" All
great writers have appreciated the significance of trifles;
but women-writers in particular have felt the importance of
apparent triviality. Jane Austen indeed was a specialist in
"small goods"; and almost every woman who came after
her inherited something of the same faculty.

Attraction for the individual rather than for the crowd is
a feature of the smaller feminine outlook. Women, said
Romney Leigh, are "personal and passionate." The choice
between the impersonal cause and the individual affection
seems a specific woman's problem. There is the charity
which begins at home and stays there; and there is the more
official charity which goes abroad to meetings. Though some
women succeed in combining both forms, a great many have
to decide for one or the other. It will be observed that most
of the Victorian women chose the home-keeping, personal
variety. They were more stirred by personalities than movements, and charity towards the individual came more in
their way than charities for the multitude. The life of a single
soul meant more to Christina Rossetti than aspirations after
the Kingdom of God.—George Eliot probably had the widest
form of sympathy. She felt the stimulus of great causes
without losing the faculty for whole-hearted private compassion. A wide horizon seemed to deepen in her the sense
of pity; this was, in her generation, a rare and difficult
achievement.—"It is you only," cried Ruskin to the women
of that day, "who can feel the depths of pain, and conceive

the way of its healing. Instead of trying to do this, you turn away from it; you shut yourselves within your park walls and garden gates; and you are content to know that there is beyond them a whole world in wilderness—a world of secrets which you dare not penetrate; and of suffering which you dare not conceive." This reproach might have been levelled with justice at the Brontes or Christina Rossetti, but not at Mrs Gaskell, George Eliot, or Mrs Browning. Mrs Gaskell's practice fitted Ruskin's ideal of womanly service. Mrs Browning went out with the best of intentions, but she was not equipped for the wilderness. George Eliot was well prepared for rough journeys. She did not, like Mrs Gaskell, enter the wilderness of which Ruskin spoke—the region of social abuses; but she passed through the deserts of human perplexity.

Charlotte Bronte, it is true, justified her personal attitude to art. Her reference to Mrs Beecher Stowe (quoted on p. 44) is deeply significant. The iron of slavery had entered her soul in childhood—and that was her qualification for speech. Charlotte distrusted anything like a "made-up" emotion. If she had been brought into personal contact with slavery, she would have written something like *Uncle Tom's Cabin*. But as things were, even if she had gone out of her way to study the slave question, she could never have written of it "from the inside." She resolved on this point:—if the experience of wider movements were sent to her she would turn it to account; if not, she would have to do without it.—It has been said that women are appreciative rather than creative. Up to a certain point Charlotte Bronte would have agreed with this statement. She would have agreed that women cannot in all ways create their intellectual environment; their intuitions are of more worth than any artificial sympathies acquired through instruction. By their intuitions they can appreciate and interpret the experience which comes to them. To the plots of her novels she added hardly anything that fell out of her experience; she created very little in the way of character or episode. She did not manufacture her materials; the originality lay in her methods of handling the raw material of experience. George Eliot both created and interpreted; but as we have suggested she was a "masculine" woman.

General Feminine Characteristics. I think it will be agreed that Mrs Gaskell and Charlotte Bronte were by far the most "womanly" of all the writers selected for this study. Without labouring the point in their favour, we may consider some of the obvious feminine characteristics of the entire group.

Beyond all controversy is the contention that the woman's vocation is closely bound up with service. She is here to make the world a more comfortable place than it would be without her. Most of these women entered on this vocation, but from different points of approach. Jane Austen provides for us the solace of a perfect courtesy; hers is the quietness of a well-bred hostess. Mrs Gaskell invites her readers to the shelter of a soothing, congenial friendship Charlotte Bronte's intimate confidences take her listeners out of themselves. From Emily Bronte we get little actual comfort, unless it be in her pictures of high windy moors where she herself sought refuge from the fret of daily care. In George Eliot we find a wide and deep compassion; it is not indeed the instinctive sympathy which Mrs Gaskell and Charlotte Bronte would have rendered to certain types of suffering. George Eliot's tenderness was based, not on impulse, but on justice. She was ready to administer the blame which all of us deserve; but she was swift to feel our crying need for pity. Mrs Browning and Anne Bronte were of that rather ineffective type known as "sweet women." Of the former particularly we feel that she was "too sweet to be wholesome." She over-emphasised one aspect of the woman's vocation. Finally, Christina Rossetti takes us into a place of shelter from the noise and strife of tongues. She soothes us with the peace of her reserved and gracious stillness.

It is strange that these women, who provide a retreat for us of larger growth, should so often appear lacking in the love for little children. It is true that there were exceptions. George Eliot loved children, and so did Christina Rossetti; Mrs Browning was an affectionate, Mrs Gaskell a wise and affectionate, mother. But the others seem to have left children very much out of account. Jane Austen used them as accessories; Charlotte Bronte understood them only when they were too old for their years; and Emily seems to have left them very much to one side; we never feel that the younger Catherine or Hareton are childlike in anything except their helplessness. This neglect is particularly surprising in Charlotte Bronte who, for all her incapacity to understand children, remained to the end most childlike and eager at heart. The explanation probably lies in the fact that the Brontes knew little of children—not until they became governesses —and they would not cherish any artificial sentiment. The woman's protective instinct, and tenderness towards frailty, found another outlet. They all loved animals. They would have loved children also, if they had been given the chance.

How far did these women share in what is specifically known as the woman's mood or temperament? And what, indeed, is the mark of that temperament?—This is a controversial—almost a perilous—question. But it is fairly safe to say that women, as a sex, are distinguished by a remarkable sensibility. We are often told—with what truth cannot be proved—that women, being more excitable than men, are at "the bottom of every row." American psychologists have recently made the discovery that women are more sensitive than men to the feeling of guilt. Moreover they are acutely sensitive to atmosphere or environment. If they are less logical than men, they are probably more imaginative. Many of these statements repeat popular conceptions, which may or may not be beyond contradiction. The fact remains that most of them have obtained wide credence; and they all contribute to the conclusion which hardly anybody would deny—that women are distinguished by a peculiarly sensitive quality. The explanation may lie in the very fact of their limitations. If they are shut out from certain experiences free to men, they will at least make the best of what they can get. They will bring to their smaller experience some vital quality which will make it glow. Women often "put more into" their ordinary living than men. We find in Charlotte Bronte a constant hunger for activity. She had no means of appeasing it; and so she did the next best thing. She forgot herself in following the activities of other people. As we have observed, she loved watching excitement.—She had to feel things living. Even her words partook of this vitality; Lucy's "sallow" dictionary and "worn-out" grammar are instances in point. As the pagan felt woods and streams filled with living tokens of a Divine presence, so Charlotte seemed to feel her words vibrating under her touch. The same quality appears in the character of her imagination, and the strange potency of her intuitions. What was true of her applies also to Emily. Both sisters seemed to have within them an alchemy which transformed and vitalised whatever came near it.

Looking backwards we see that if Jane Austen possessed any of this feminine love of excitement, she held it strictly within bounds; there *was* excitement in her favourite game of matrimony, though she kept so cool about it. Mrs Gaskell also was cautious lest her feelings should evaporate in words; she closed them in behind the doorways of speech, that they might grow in secret to a greater fullness of life. She nurtured them, moreover, in the health-giving atmosphere of intimate family affections. The woman's heart in her went out to the graces and comforts of home. Looking forward again, we see George Eliot not excitable certainly, but deeply sensitive. She was acutely aware of her environment, and this is a feminine quality. A woman cares far more than a man for the furnishings not only of her rooms, but of her entire life. Lamb, as we know, was prone to tease Wordsworth about his dependence on the backgrounds of Nature. "The earth, sea, and sky," he remarked, "...is but as a house to dwell in." Manlike, he declared himself indifferent to the fittings of the house, so long as he found within it congenial company. But George Eliot had the woman's concern in all questions of "furniture." She always saw her figures moving across a background—either of Nature or of human association; and she saw to it that the background was in keeping. This was a womanly characteristic which she shared with Jane Austen, so fully awake to the "feeling" of things; and also with the Brontes who possessed it as all other qualities, with a greater degree of intensity. The "atmosphere" of an episode was taken to their hearts; they endowed it with their own unique emotions.

Finally we recall the sensitive quality of Christina Rossetti's poetry. This we have treated so fully that there is no need for much further comment. If it be true that the woman is by nature dependent on individual experience, it is evident that she is fitted for the lyric cry of personal feeling. In this expression of the solitary, inner life, Christina rose to heights which have rarely—if ever—been surpassed. There was, moreover, something specifically feminine in her type of religious outlook. This is not to say that all, or indeed many, women share the same outlook; it simply means that a stranger, ignorant of her sex, would detect in her religious poems an indefinite quality, unlike anything found in the similar work of men. This would be her personal clinging quality of devotion—a quality found, it is true, in the mysticism of several men, but never in quite the same fashion. Christina sounded the same melodies, but pitched them in a different key; and something in this alteration of the pitch produced an indescribable change in the character of the emotion.

It would be a rash conjecture to assume that women of the future will proceed along Victorian lines. At that time there was in the air an antagonism which made women afraid to be themselves. In their struggle for self-expression they frequently, and quite naturally, failed to discriminate between equality and identity with man. They were apt to accept the male standard, instead of creating a new one for themselves. Now that the day of antagonism is over, it is much easier for women to be unaffected. Moreover, many of the restrictions laid upon women are passing away; and with the new liberty comes the new possibility. We can never measure the consequences of freedom. The descendants of great liberators often move far from the outlook and ideals of their ancestors. But if they belong to the true stock, there always clings to them some worthy survival of the old tradition. It was in the plan of the fathers that the sons should move onwards. They accept their inheritance of progress, but no matter how far they may travel, they retain a portion of their birthright; and the blood stirs within them as they look back proudly to the distant hills of home.

INDEX

Addison, 26, 53, 113
Aristotle, 162
Arnold, Matthew, 45, 186, 213
Athenaeum, 215
Augustine, 239
Austen, Jane, 1–27
General references: 29–32, 39, 41, 44, 49, 120, 125, 142, 157–8, 162, 187–9, 206, 275–6, 278–9, 281–3
Works: *Emma*, 1–2, 4–7, 11–12, 17–20, 111, 198; *Mansfield Park*, 1–3, 7–8, 10, 13, 16–18, 22–24; *Northanger Abbey*, 1, 9–10, 14–18, 21, 23–4, 189; *Persuasion*, 1, 23–25, 188; *Pride and Prejudice*, 1, 2, 6–8, 11, 17, 19, 21, 23–4, 30, 118; *Sense and Sensibility*, 1, 7–8, 14, 18, 21–22

Bagehot, W., 173
Bennett, Arnold, 193
Benson, A. C., 236
Blake, 39, 90
Boccaccio, 215
Borrow, George, 39
Brock, C. E., 35
Brontes, The, 28–99
General references: 26, 103, 104, 210, 229–30, 276, 280, 283
Bronte, Anne, 35–7
General reference: 281
Works: *Agnes Grey*, 35; *The Tenant of Wildfell Hall*, 33, 35, 36, 47, 52
Bronte, Charlotte, 38–76
General references: 2–4, 13, 15, 17, 19, 25, 77–80, 84, 96–8, 100 *n.*, 103, 129–30, 139, 142, 151, 154, 157–60, 166, 168, 172, 174, 204–6, 230, 249, 276–8, 280–3
Works: *Jane Eyre*, 29, 31, 38–41, 43–44, 48–53, 55, 57–73, 98, 103, 105, 112, 125, 178, 204–6, 212; *Shirley*, 30, 43–4, 49, 52, 55–8, 61, 65–6, 68–70, 77, 159; *The Moores*, 49, 55, 64, 65; *The Professor*, 52, 55; *Villette*, 38, 43–52, 54–5, 59, 61, 63–66, 69–74, 98, 138, 196, 204, 283
Bronte, Emily, 77–99
General references: 45, 142, 229, 276, 278, 281–3
Works: *Wuthering Heights*, 36, 43, 46, 48, 52, 55, 78–87, 88–9, 98–9; *Poems*, 87–97
Reference, among other poems, to: *Death*, 95; *Remembrance*, 95; *Self-Interrogation*, 94; *The Old Stoic*, 95; *The Philosopher*, 94; *The Prisoner*, 96; *The Visionary*, 90
Brooke, Rupert, 236
Browning, Mrs E. B., 209–32
General references: 42, 246–51, 263, 277, 279–81
Works:
Reference, among other poems, to: *Aurora Leigh*, 211–2, 214–6, 228, 247–51; *Casa Guidi Windows*, 213, 218–19, 226; *Catarina to Camoens*, 226; *Drama of Exile*, 218, 221–3, 246; *Sonnets from the Portuguese*, 210, 225–7, 247; *The Cry of the Children*, 217; *The Dead Pan*, 223
Browning, Robert, 197, 202–3, 209–10, 212, 215, 217, 221, 224–8, 231–2, 238–9, 250–1, 256, 258, 271
Bunyan, 30, 244
Burne-Jones, Mrs, 164
Burney, Frances, 1, 26
Burns, 76, 256

Carlyle, Jane Welsh, 168, 186

Carlyle, Thomas, 38, 41, 228, 239
Cayley, C. B., 235, 237, 273
Cervantes, 14, 72
Chaucer, 11
Chesterton, G. K., 41, 53, 113
Coleridge, 32, 230–1, 245
Collinson, James, 234
Colvin, Sir Sidney, 242
Cornhill Magazine, 156, 216
Crabbe, 160
Crashaw, 244
Cromwell, 74
Cross, J. W., 164, 185

Dante, 79, 156, 168, 183, 239, 240–2, 244–5, 254
De Quincey, 49
Dickens, 40–1, 47, 112–3, 136, 148–9, 160, 168, 180, 189–90, 197–8, 206–7, 230, 257
Disraeli, 148
Dobell, S., 54

Eliot, George, 162–208
    General references: 10, 21, 26, 38, 40, 44, 56, 59, 62, 64, 124, 127, 129, 149, 153, 155, 158–9, 212, 230, 249, 277–81, 283
    Works: *Adam Bede*, 163, 168–9, 174, 176–9, 181, 186, 188, 190–1, 194–7, 199, 204; *Armgart*, 167–8, 184–5, 203; *Daniel Deronda*, 164, 167–8, 171, 173, 176, 179, 181, 183, 185, 189, 194, 196, 198, 199–200, 208; *Felix Holt*, 164, 167, 170, 174–5, 185, 189, 192–3, 199; *Middlemarch*, 164, 170, 172, 175, 177, 182, 188–90, 193–4, 197–9; *Romola*, 164, 167–8, 170, 174–5, 181, 192, 194–6, 198–9, 205; *Scenes of Clerical Life*, 163, 173, 175, 187–8, 190–1, 195; *Silas Marner*, 163, 182, 189, 191–2, 197; *The Legend of Jubal*, 184, 187, 203; *The Mill on the Floss*, 163, 167, 172, 174–5, 178–80, 188–9, 192, 194, 196–8, 200, 205, 207; *The Spanish Gypsy*, 164, 169, 176, 181, 182, 184, 200–3; *Theophrastus Such*, 164, 172, 176, 191

Elton, Professor O., 207
Emerson, R. W., 32, 156, 159, 169

Fuller, Margaret, 170

Gaskell, Mrs E. C., 100–61
    General references: 25, 45, 47–8, 52, 54, 57–8, 78, 166, 191, 230, 276, 278, 280–1, 283
    Works: *Bessy's Troubles at Home*, 138; *Company Manners*, 107; *Cousin Phillis*, 105–6, 116–7, 121, 132–3, 137–42, 154–5, 158–9; *Christmas Storms and Sunshine*, 107; *Cranford*, 105, 108–13, 118, 120–2, 125–7, 129–30, 136–7, 141, 149–50, 158, 160; *Crowley Castle*, 139; *Curious, if True*, 115, 120; *French Life*, 107, 115, 120, 137, 139, 154–5; *Half a Lifetime Ago*, 129; *Libbie Marsh's Three Eras*, 138, 145, 151; *Lois the Witch*, 105, 130; *Mary Barton*, 104, 108, 122–4, 128, 136, 139–40, 145–6, 148–51, 156–8; *Mr Harrison's Confessions*, 108–9, 120, 125; *My French Master*, 127; *My Lady Ludlow*, 112–4, 120, 130, 132, 137, 150, 154; *North and South*, 104, 106, 113, 128, 137–8, 140, 142, 147–50, 153–4, 159; *Ruth*, 104–6, 112–3, 115, 120, 127–8, 139–40, 152–3, 160; *Sketches Among the Poor*, 145, 160; *Sylvia's Lovers*, 103–6, 115–6, 120–1, 131–2, 138–40, 142, 157–9; *The Crooked Branch*, 130, 154; *The Heart of John Middleton*, 124; *The Life of Charlotte Bronte*, 129–30, 138–9, 151 (Quoted *passim* on section on Charlotte Bronte); *The Manchester Marriage*, 115; *The Moorland Cottage*, 103, 108, 136, 152, 160; *The Old Nurse's Story*, 105, 157; *The Poor Clare*, 129, 154, 157; *Wives and Daughters*, 106–8, 117–21, 132–7, 140–4, 146, 150, 152, 155–7, 160

Goldsmith, 5, 26
Gosse, Edmund, 245, 260, 264
Greek Drama, 181
Greenwood, Frederick, 156

Hardy, Thomas, 19
Harrison, Frederic, 60, 166
Hazlitt, W., 32
Hemans, Mrs F., 219
Herbert, G., 244

Imitation of Christ, The, 174, 239, 243-4
Israels, Josef, 169

Jack, Professor, 70, 78
Johnson, Dr S., 172

Keats, 92, 104, 187, 190, 242, 246, 255, 270
Kenyon, J., 217
Kingsley, C., 52-3
Kipling, R., 218

Lamb, C., 19, 42, 126, 130, 145, 151, 161, 170, 283
— Mary, 145
Lewes, G. H., 45, 56, 63, 163-4, 166, 178-9
Lockhart, 50

Maeterlinck, 71
Marlowe, 222
Masefield, 184
Merivale, C., 53
Meynell, Mrs A., 219, 263, 272
Milton, 28, 79, 90, 172, 215, 221-4, 240, 242, 250

Newman, J. H., 239
Nicoll, Sir W. Robertson, 52-3, 60
Nightingale, Florence, 211

Plato, 254, 257
Pope, 26

Quintilian, 119

Radcliffe, Mrs, 15
Raleigh, Sir W., 19, 29
Rossetti, Christina, 233-74
General references: 34, 86, 91, 209 *n*., 213, 215, 219, 228, 229-30, 276, 278-81, 284
Works:
Reference, among other poems, to: *A Better Resurrection*, 264; *A Birthday*, 264; *Advent*, 258-9; *An Old-World Thicket*, 265, 270; *At Home*, 241, 257; *Birds of Paradise*, 259, 269; *Despised and Rejected*, 265; *Dream Love*, 258, 269; *Dreamland*, 245, 257-8, 260; *Echo*, 257; *Fata Morgana*, 255-6, 270; *From House to Home*, 238, 256; *Goblin Market*, 256-7, 270; *Heaven Overarches*, etc., 237-8; *Introspective*, 235-6, 264, 270; *Marvel of Marvels*, 237, 259, 271; *Monna Innominata*, 237, 247, 260, 262-3, 272; *My Love, Whose Heart is Tender*, 237, 270-1; *Passing Away*, 265, 270; *Remember*, 261, 263; *Repining*, 251, 255; *Sleep at Sea*, 256, 268; *The Heart Knoweth*, etc., 262; *The Love of Christ*, etc., 265; *The Prince's Progress*, 252, 255, 269; *The Royal Princess*, 251-2; *Twice*, 261-2; *Uphill*, 262; *When I am Dead*, etc., 241, 258
Rossetti, D. G., 79, 233, 241, 252-3
— W., 235, 244, 252, 254, 265
Ruskin, 31, 41, 109, 122, 217, 226, 230, 251, 279-80

Saintsbury, Professor G., 268
Sand, George, 156
Scott, W., 39, 43, 168, 173, 206
Shakespeare, 19, 23, 42, 48, 50, 81, 87, 167, 170-1, 181, 192, 196, 207, 208, 213-4, 230-1, 263, 278-9
Shelley, 3, 60, 245-6
Sheridan, 26
Shorter, Clement, 77
Southey, 54, 276
Stephen, Sir L., 162-3, 168, 171
Stevenson, R. L., 12, 101, 172
Stowe, Mrs H. B., 44, 166, 280
Strauss, 163, 173
Swinburne, 79, 84, 219

Tennyson, 19, 34, 90–1, 191, 203, 213, 229, 239, 251–2, 270
Thackeray, 19, 21–2, 26, 30, 39, 41–2, 47, 96–7, 168, 191, 206, 216, 230
Thomas à Kempis, 239 (*see also* under *Imitation of Christ*)
Thompson, Francis, 219, 272
Thomson, Hugh, 35
Thorwaldsen, 173
Times, The, 170
Tolstoi, 122

Vachell, H. A., 1'9
Vaughan, 244

Ward, Sir A. W., 100, 115
Watts, G. F., 234, 253
Webster, J., 201
Wells, H. G., 207
Westminster Review, 163
Wordsworth, 32, 88, 103, 145, 166–7, 195, 267, 283

Young, E., 176, 187